RECORD OF
GRANCREST
— WAR —

4

D1320061

Original Story by **Ryo Mizuno**
Story & Art by **Makoto Yotsuba**
Character Design by **Miyuu**

· Story ·

Previously...

In a world where chaos is the most powerful force, the people are terrified of the threat it poses. They live under the protection of lords, who are the only ones capable of wielding crests that can quell chaos.

However, the lords use their crests to fight each other in petty battles over territory, and the continent has been plunged into a war-torn era.

Siluca Meletes, the talented mage whose abilities were on display at the Grand Hall Tragedy, voids her upcoming contract with the lecherous Count Villar of Altirk in order to enter a contract with a wandering lord named Theo. Together, they defeat a feudal lord, making Theo the lord of that territory. The two then declare allegiance to the Fantasia Union and defeat Lord Lassic, who opts to serve Theo. Their actions earn them the trust of the citizens and, more importantly, give them the allegiance of the independent lords, who back their claim against the King of Sievis.

Theo is soon promoted to a Sub-Viscount. Siluca heads to Waldlind to negotiate their return to the Factory Alliance. However, the negotiations with her adoptive father, Aubest, and Marrine Kreische, the leader of the Alliance, fall through. Inevitably, this leads to Waldlind declaring war. In desperation, Siluca seeks help from the Fantasia Union superpower Altirk, despite the fact that she broke her previous contract with them.

Predictably, Earl Villar refuses to even see her, leaving Theo and Siluca in a terrible predicament as the powerful Waldlind military attacks!

Key ·

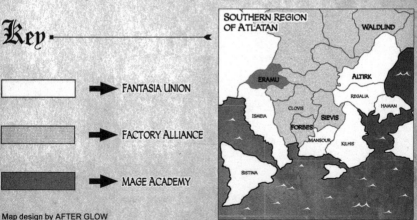

FANTASIA UNION

FACTORY ALLIANCE

MAGE ACADEMY

SOUTHERN REGION
OF ATLATAN

WALDLIND

ERAMU

ALTIRK

REGALIA

HAMAN

ISMEIA

CLOVIS

SIEVIS

FORBES

MANSOUR

KILHIS

SISTINA

Map design by AFTER GLOW

Characters

Theo

A wandering lord who hopes one day to free his homeland from tyranny. He enters into a contract with Siluca. He cares about his people and has great instincts.

Siluca Meletes

A mage thought at school to be a genius. She believes that Theo could be an ideal lord and decides to serve him.

Irvin

A brilliant Artist who used to serve an Archduke. Seeing potential in Siluca due to her ability to "treat him roughly," he chooses to serve her.

Aishela

A female warrior and Artist who loves Siluca very much. She is distrustful of Theo. Her skill with pole weapons is both beautiful and deadly.

Lassic David

The independent lord of Sievis. Full of ambition, he invaded Theo's territory but was defeated. Seeing potential in Theo, he decides to serve him in hopes of fulfilling his own goals.

Moreno Dortous

A mage who serves Lassic. He believes Lassic to have the makings of an emperor and advises him with that in mind.

Marrine Kreische

The Lord of Waldlind and leader of the Factory Alliance. Her life was saved by Siluca during the Great Hall Tragedy.

Aubest Meletes

The high mage of Waldlind. His decisions are made with cold logic and calculations. He is also the adoptive father of Siluca and Aishela.

Priscilla

A priestess in the Order of the Crest. She arrived hoping to convert Theo and decided to stay. She is often at odds with Siluca.

Contents

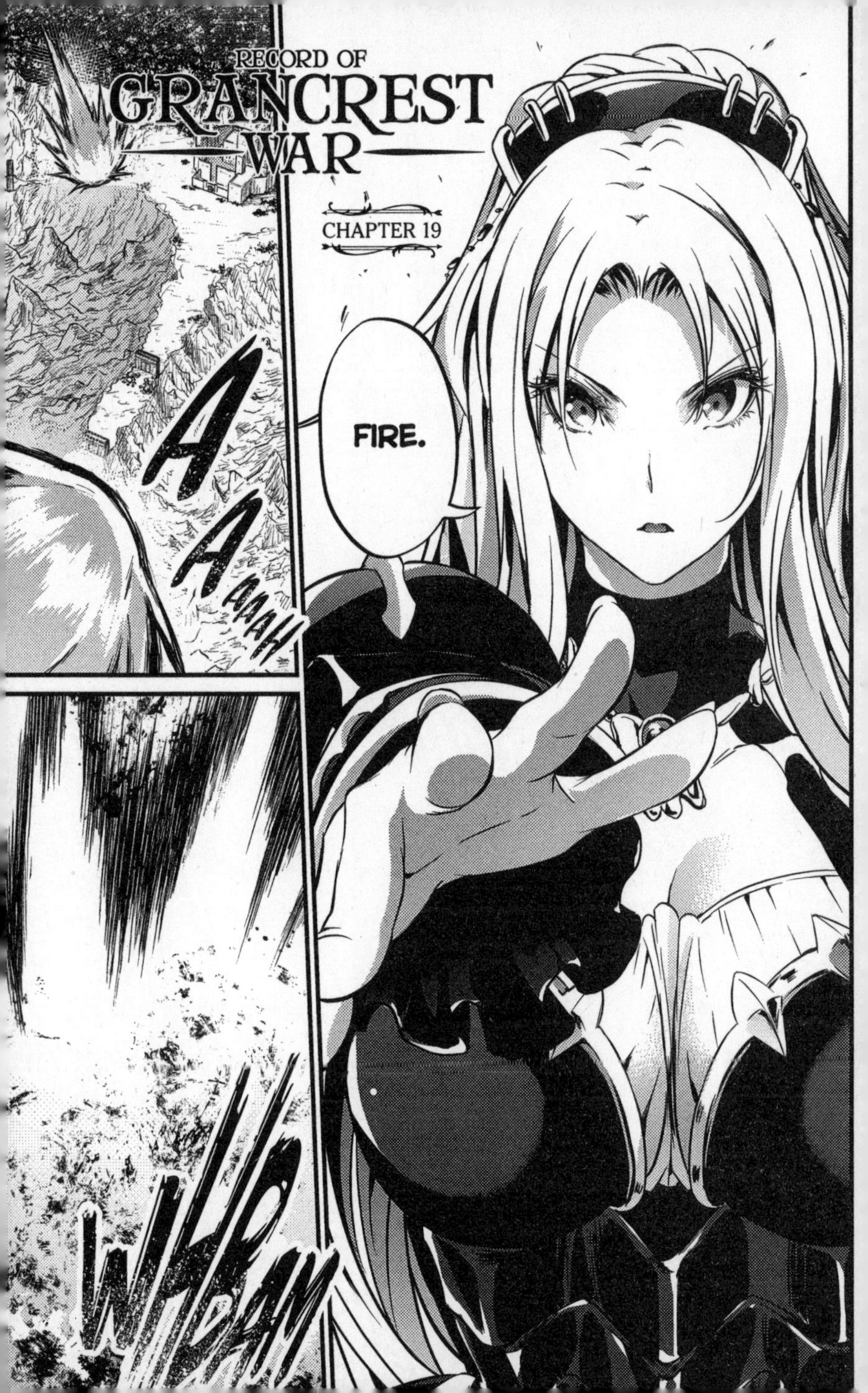
RECORD OF
GRANCREST
WAR
CHAPTER 19
FIRE.
AAAAAH

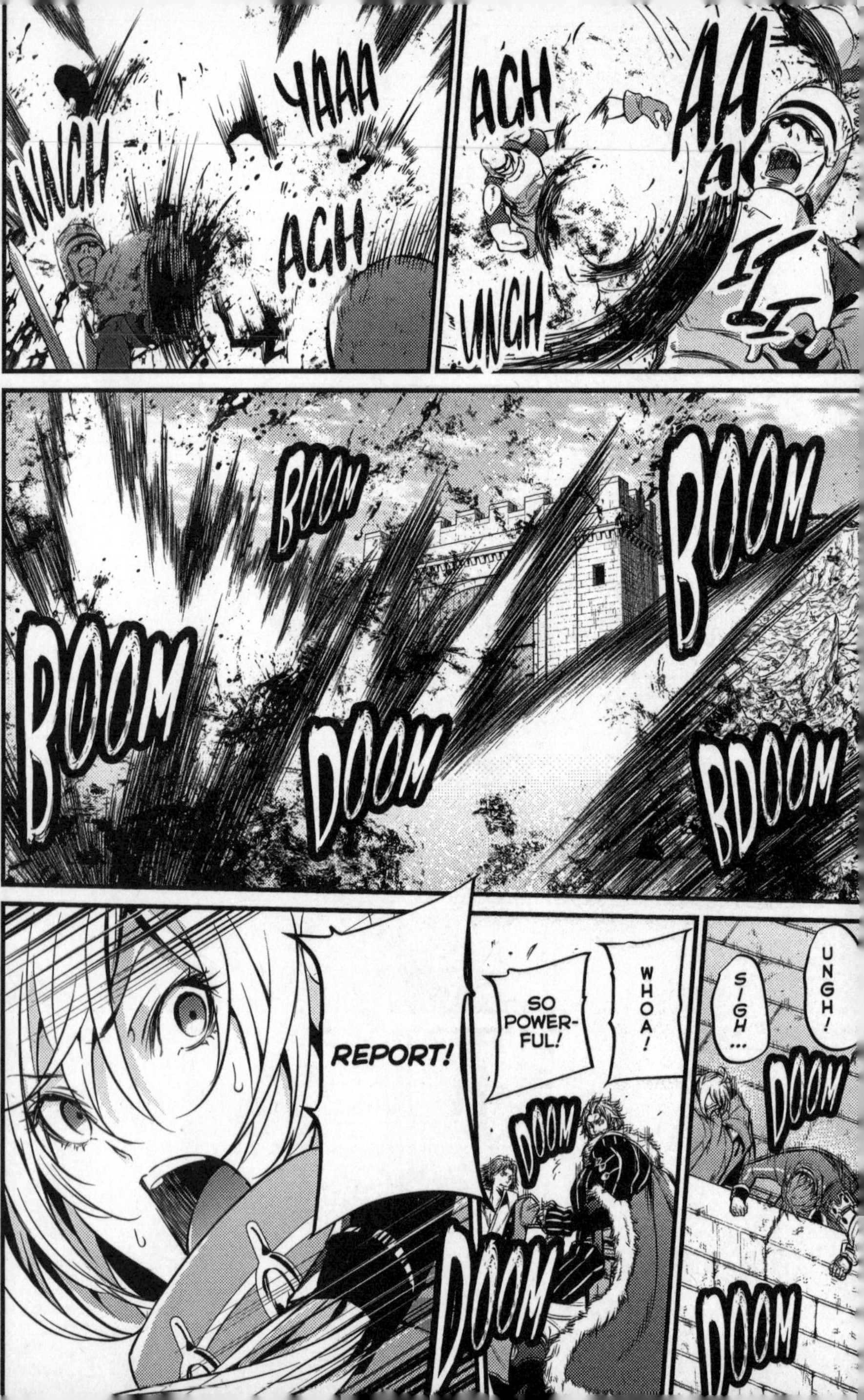
AAAIII
ACH
UNGH
YAAA
ACH
NNCH
BOOM
BOOM
BDOOM
DOOM
BOOM
UNGH!
SIGH...
DOOM
DOOM
WHOA!
SO POWERFUL!
DOOM
DOOM
REPORT!

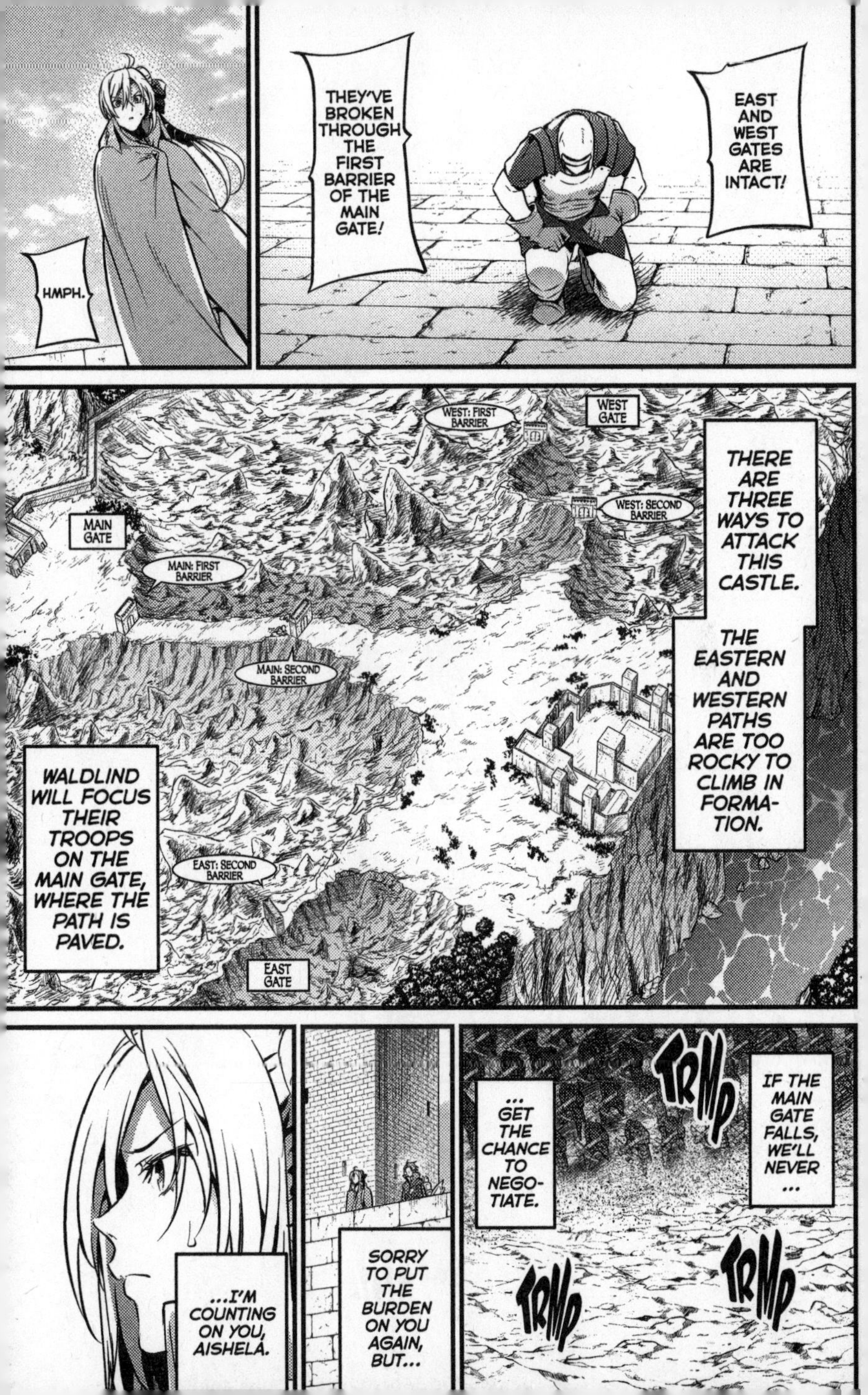
EAST AND WEST GATES ARE INTACT!
THEY'VE BROKEN THROUGH THE FIRST BARRIER OF THE MAIN GATE!
HMPH.
THERE ARE THREE WAYS TO ATTACK THIS CASTLE.
THE EASTERN AND WESTERN PATHS ARE TOO ROCKY TO CLIMB IN FORMATION.
WEST GATE
WEST: FIRST BARRIER
WEST: SECOND BARRIER
MAIN GATE
MAIN: FIRST BARRIER
MAIN: SECOND BARRIER
EAST: SECOND BARRIER
EAST GATE
WALDLIND WILL FOCUS THEIR TROOPS ON THE MAIN GATE, WHERE THE PATH IS PAVED.
TRMP
IF THE MAIN GATE FALLS, WE'LL NEVER ...
... GET THE CHANCE TO NEGOTIATE.
TRMP
TRMP
SORRY TO PUT THE BURDEN ON YOU AGAIN, BUT...
...I'M COUNTING ON YOU, AISHELA.

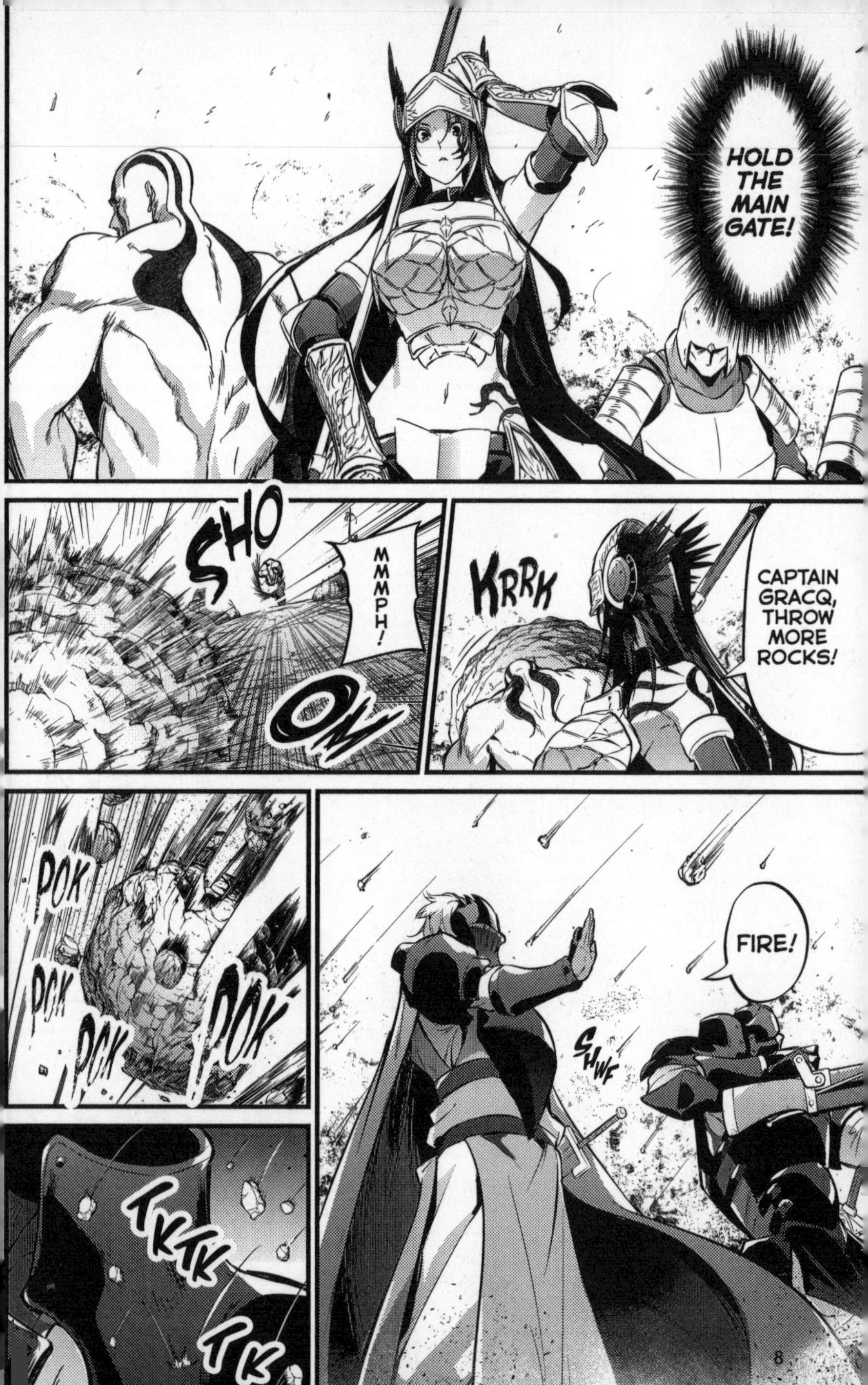
HOLD THE MAIN GATE!
CAPTAIN GRACQ, THROW MORE ROCKS!
KRRK
MMMPH!
SHOOM
FIRE!
SHWF
POK
POK
POK
POK
TKTK
TK

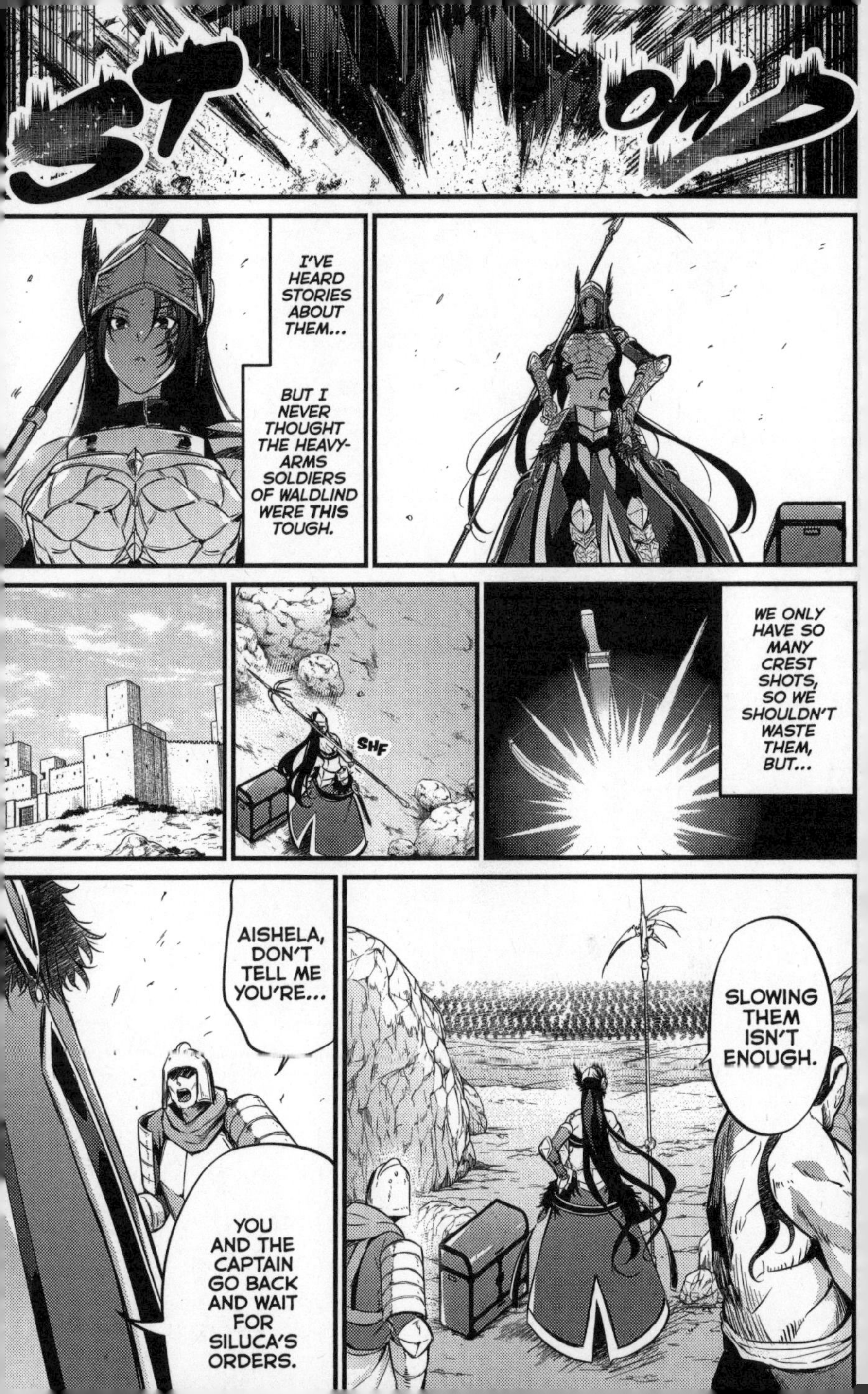
I'VE HEARD STORIES ABOUT THEM...
BUT I NEVER THOUGHT THE HEAVY-ARMS SOLDIERS OF WALDLIND WERE THIS TOUGH.
WE ONLY HAVE SO MANY CREST SHOTS, SO WE SHOULDN'T WASTE THEM, BUT...
SHF
SLOWING THEM ISN'T ENOUGH.
AISHELA, DON'T TELL ME YOU'RE...
YOU AND THE CAPTAIN GO BACK AND WAIT FOR SILUCA'S ORDERS.

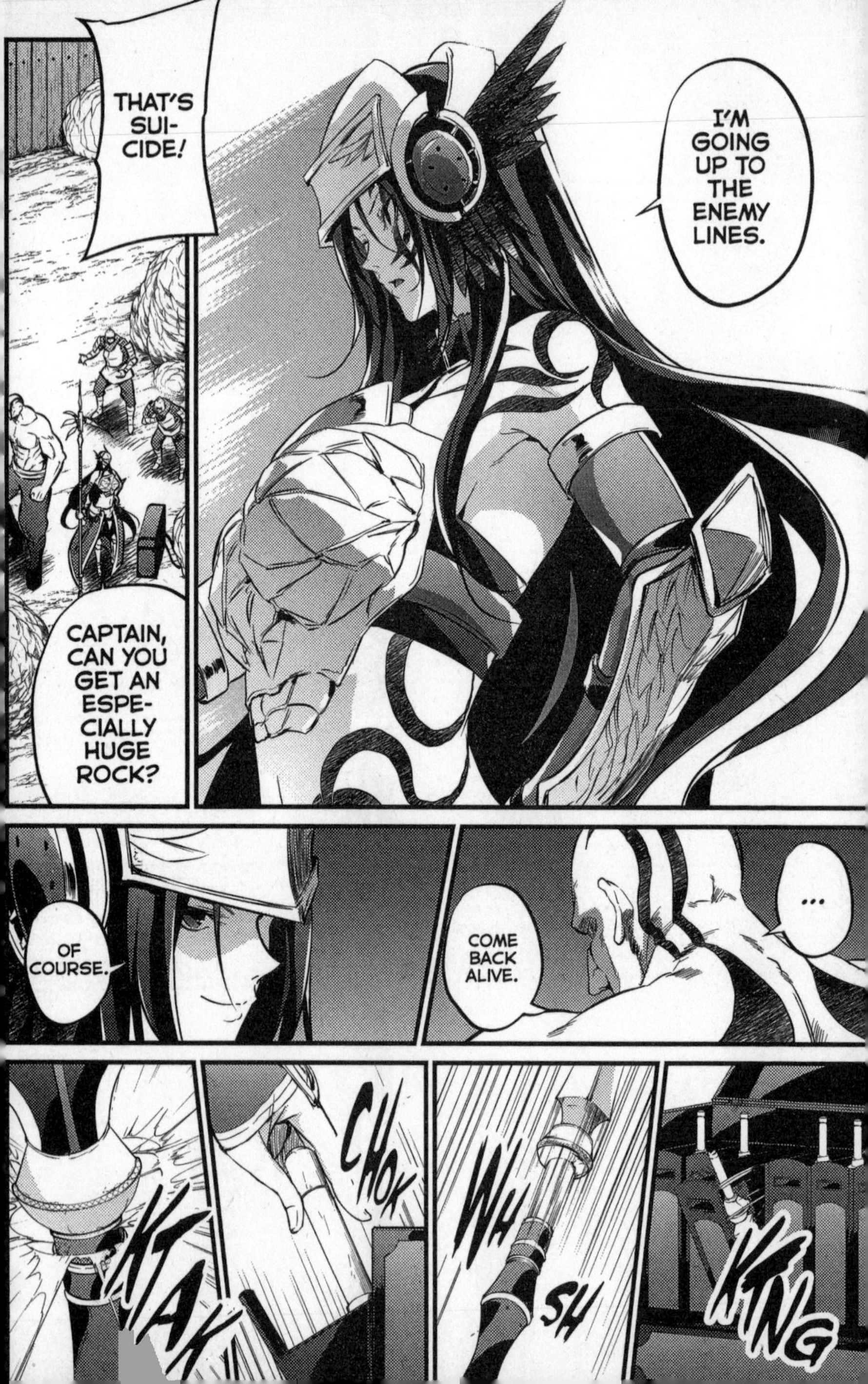
I'M GOING UP TO THE ENEMY LINES.
THAT'S SUI-CIDE!
CAPTAIN, CAN YOU GET AN ESPE-CIALLY HUGE ROCK?
...
COME BACK ALIVE.
OF COURSE.
KLING
WHSH
CHOK
KTAK

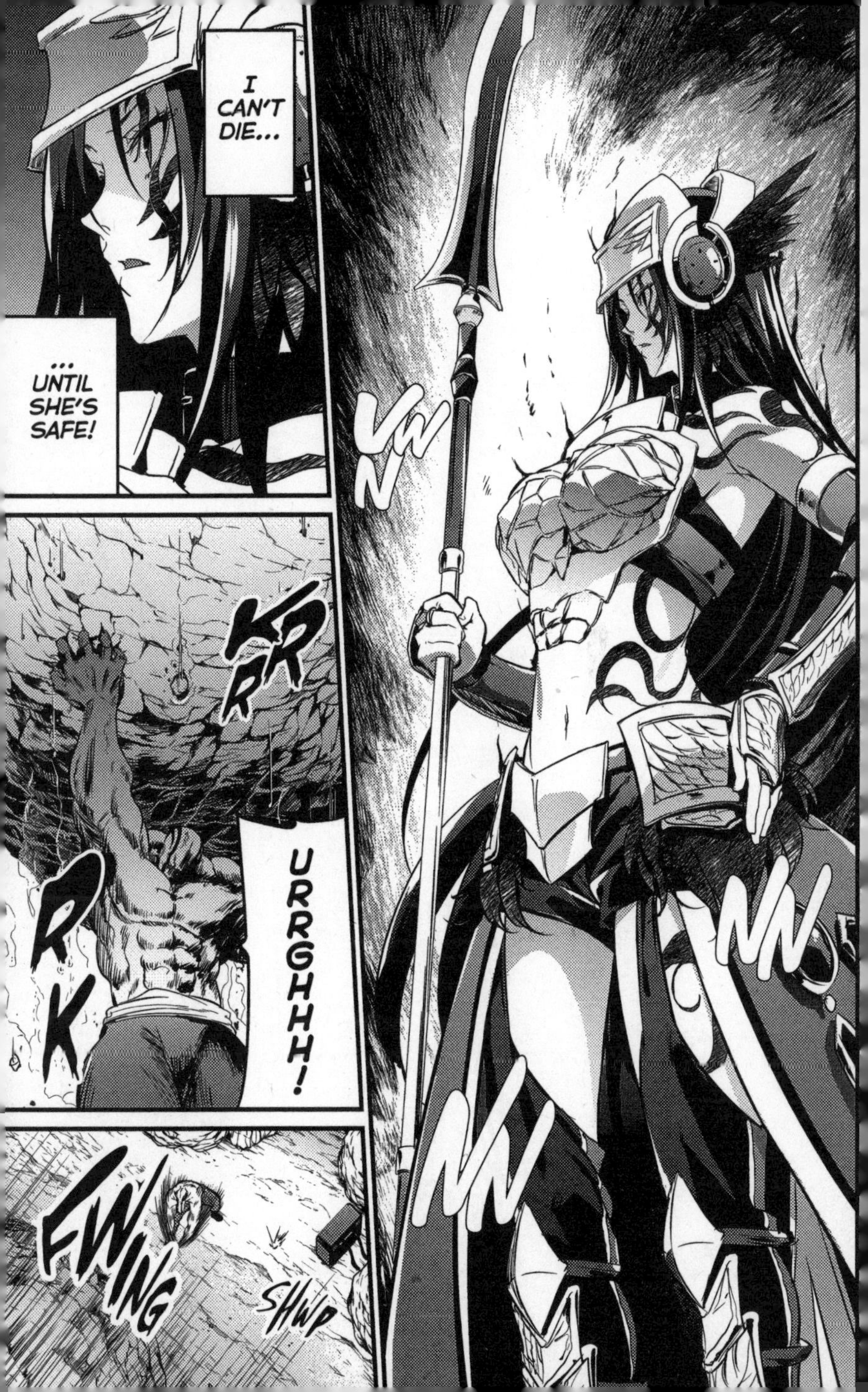

VWN
NNN
NNN
I CAN'T DIE...
... UNTIL SHE'S SAFE!
KRRR
URRGHHH!
RK
FWING
SHWP

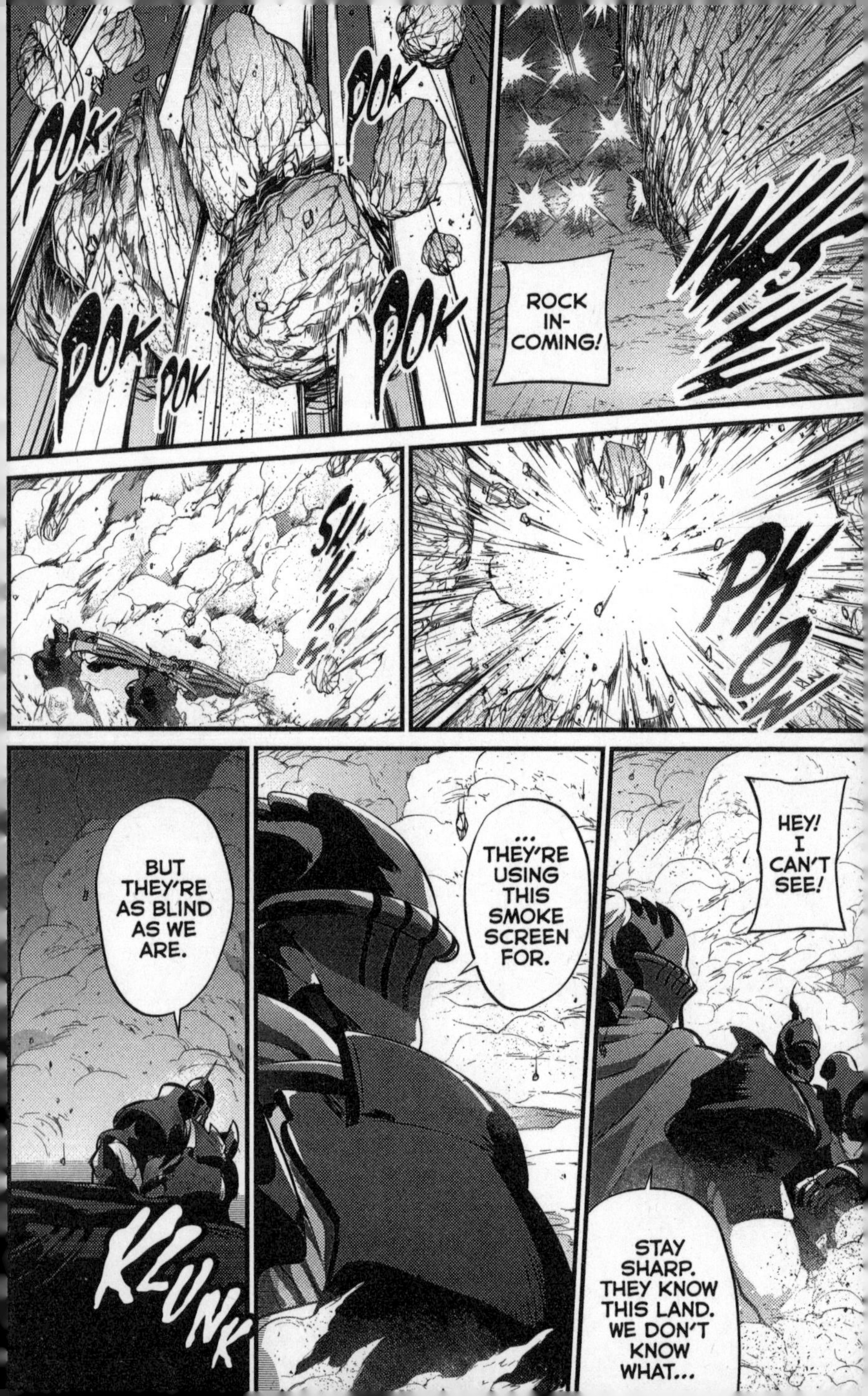
ROCK IN-COMING!
POK
POK
POK
POK
POK
HEY! I CAN'T SEE!
STAY SHARP. THEY KNOW THIS LAND. WE DON'T KNOW WHAT...
... THEY'RE USING THIS SMOKE SCREEN FOR.
BUT THEY'RE AS BLIND AS WE ARE.
KLUNK

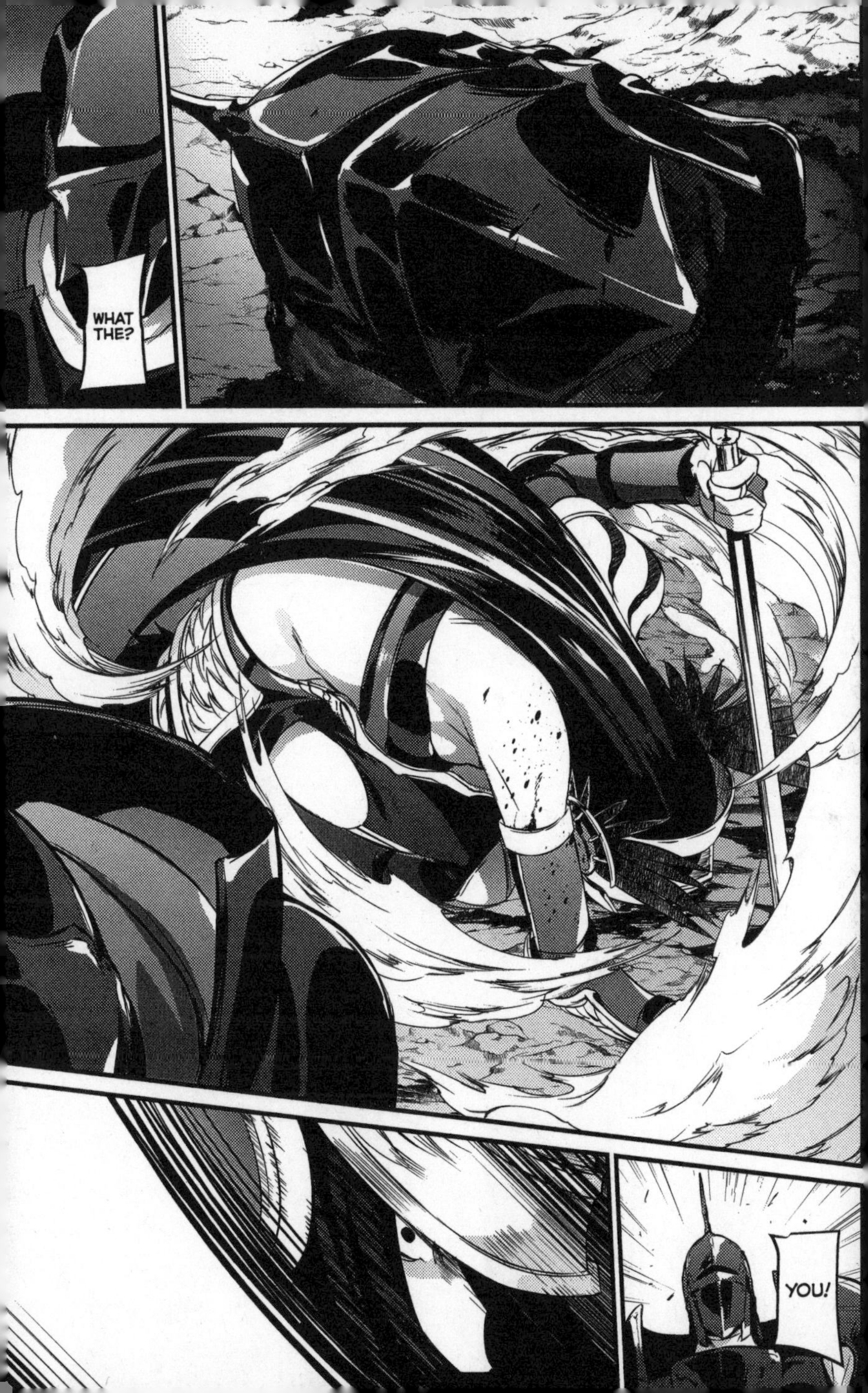
WHAT THE?
YOU!

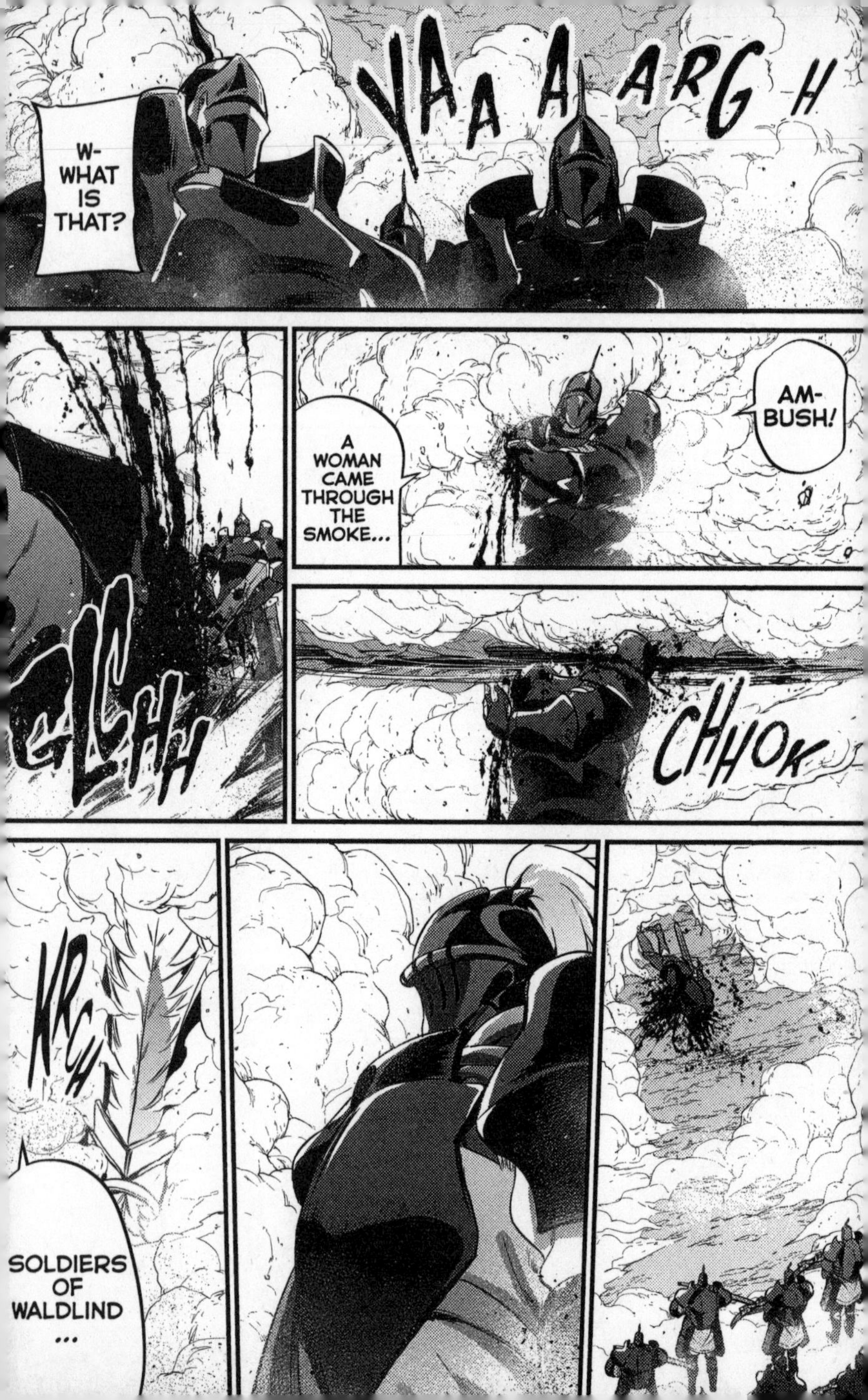
YAAAARGH
W-WHAT IS THAT?
AM-BUSH!
A WOMAN CAME THROUGH THE SMOKE...
CHHOK
GLCHH
KRCH
SOLDIERS OF WALDLIND ...

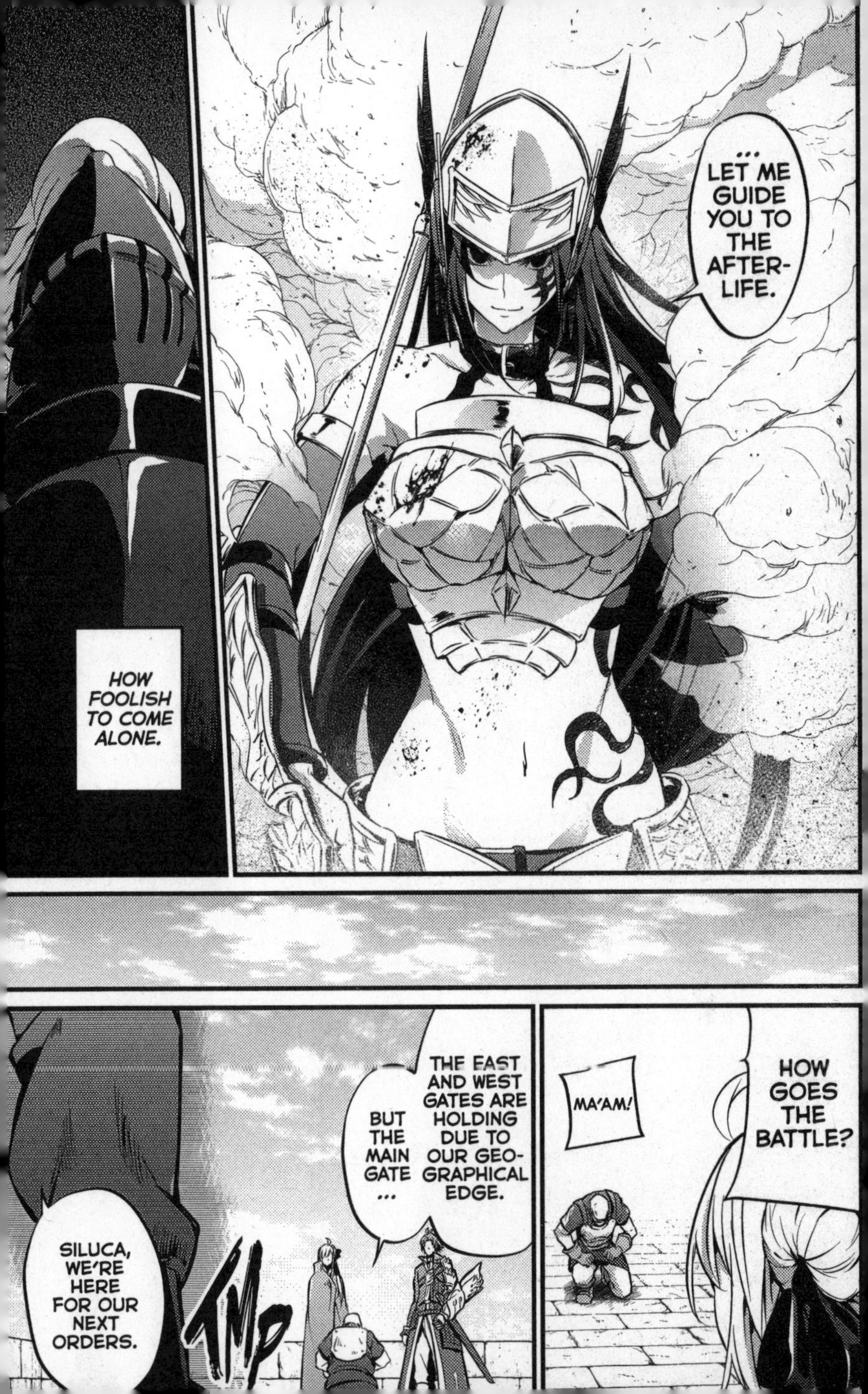
...LET ME GUIDE YOU TO THE AFTER-LIFE.
HOW FOOLISH TO COME ALONE.
HOW GOES THE BATTLE?
MA'AM!
THE EAST AND WEST GATES ARE HOLDING DUE TO OUR GEO-GRAPHICAL EDGE.
BUT THE MAIN GATE...
TMP
SILUCA, WE'RE HERE FOR OUR NEXT ORDERS.

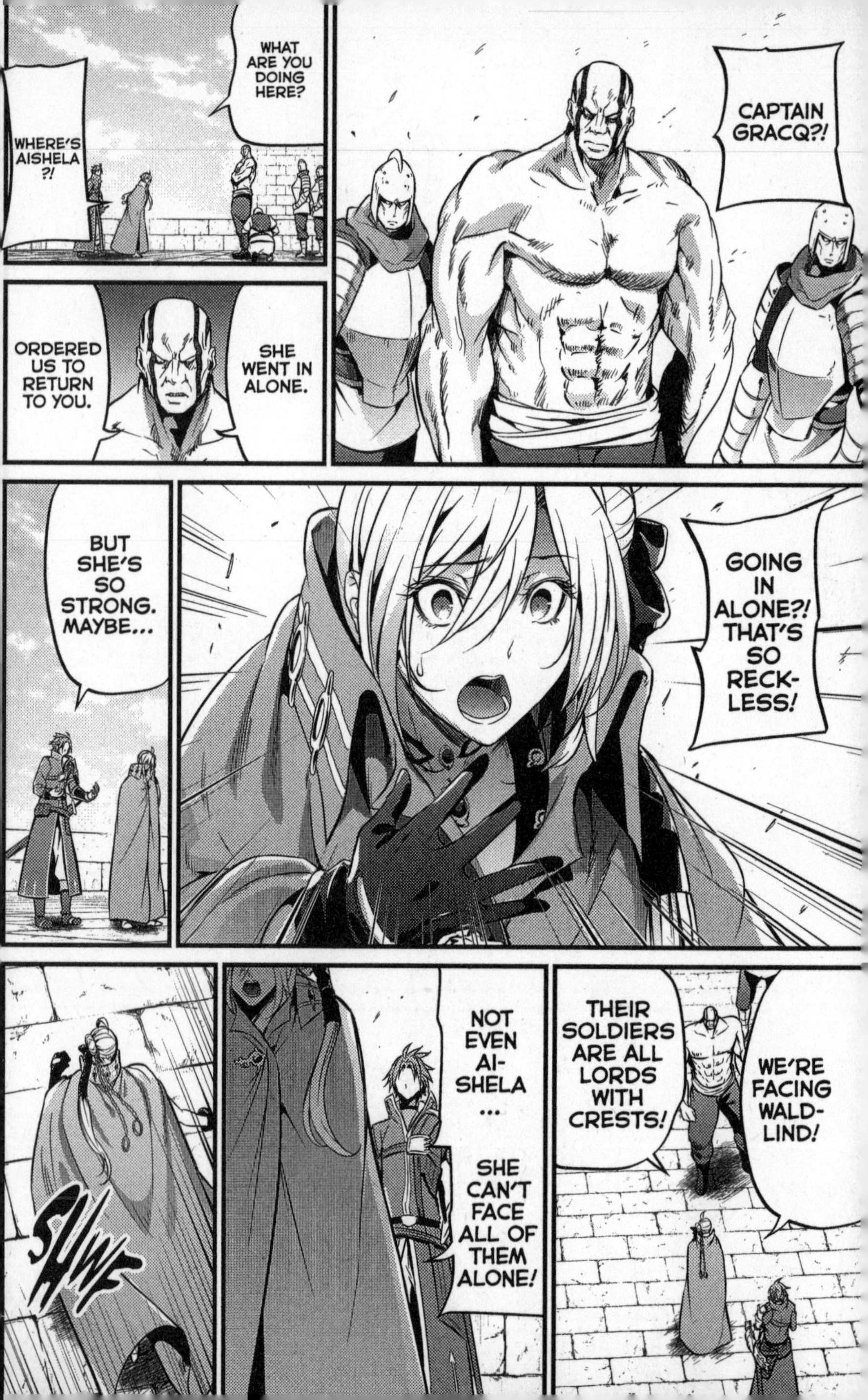
CAPTAIN GRACQ?!
WHAT ARE YOU DOING HERE?
WHERE'S AISHELA?!
SHE WENT IN ALONE.
ORDERED US TO RETURN TO YOU.
GOING IN ALONE?! THAT'S SO RECK-LESS!
BUT SHE'S SO STRONG. MAYBE...
WE'RE FACING WALD-LIND!
THEIR SOLDIERS ARE ALL LORDS WITH CRESTS!
NOT EVEN AI-SHELA...
SHE CAN'T FACE ALL OF THEM ALONE!
SHWF

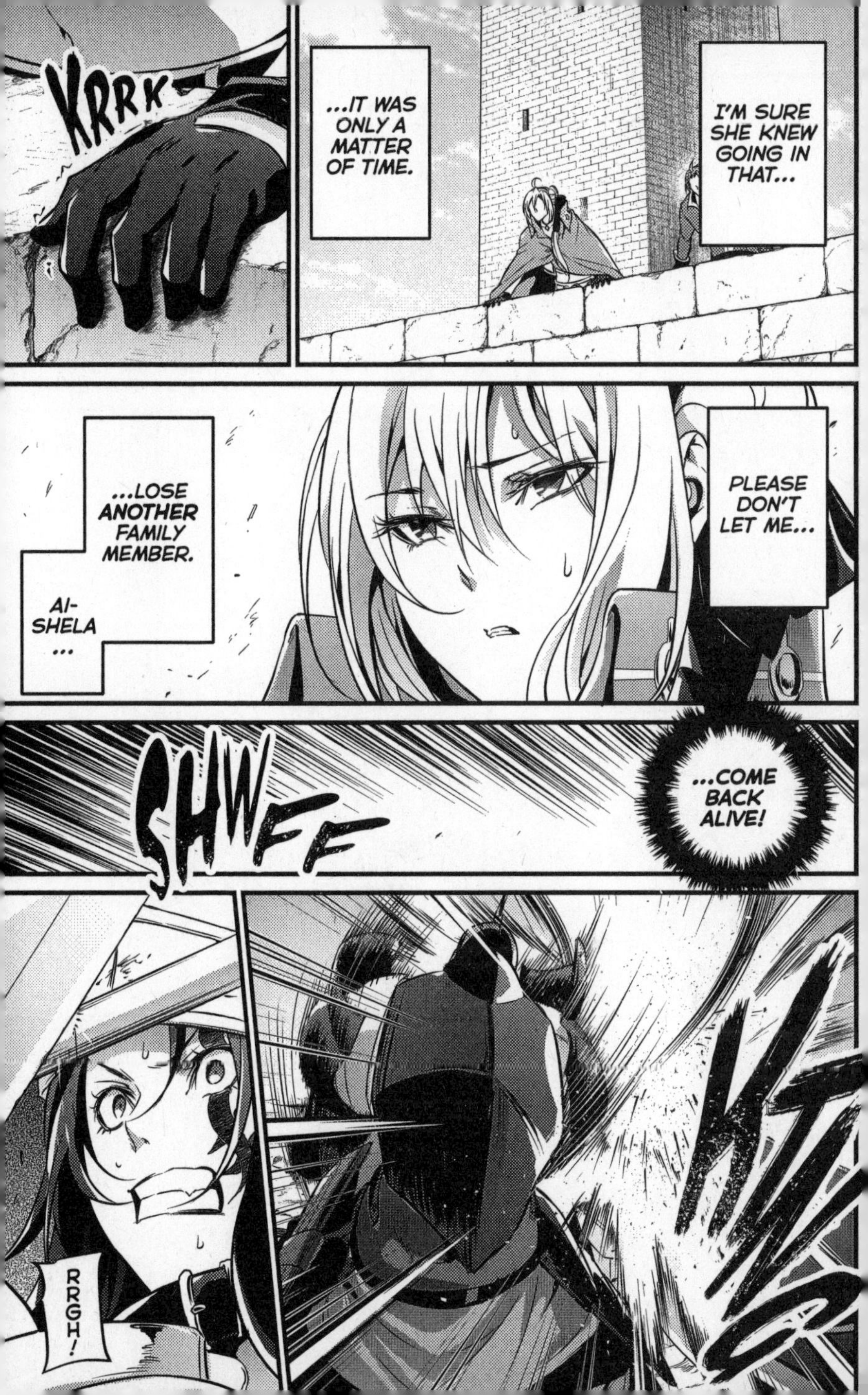
I'M SURE SHE KNEW GOING IN THAT...
...IT WAS ONLY A MATTER OF TIME.
KRRK
PLEASE DON'T LET ME...
...LOSE ANOTHER FAMILY MEMBER.
AI-SHELA...
...COME BACK ALIVE!
SHWFF
RRGH!

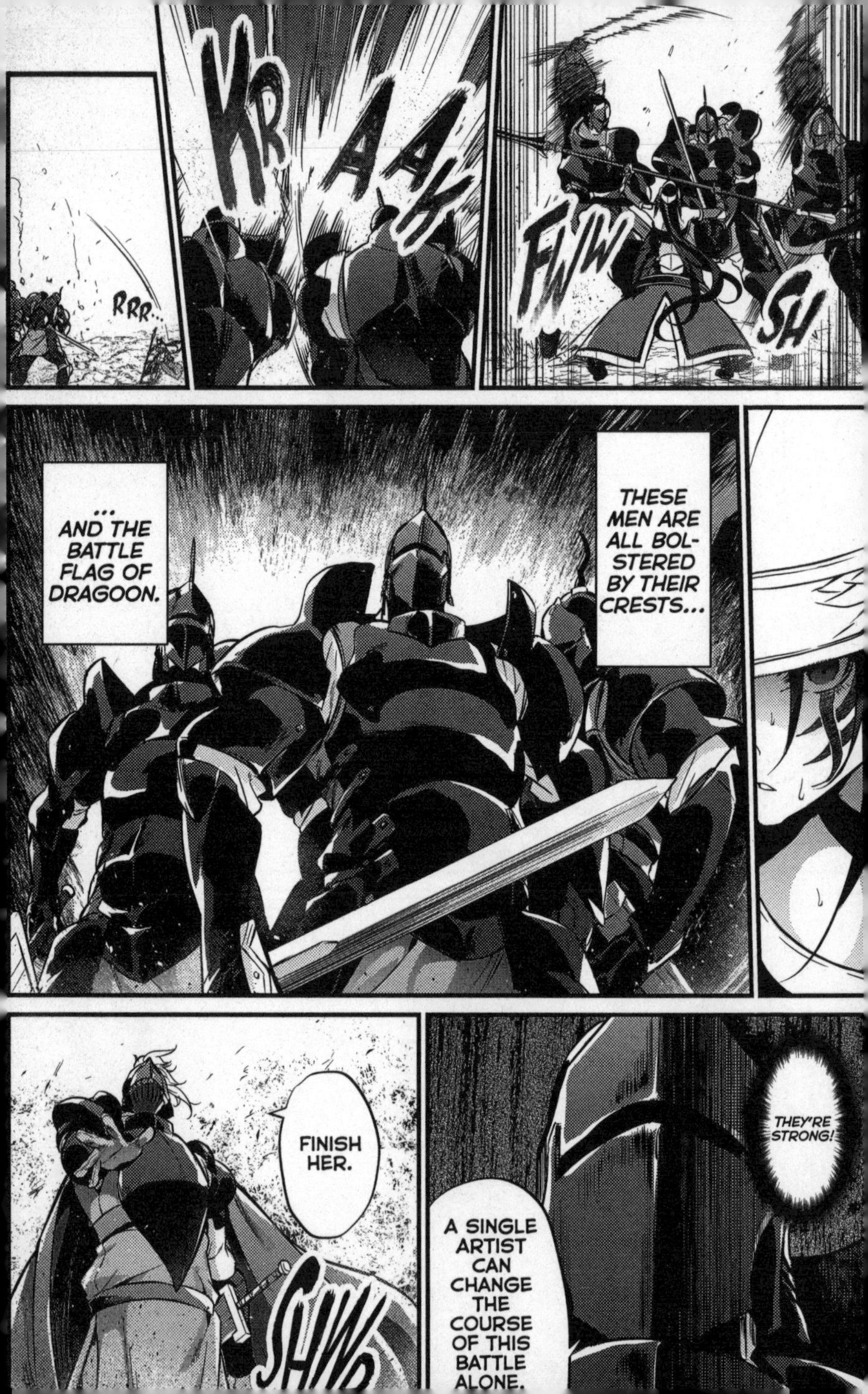
FWW
SH
KRAAK
RRR...
THESE MEN ARE ALL BOLSTERED BY THEIR CRESTS...
... AND THE BATTLE FLAG OF DRAGOON.
THEY'RE STRONG!
A SINGLE ARTIST CAN CHANGE THE COURSE OF THIS BATTLE ALONE.
FINISH HER.
SHIN

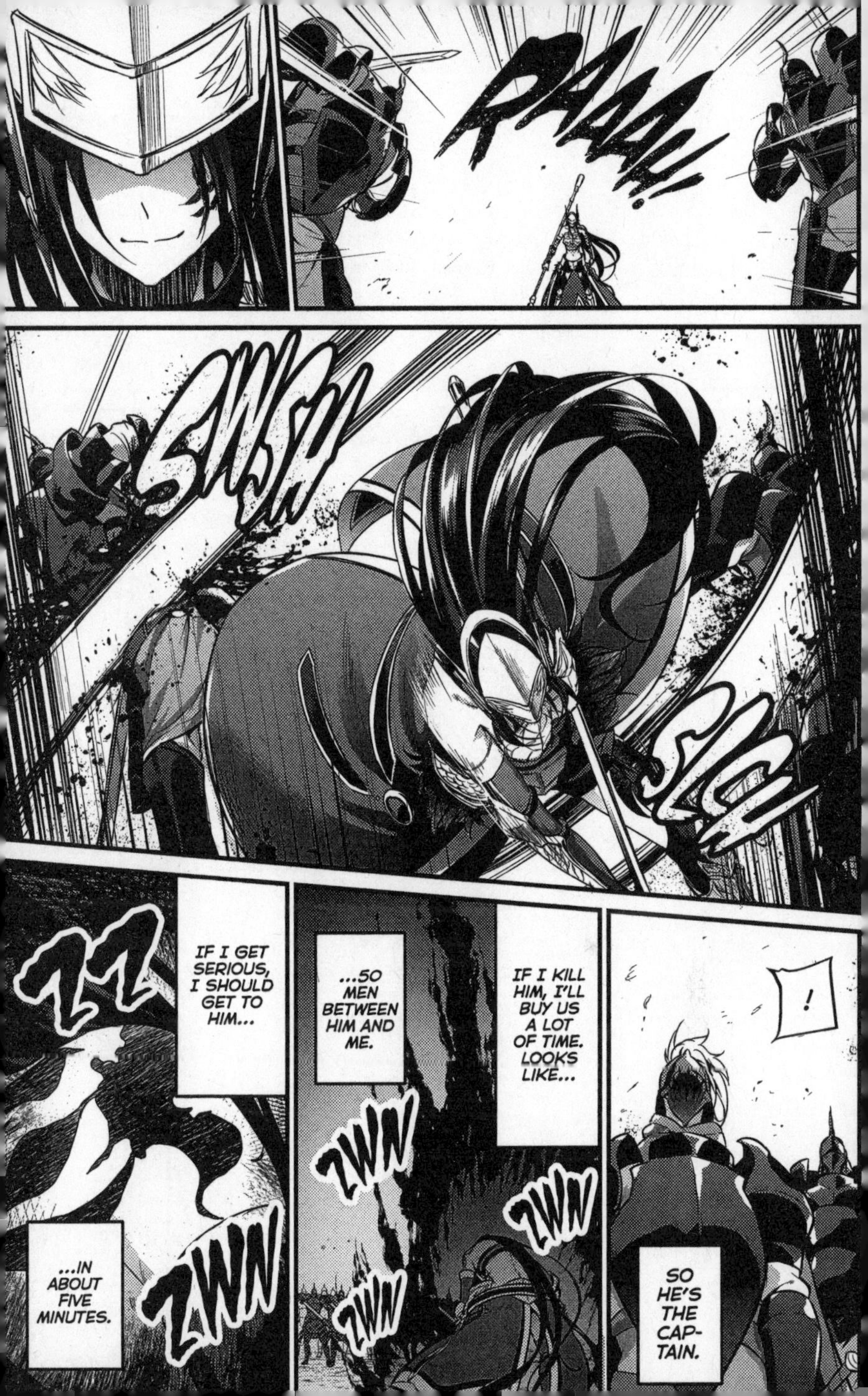
RAAAH!!
SWISH
!
SO HE'S THE CAP-TAIN.
IF I KILL HIM, I'LL BUY US A LOT OF TIME. LOOKS LIKE...
ZWN
...50 MEN BETWEEN HIM AND ME.
ZWN
ZWN
IF I GET SERIOUS, I SHOULD GET TO HIM...
ZZ
...IN ABOUT FIVE MINUTES.
ZWN

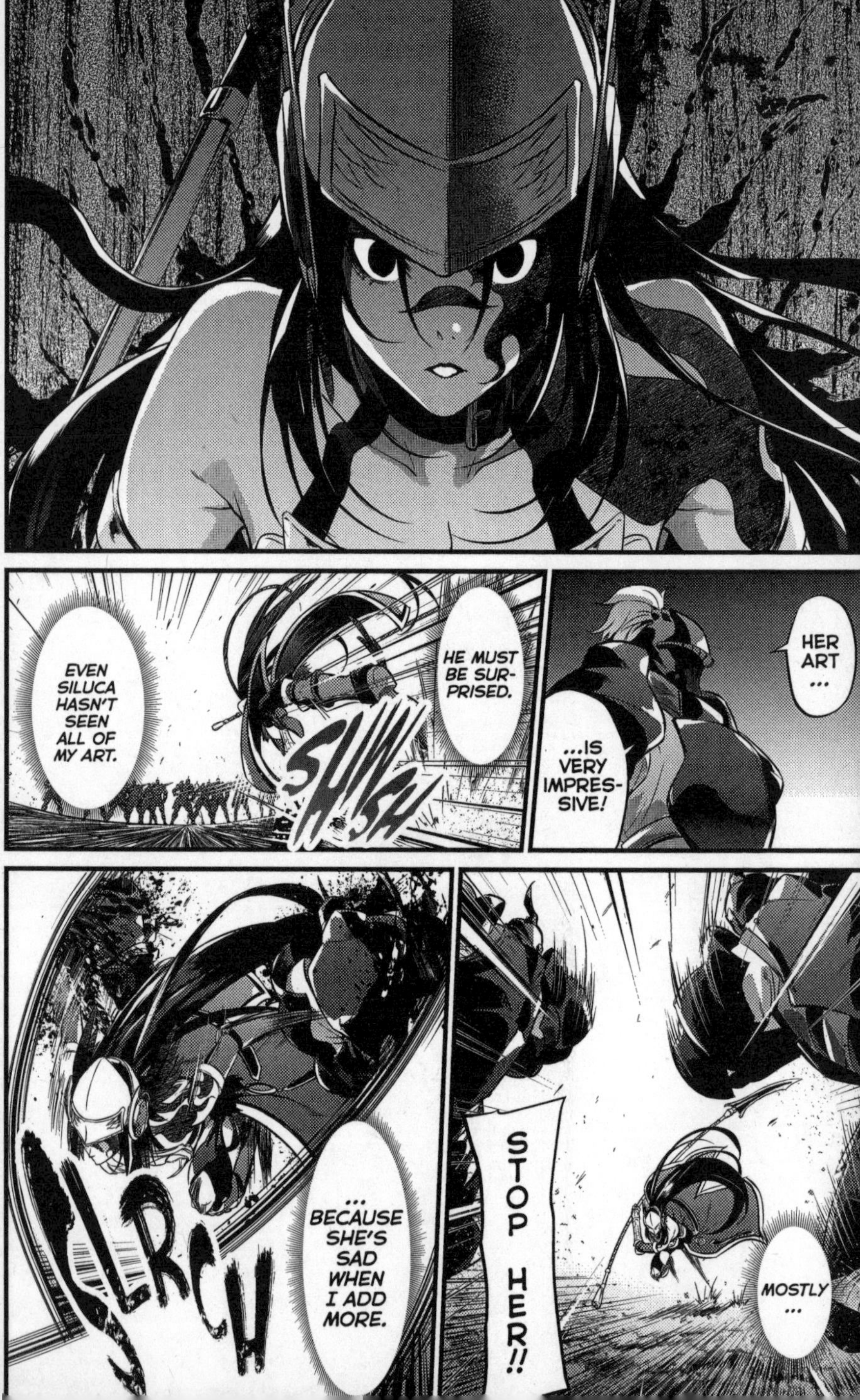
HER ART ...
...IS VERY IMPRESSIVE!
HE MUST BE SURPRISED.
SHISH
EVEN SILUCA HASN'T SEEN ALL OF MY ART.
STOP HER!!
MOSTLY ...
... BECAUSE SHE'S SAD WHEN I ADD MORE.
SLRCH

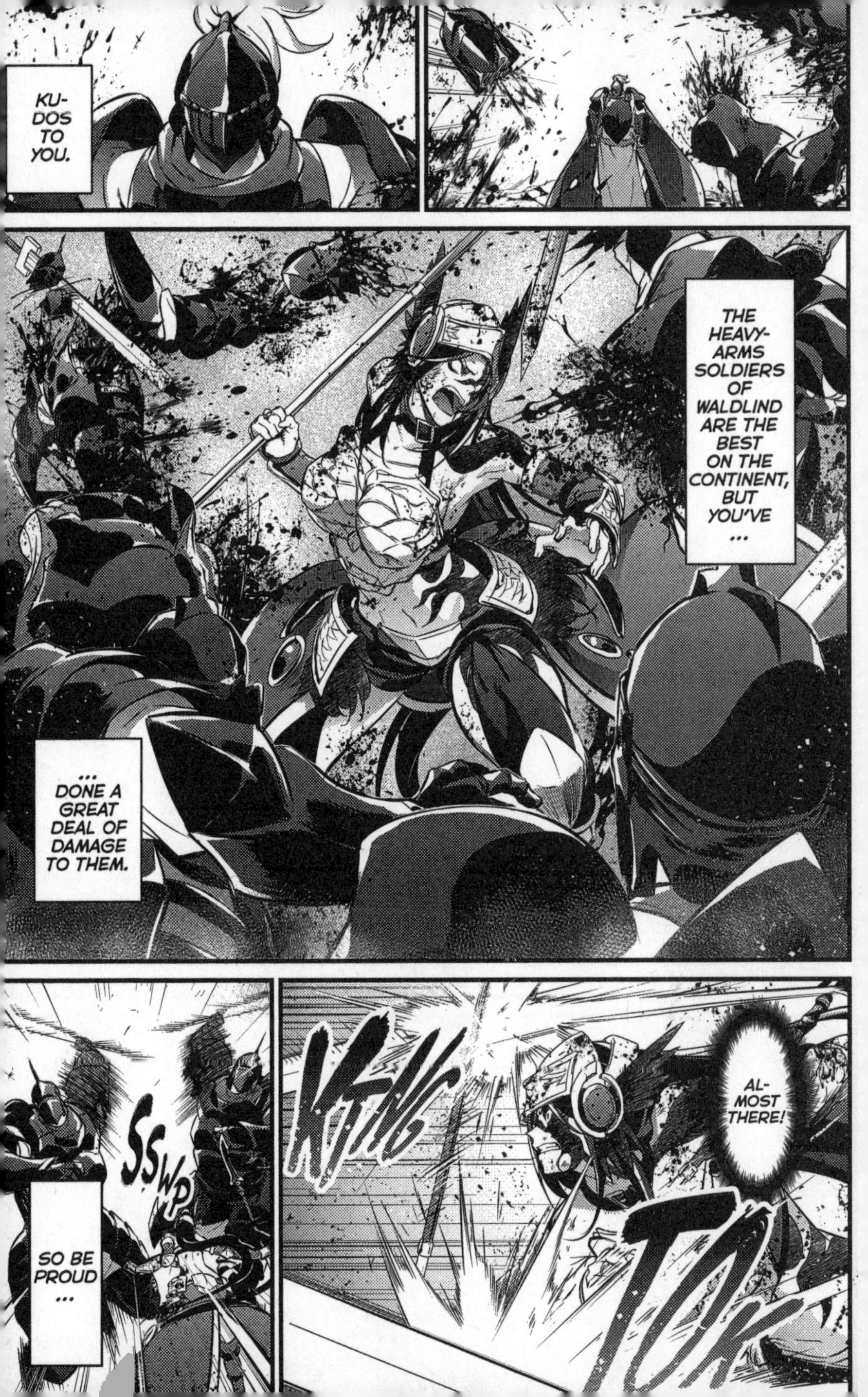
KU-DOS TO YOU.
THE HEAVY-ARMS SOLDIERS OF WALDLIND ARE THE BEST ON THE CONTINENT, BUT YOU'VE ...
... DONE A GREAT DEAL OF DAMAGE TO THEM.
AL-MOST THERE!
SSWP
SO BE PROUD ...

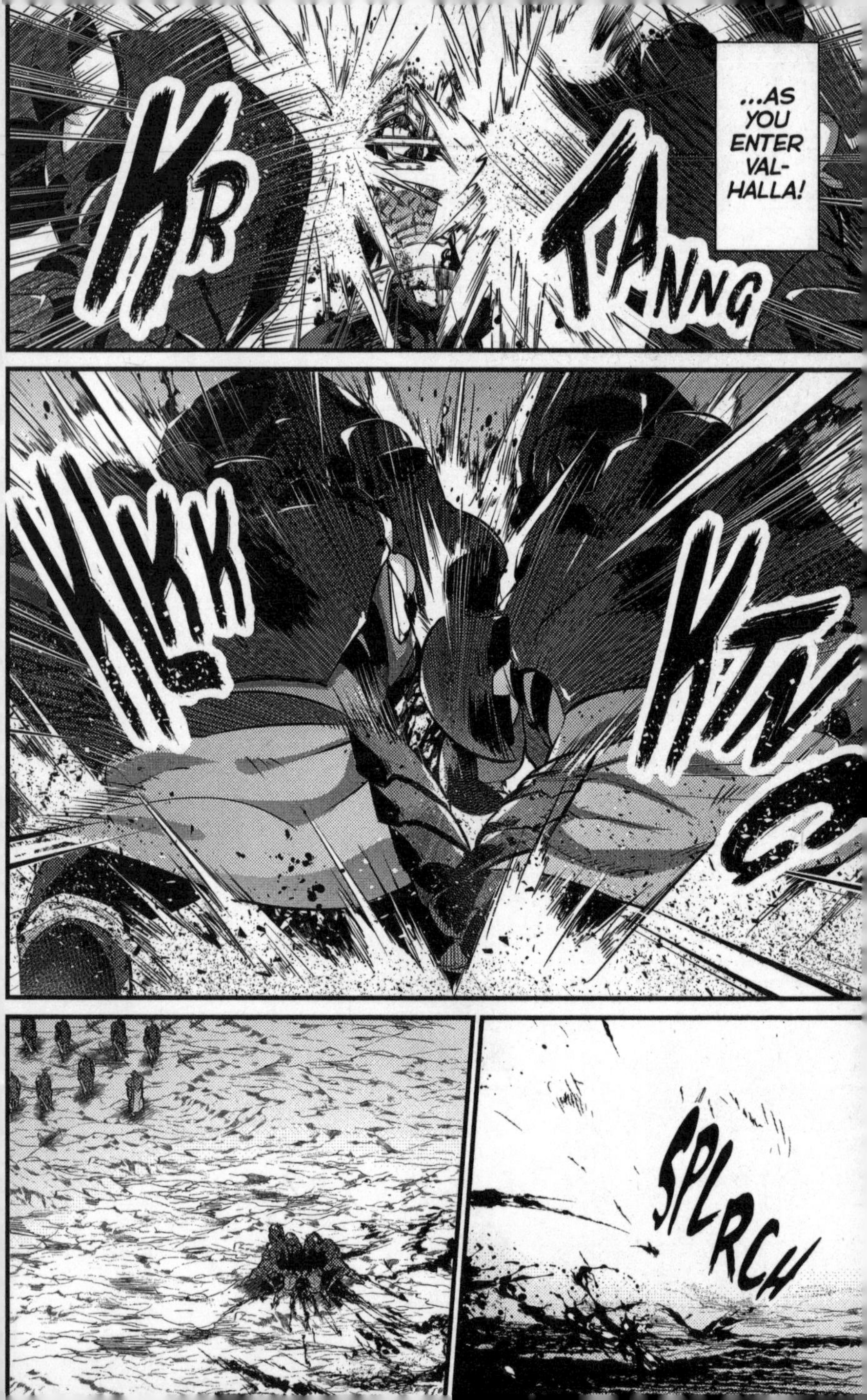
...AS YOU ENTER VAL-HALLA!
KR TANNG
SPLRCH

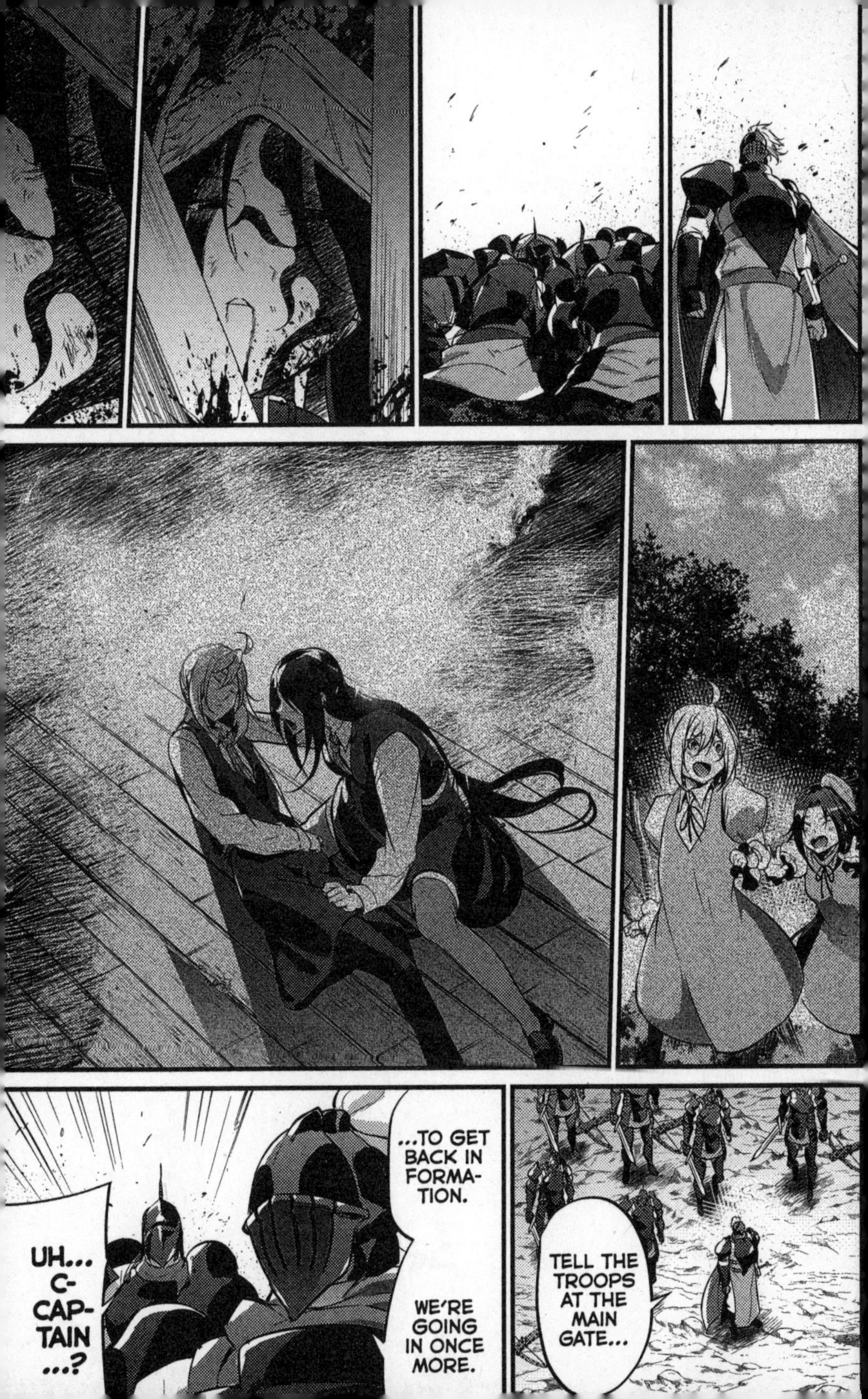
TELL THE TROOPS AT THE MAIN GATE...
...TO GET BACK IN FORMATION.
WE'RE GOING IN ONCE MORE.
UH... C-CAPTAIN...?

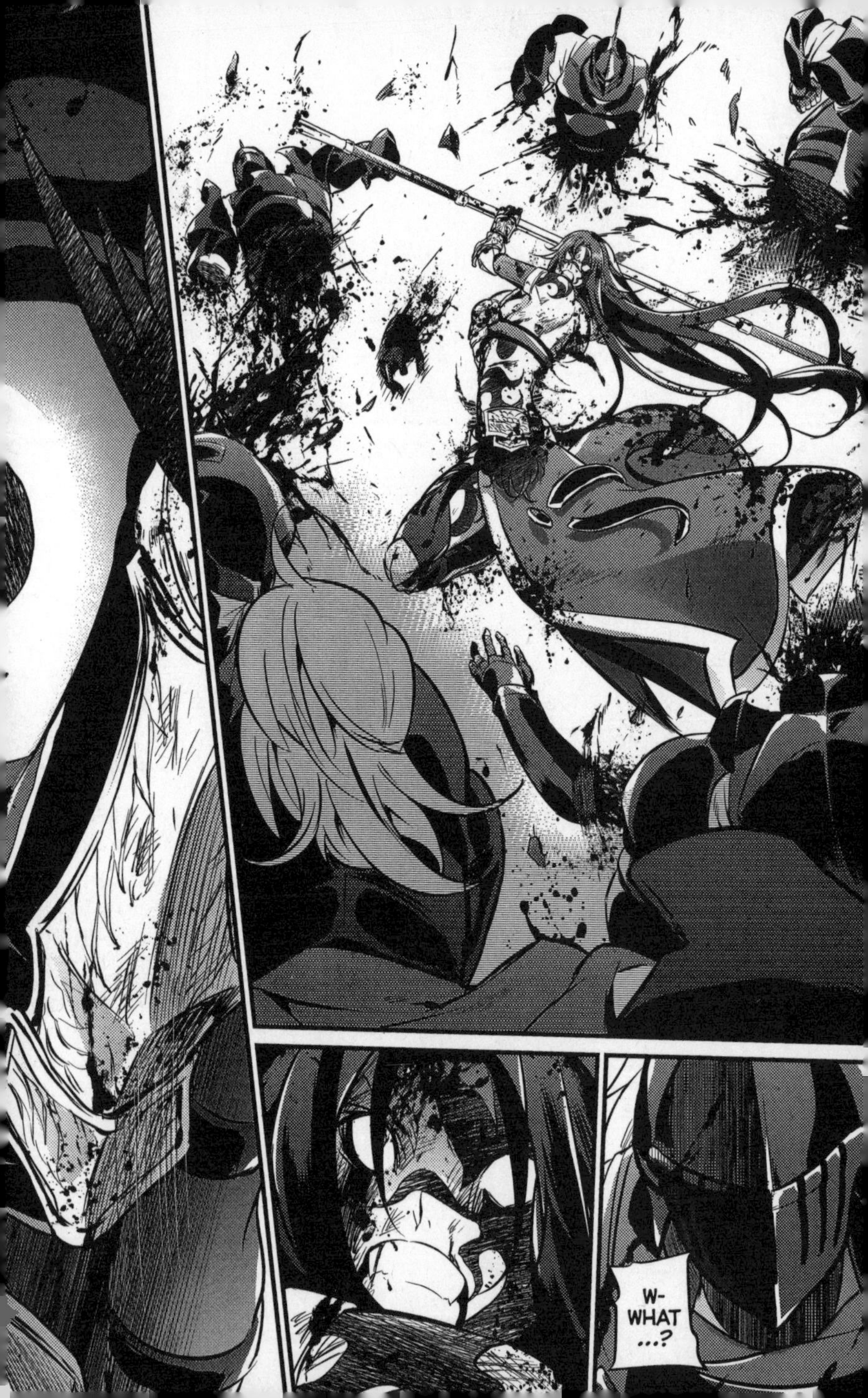
W-
WHAT
...?

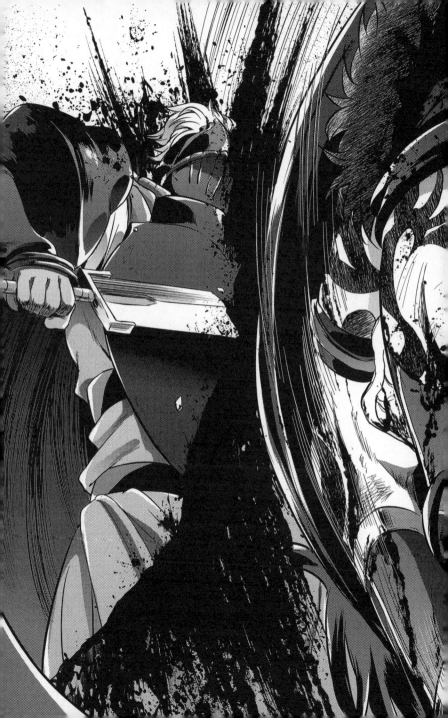

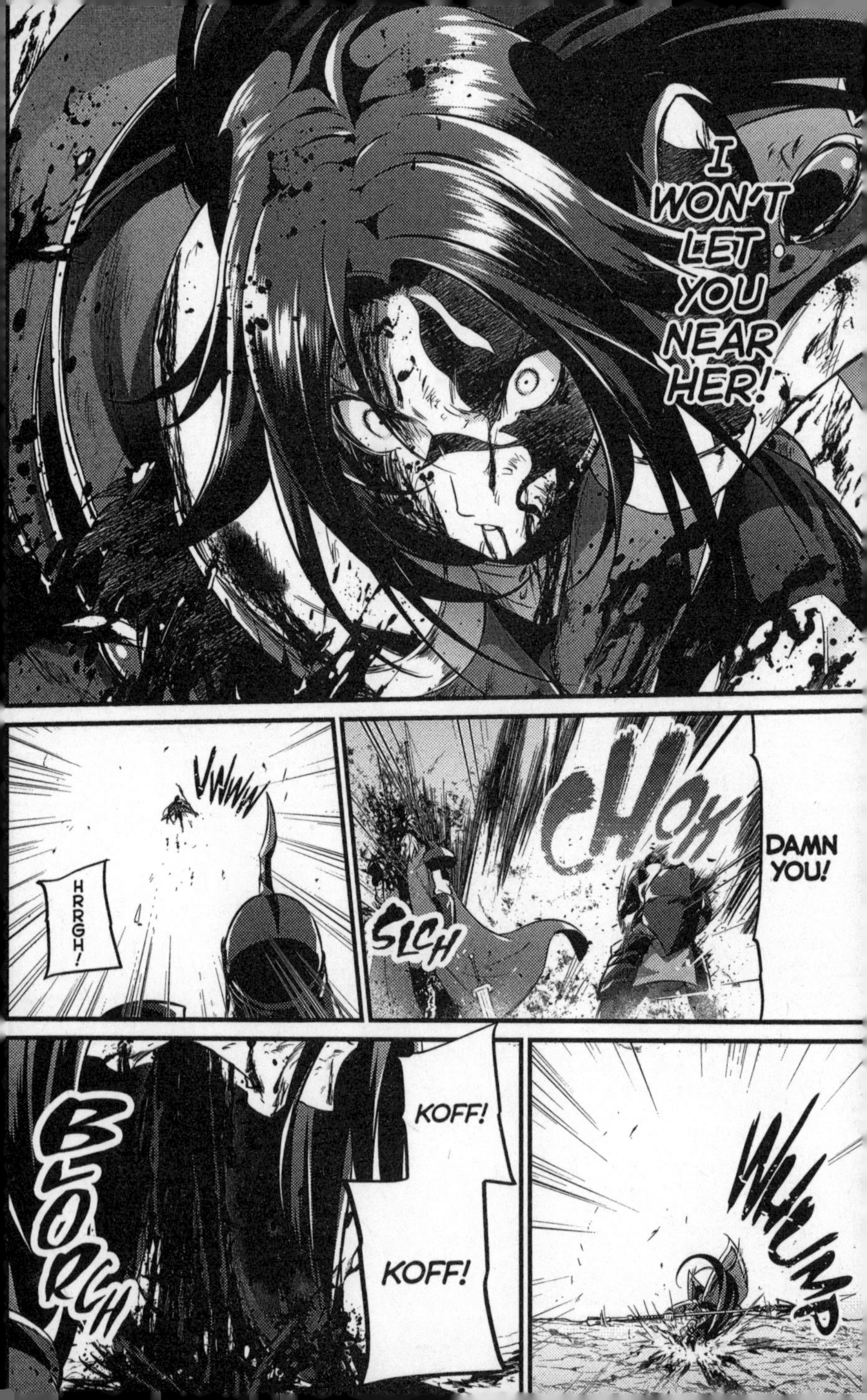
I WON'T LET YOU NEAR HER!
DAMN YOU!
SLCH
VWWW
HRRGH!
WHUMP
KOFF!
KOFF!

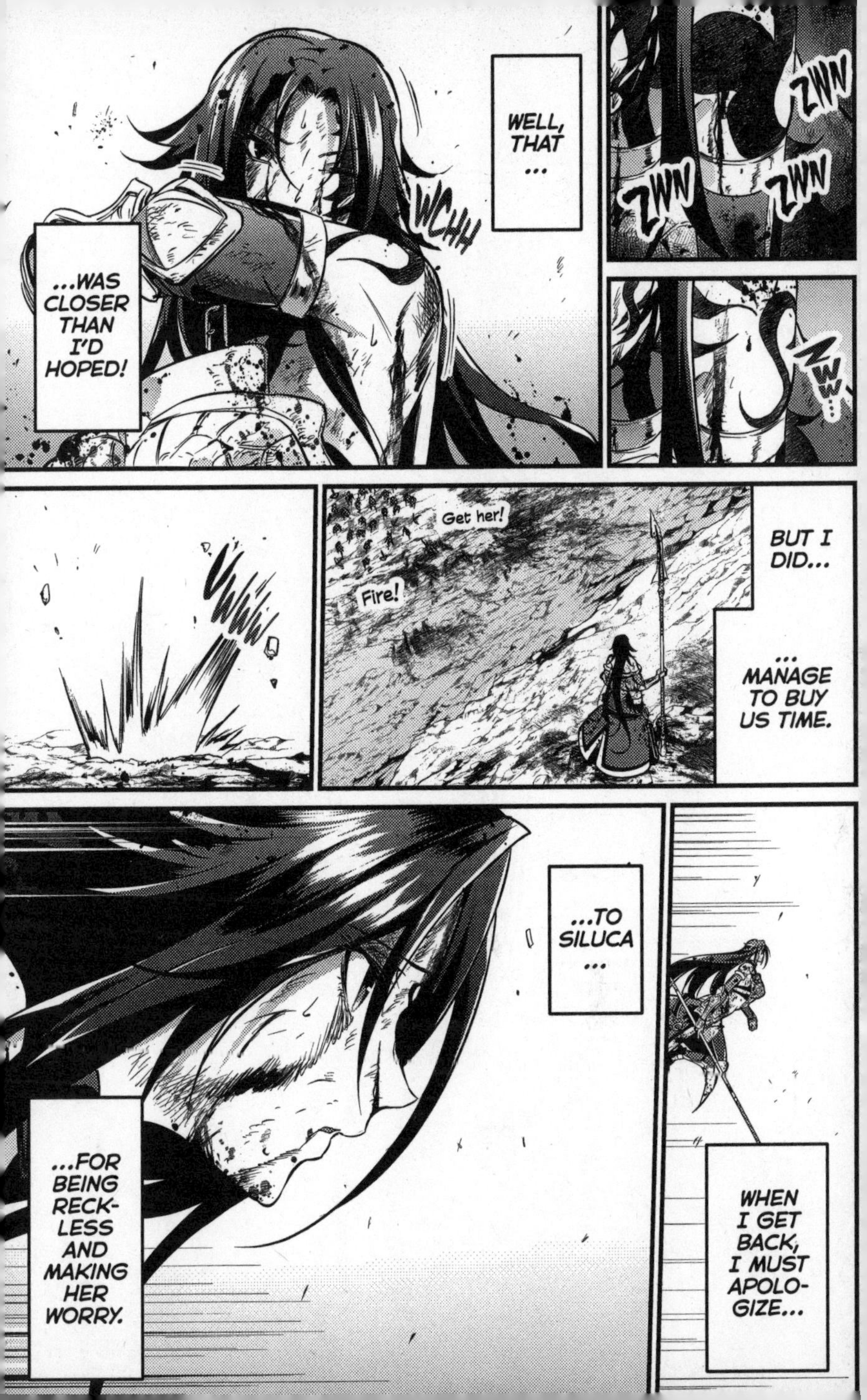
ZWN
ZWN
ZWN
ZWW...
WELL, THAT ...
WCHH
...WAS CLOSER THAN I'D HOPED!
BUT I DID...
Get her!
Fire!
... MANAGE TO BUY US TIME.
WHEN I GET BACK, I MUST APOLO-GIZE...
...TO SILUCA ...
...FOR BEING RECK-LESS AND MAKING HER WORRY.

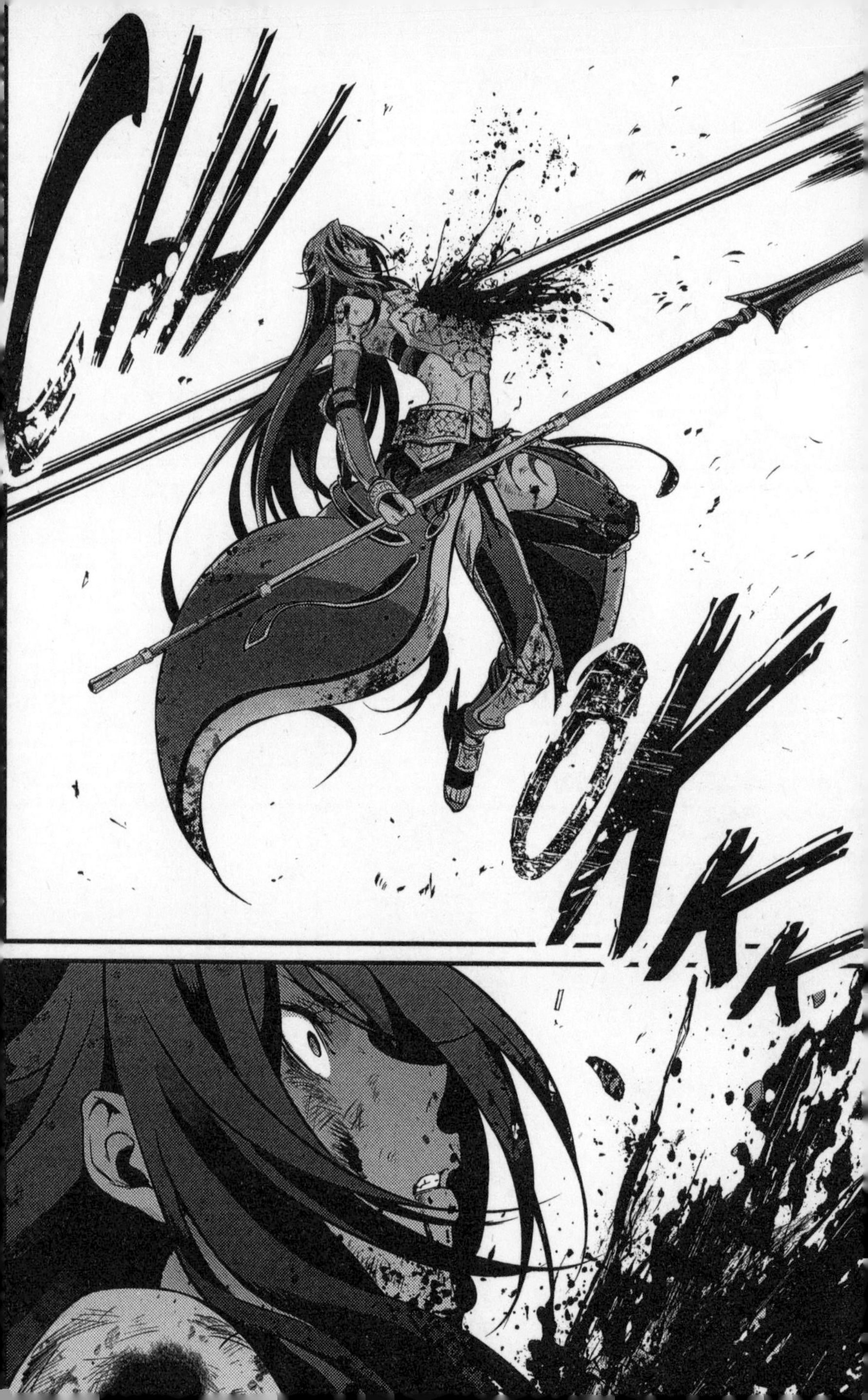
CHHOKK

RECORD OF
GRANCREST
—WAR—

RECORD OF
GRANCREST
WAR

M-MUST FOCUS THE CHAOS...

...AND REPAIR MY WOUNDS...

I NEED TO HEAL.

N-NOT... ENOUGH ...

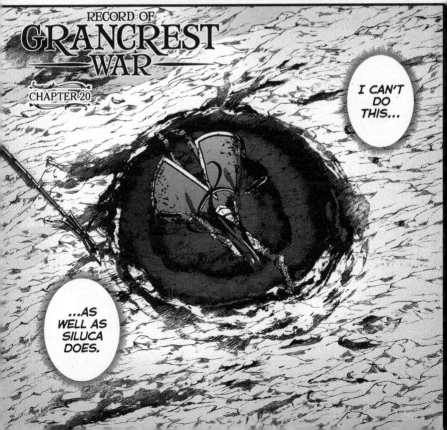

RECORD OF GRANCREST WAR

CHAPTER 20

I CAN'T DO THIS...

...AS WELL AS SILUCA DOES.

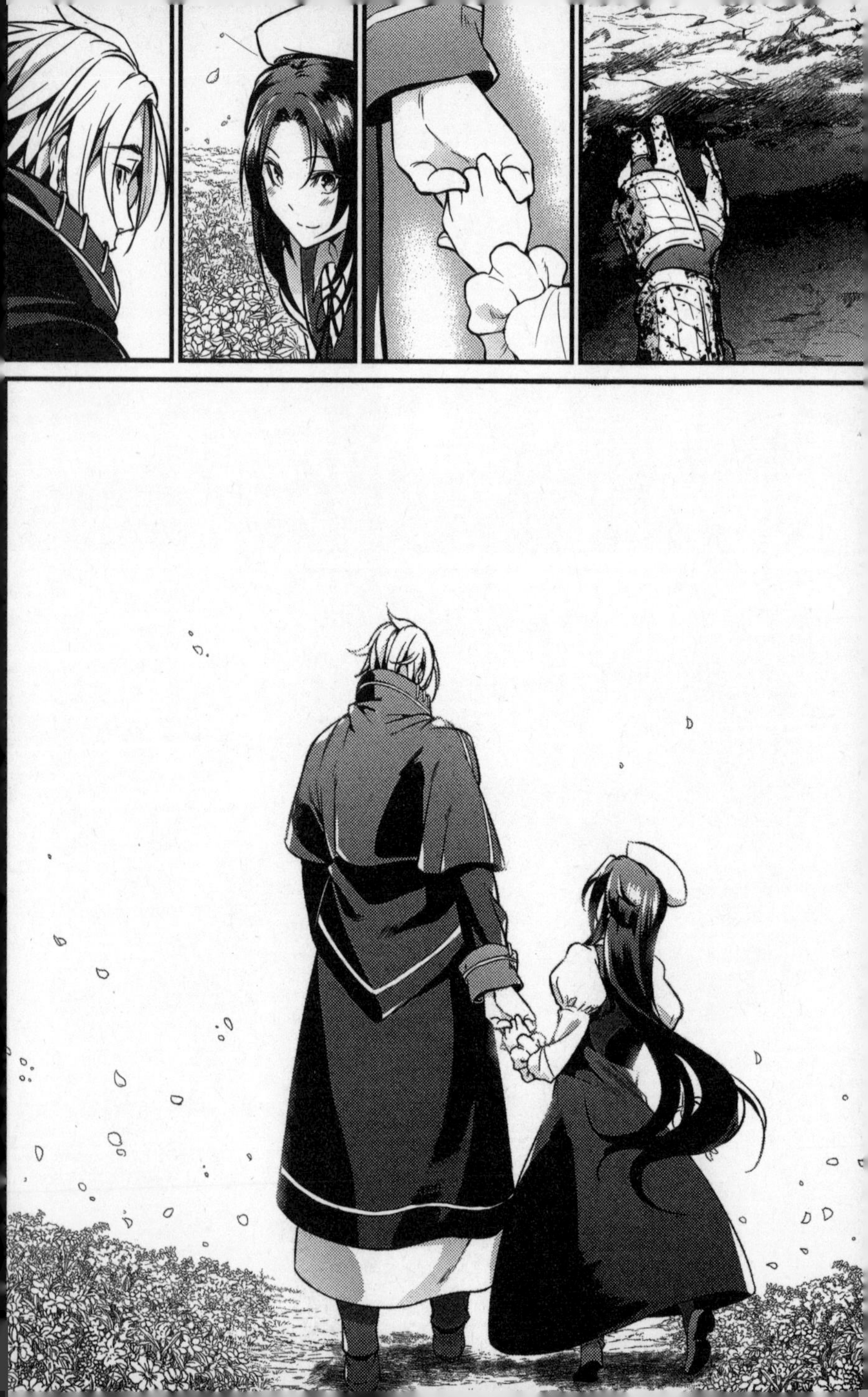

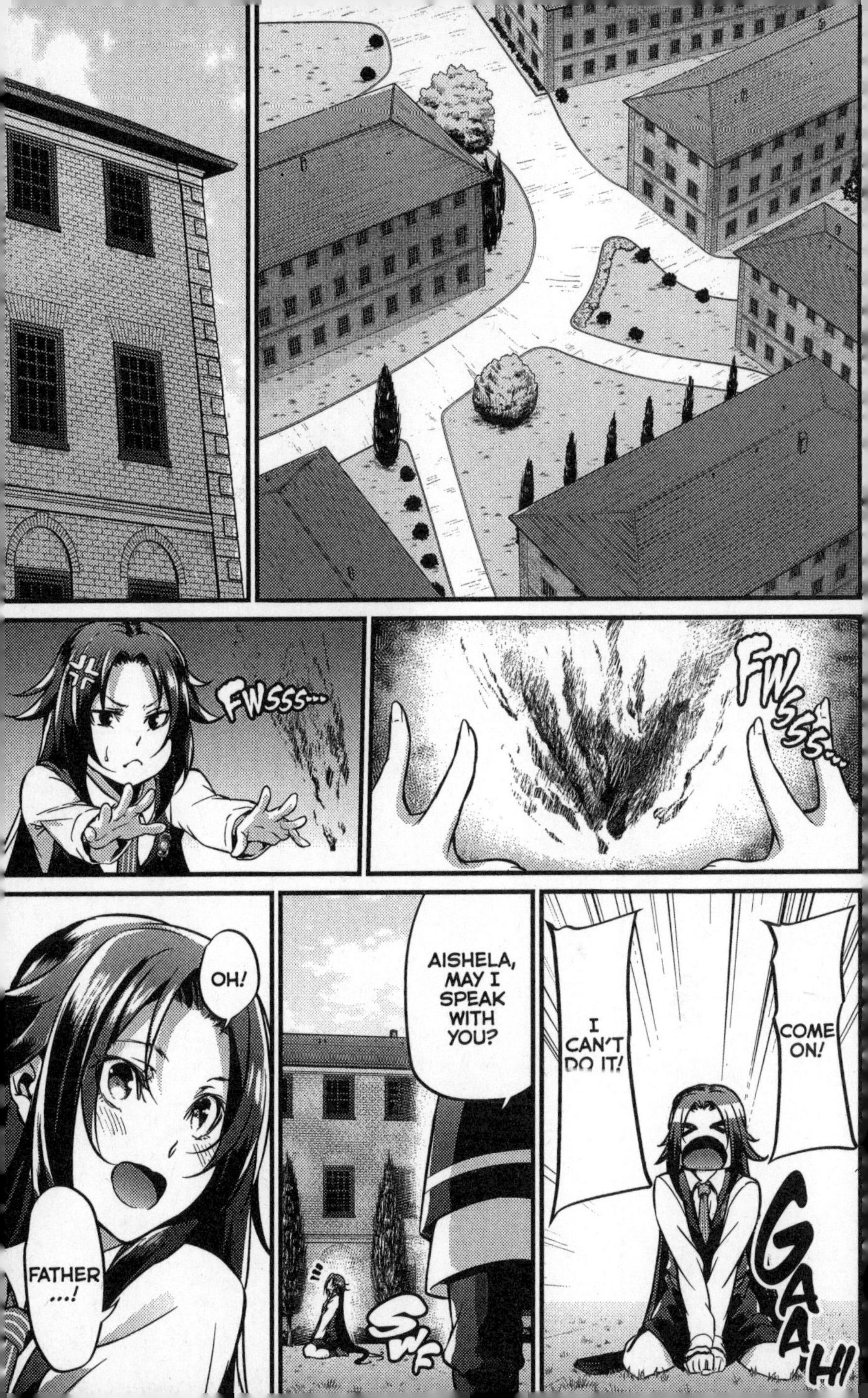
FWSSS...
FWSSS...
COME ON!
I CAN'T DO IT!
GAAH!!
AISHELA, MAY I SPEAK WITH YOU?
SWF
OH!
FATHER...!

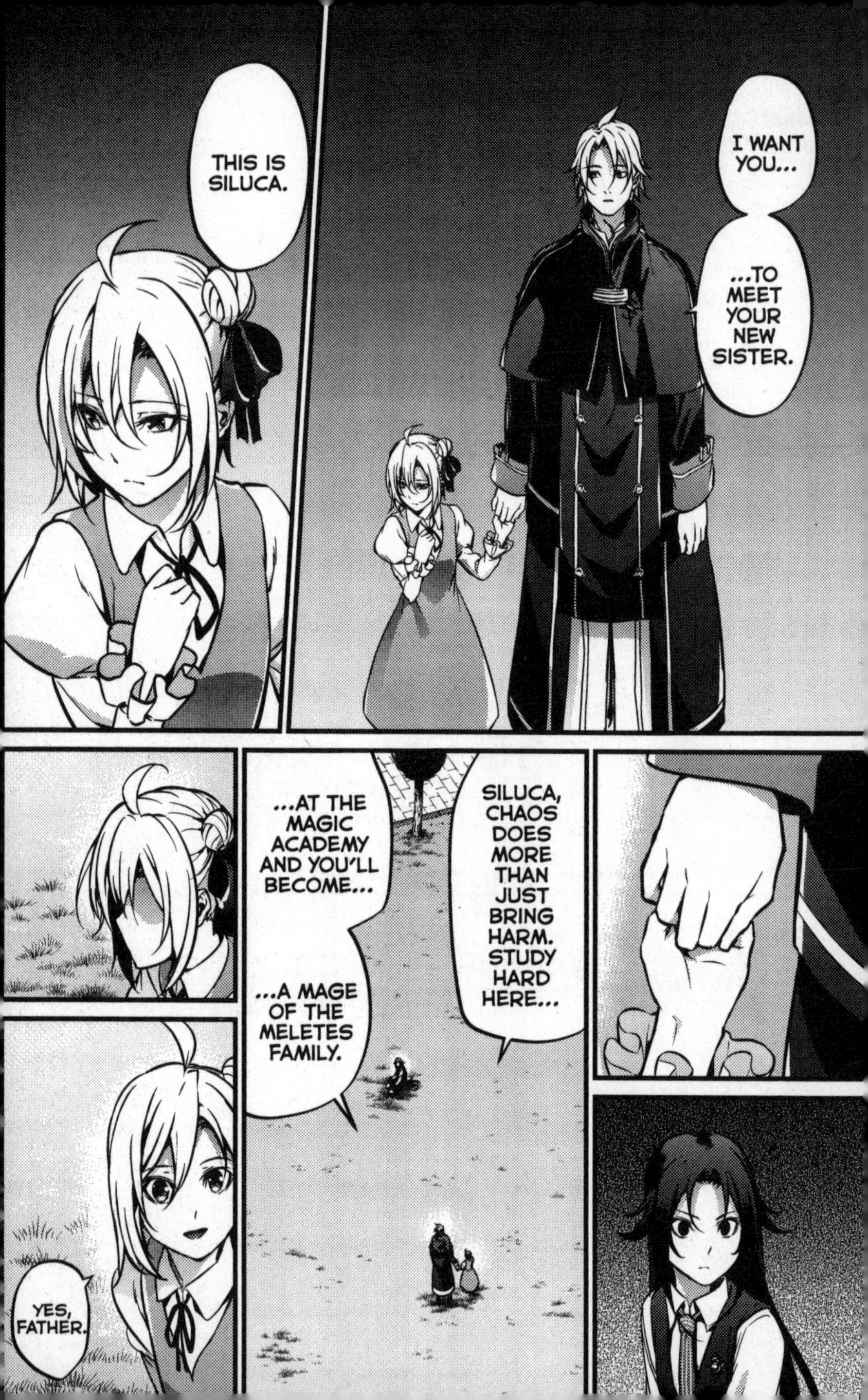
I WANT YOU...
...TO MEET YOUR NEW SISTER.
THIS IS SILUCA.
SILUCA, CHAOS DOES MORE THAN JUST BRING HARM. STUDY HARD HERE...
...AT THE MAGIC ACADEMY AND YOU'LL BECOME...
...A MAGE OF THE MELETES FAMILY.
YES, FATHER.

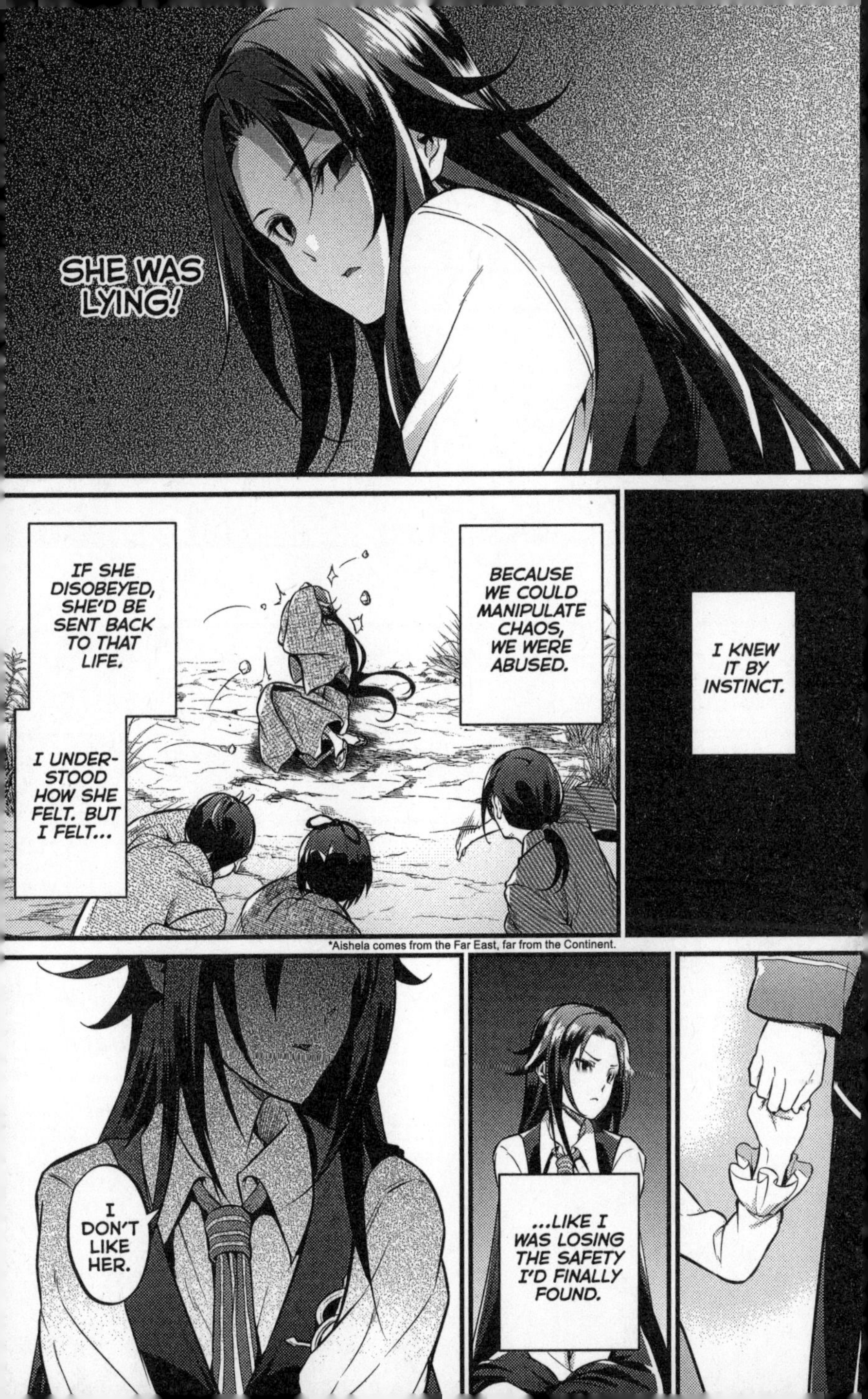
SHE WAS LYING!
I KNEW IT BY INSTINCT.
BECAUSE WE COULD MANIPULATE CHAOS, WE WERE ABUSED.
IF SHE DISOBEYED, SHE'D BE SENT BACK TO THAT LIFE.
I UNDER-STOOD HOW SHE FELT. BUT I FELT...
...LIKE I WAS LOSING THE SAFETY I'D FINALLY FOUND.
I DON'T LIKE HER.
*Aishela comes from the Far East, far from the Continent.

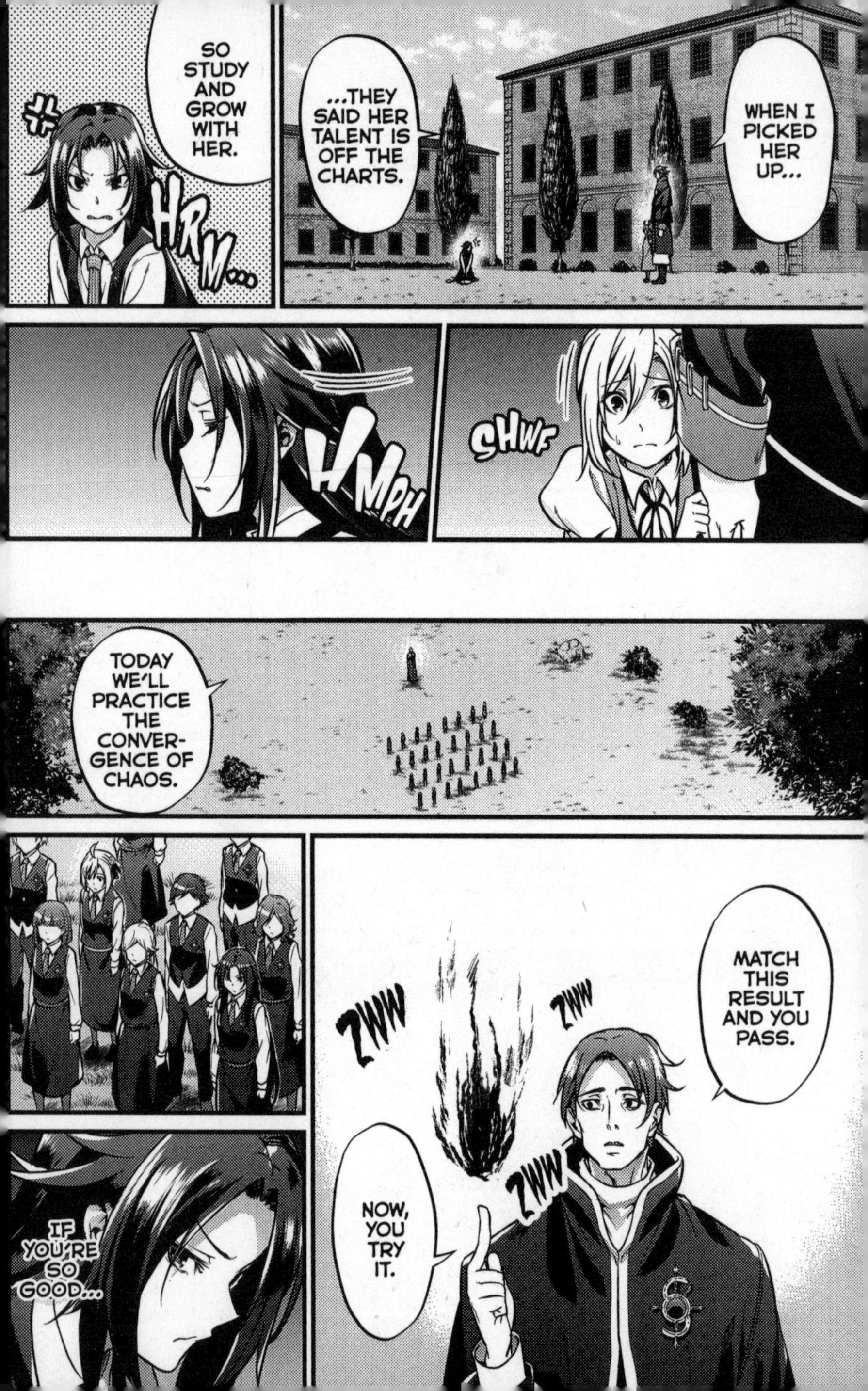
WHEN I PICKED HER UP...
...THEY SAID HER TALENT IS OFF THE CHARTS.
SO STUDY AND GROW WITH HER.
HRM...
SHWF
HMPH
TODAY WE'LL PRACTICE THE CONVERGENCE OF CHAOS.
MATCH THIS RESULT AND YOU PASS.
ZWW
ZWW
ZWW
NOW, YOU TRY IT.
IF YOU'RE SO GOOD...

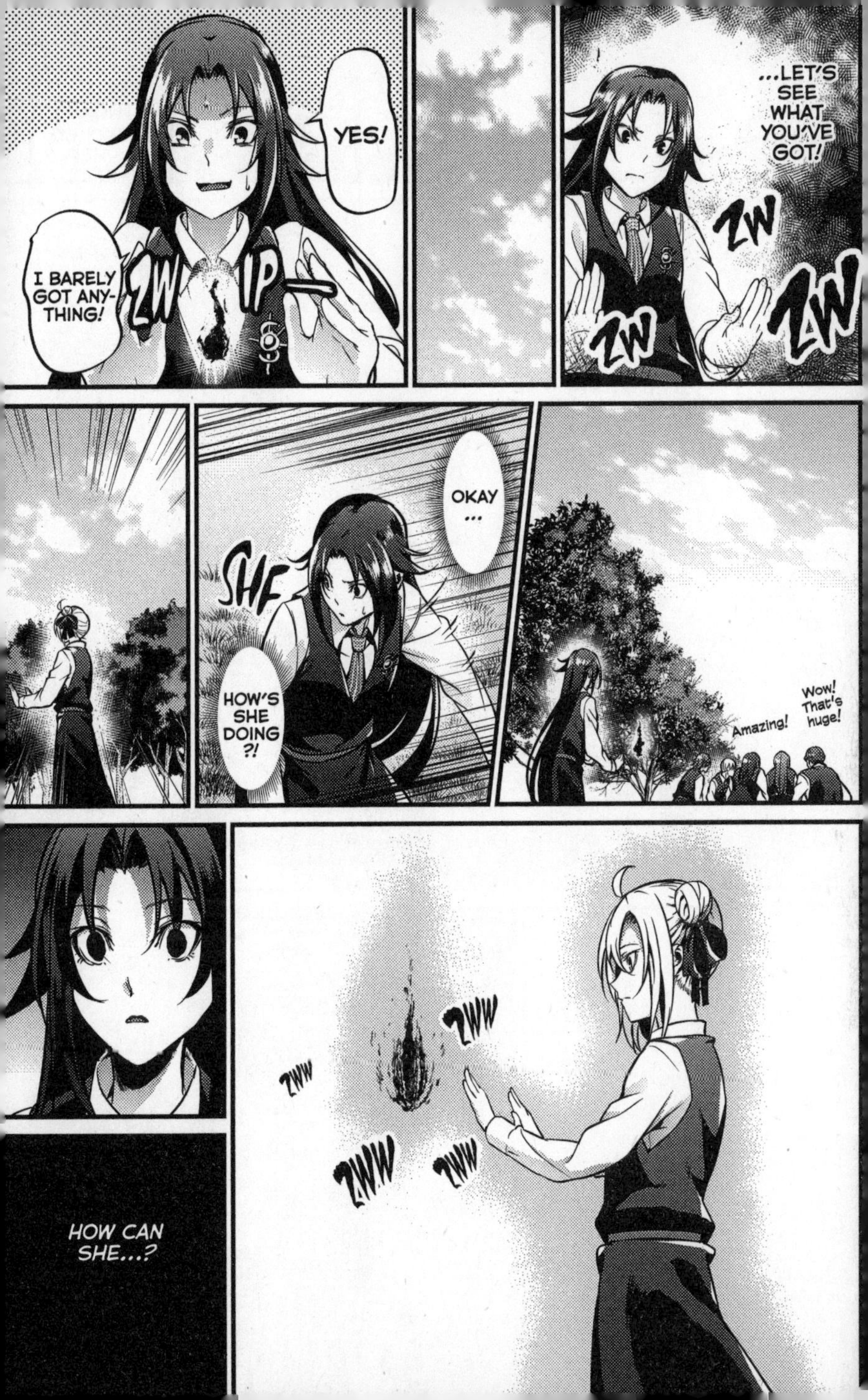

...LET'S SEE WHAT YOU'VE GOT!
ZW
ZW
ZW
YES!
ZWIP
I BARELY GOT ANYTHING!
Wow! That's huge!
Amazing!
OKAY ...
SHF
HOW'S SHE DOING ?!
ZWW
ZWW
ZWW
ZWW
HOW CAN SHE...?

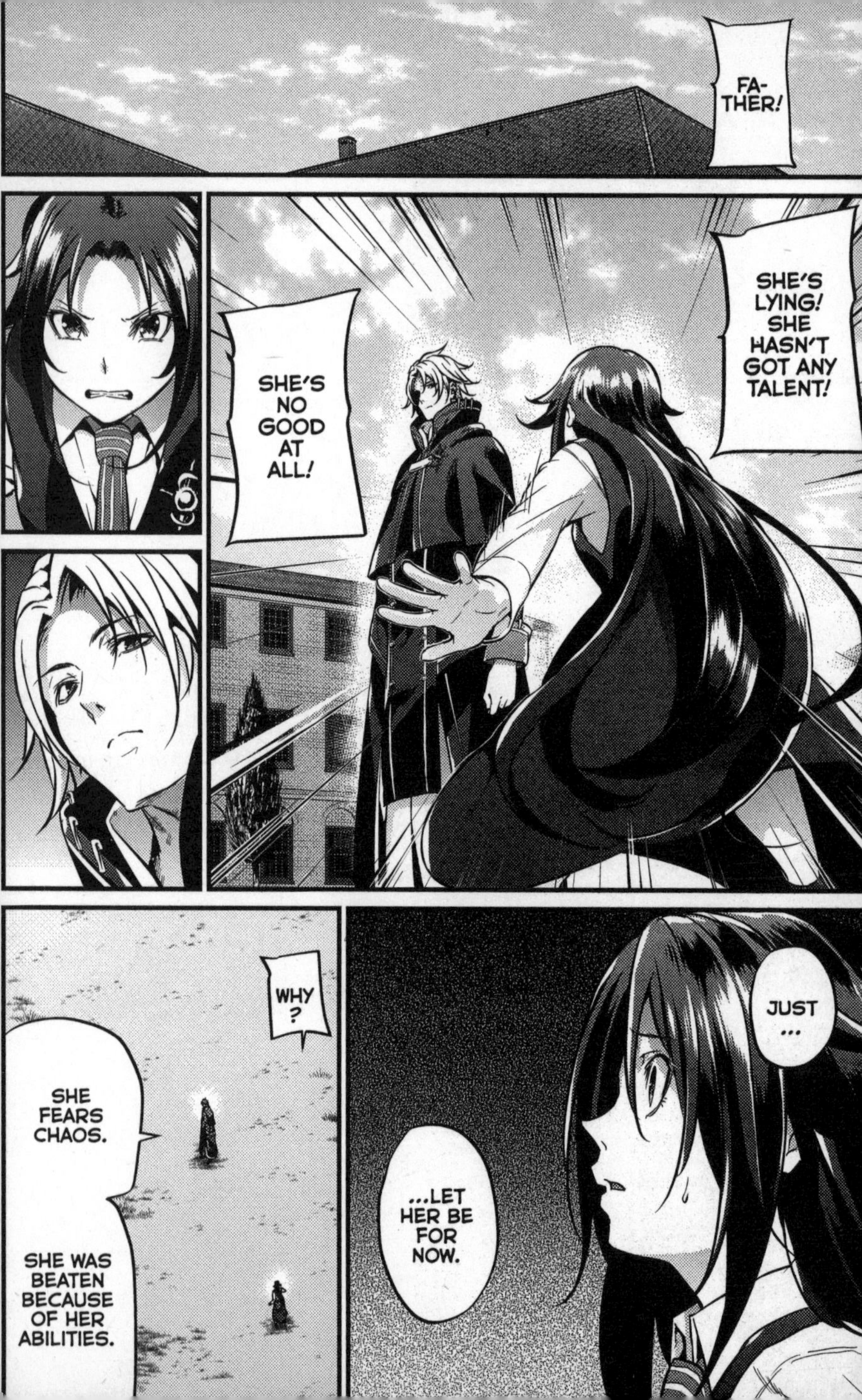
FA-THER!
SHE'S LYING! SHE HASN'T GOT ANY TALENT!
SHE'S NO GOOD AT ALL!
JUST...
...LET HER BE FOR NOW.
WHY?
SHE FEARS CHAOS.
SHE WAS BEATEN BECAUSE OF HER ABILITIES.

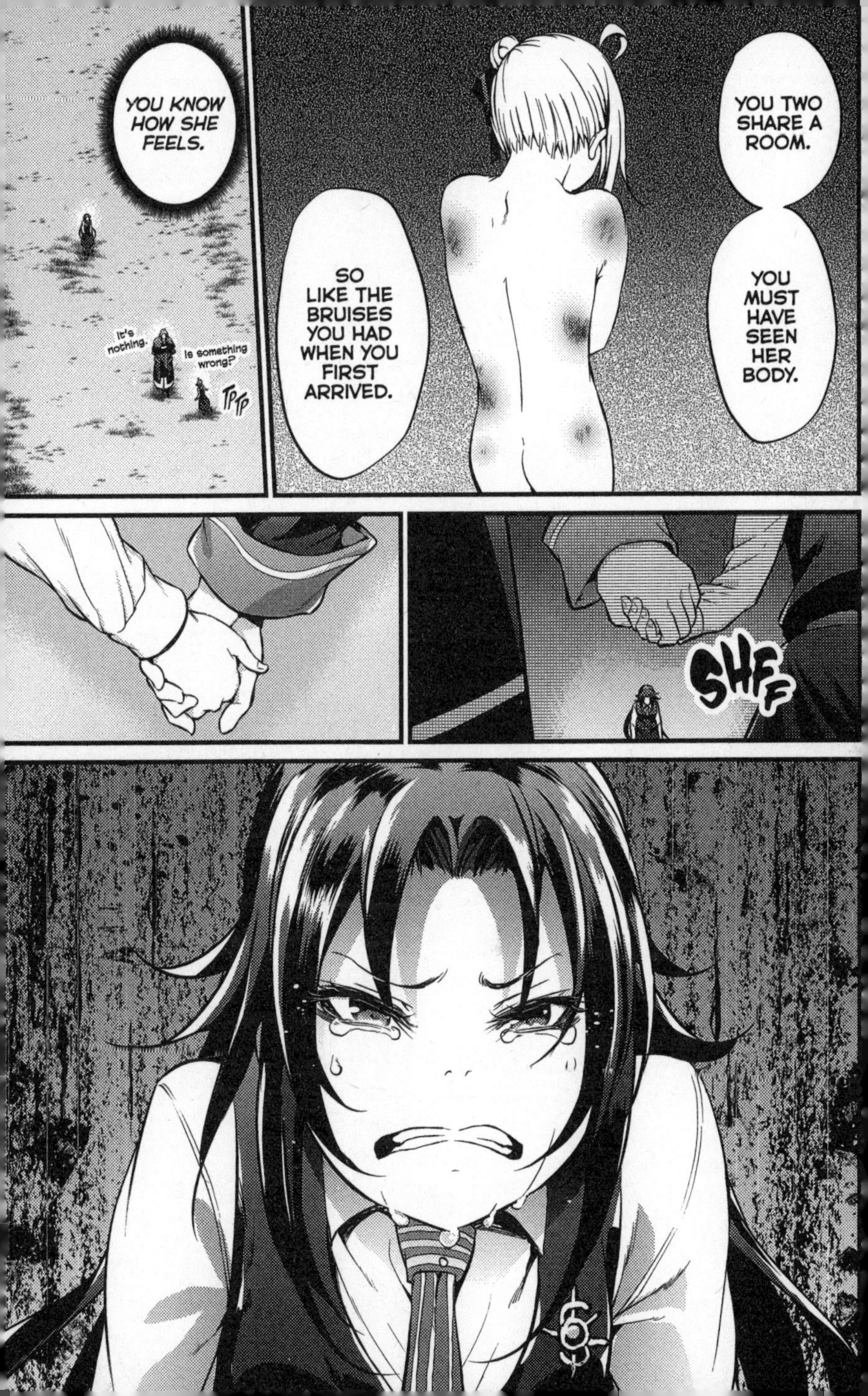
YOU TWO SHARE A ROOM.
YOU MUST HAVE SEEN HER BODY.
SO LIKE THE BRUISES YOU HAD WHEN YOU FIRST ARRIVED.
YOU KNOW HOW SHE FEELS.
Is something wrong?
It's nothing.
TP TP
SHFF

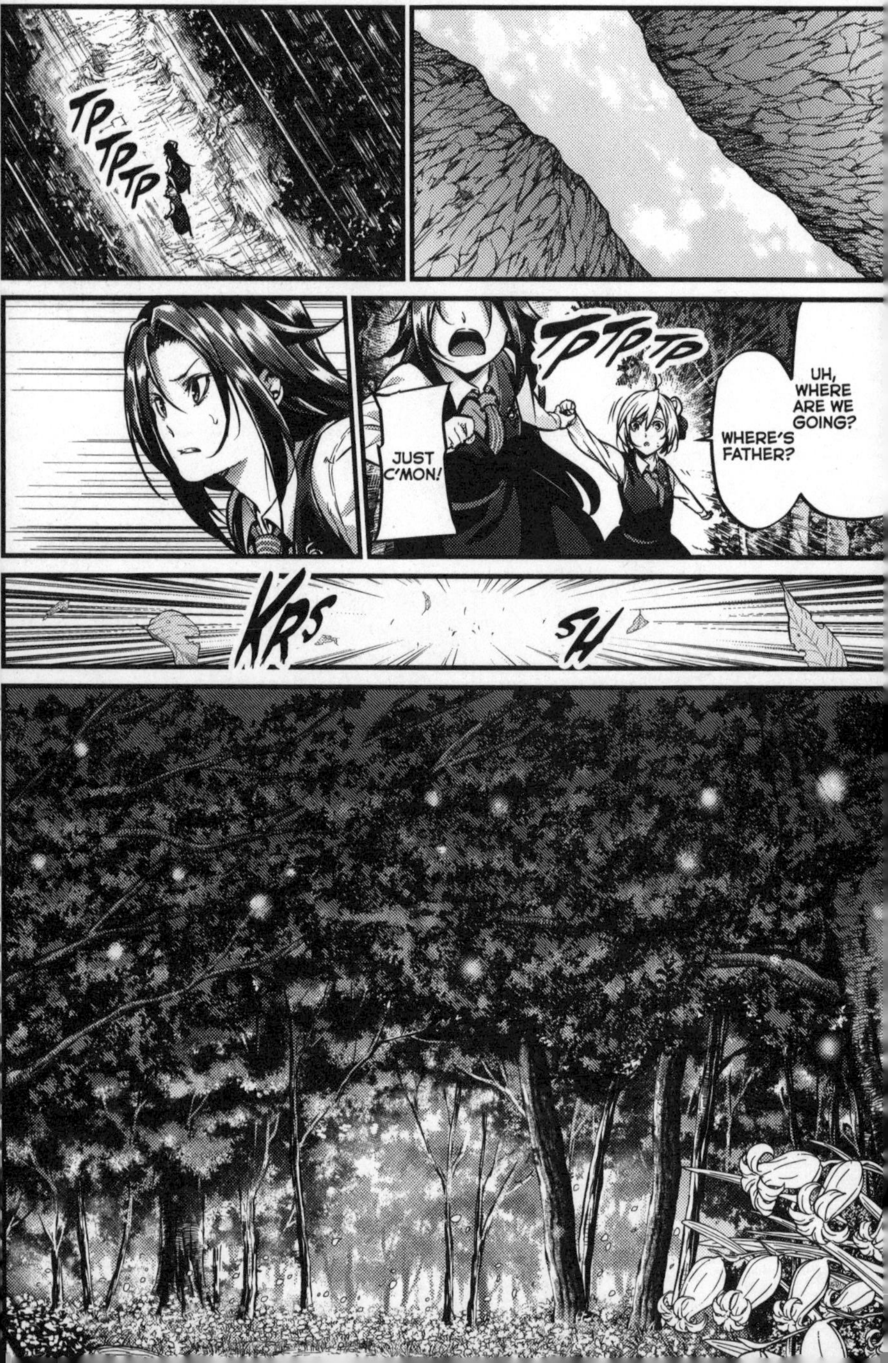
TPTPTP
UH, WHERE ARE WE GOING?
WHERE'S FATHER?
JUST C'MON!
KRSSH

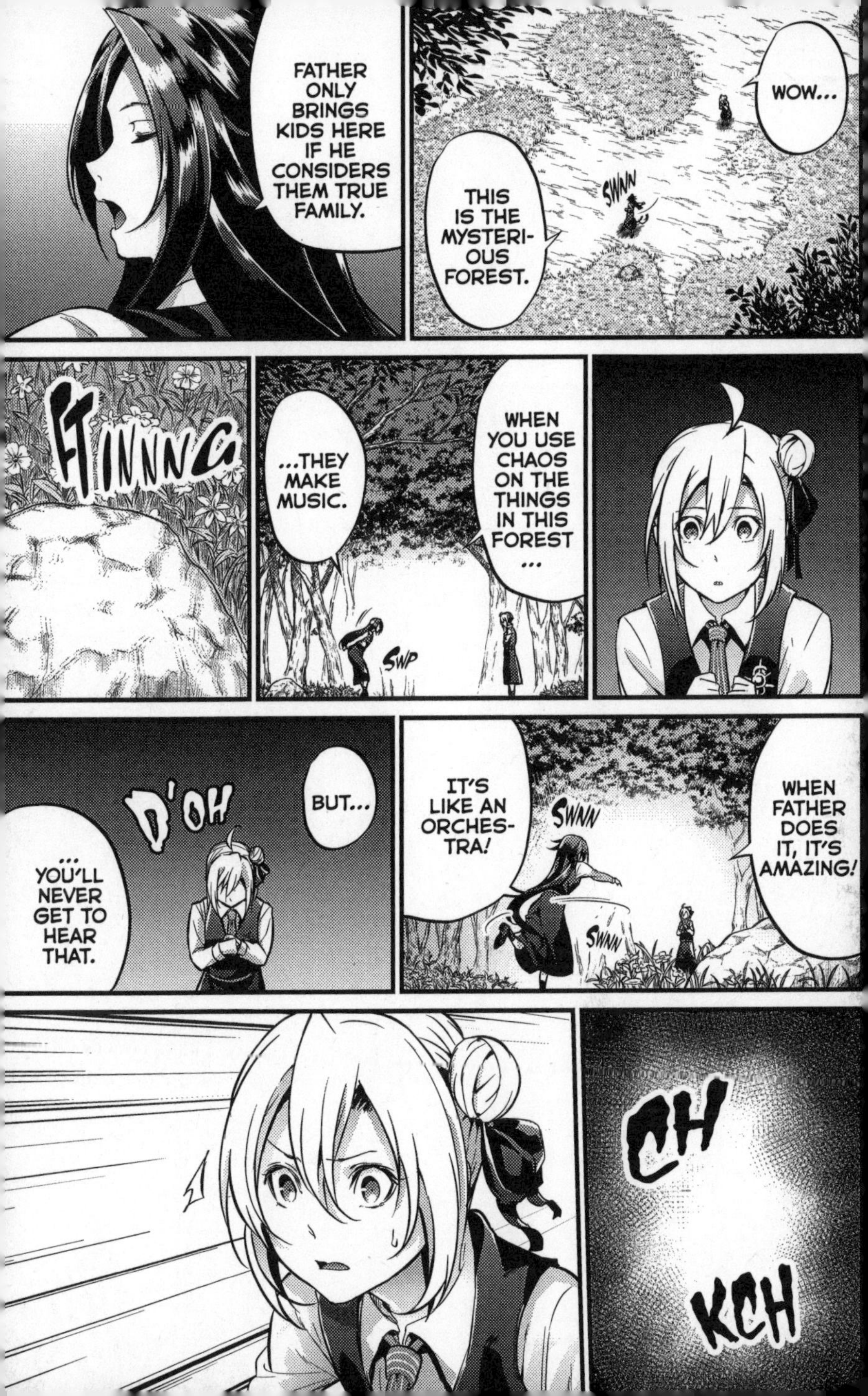
WOW...
SWNN
THIS IS THE MYSTERIOUS FOREST.
FATHER ONLY BRINGS KIDS HERE IF HE CONSIDERS THEM TRUE FAMILY.
WHEN YOU USE CHAOS ON THE THINGS IN THIS FOREST...
...THEY MAKE MUSIC.
SWP
FTINNG
WHEN FATHER DOES IT, IT'S AMAZING!
IT'S LIKE AN ORCHESTRA!
SWNN
SWNN
BUT...
D'OH
...YOU'LL NEVER GET TO HEAR THAT.
CH
KCH

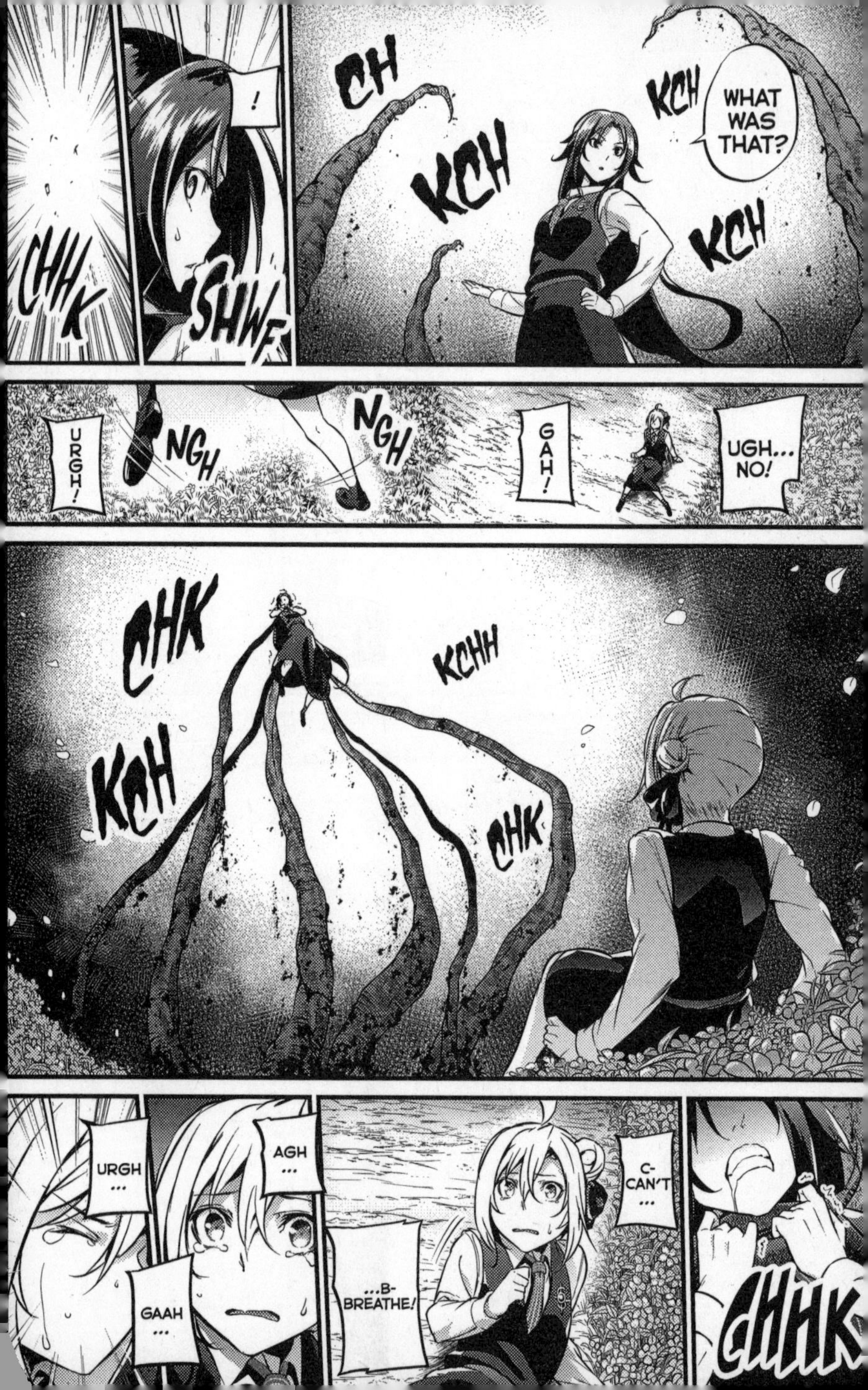
WHAT WAS THAT?
KCH
CH
KCH
KCH
!
SHWF
CHHK
UGH... NO!
GAH!
NGH
NGH
URGH!
KCHH
CHK
KCH
CHK
CHHK
C-CAN'T...
...B-BREATHE!
AGH...
GAAH...
URGH...

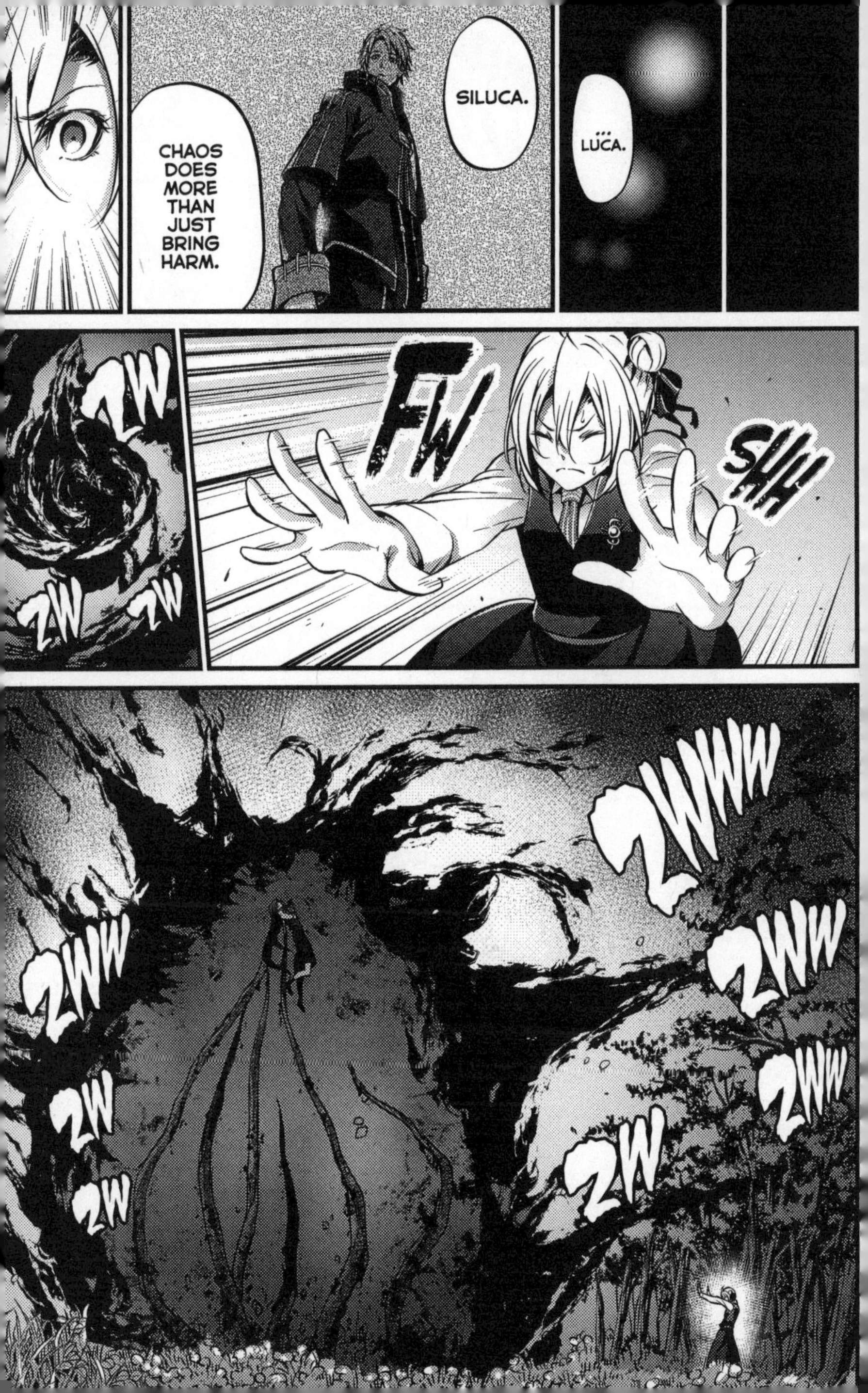

... LUCA.
SILUCA.
CHAOS DOES MORE THAN JUST BRING HARM.
SHH
FW
ZW
ZW
ZW
ZWWW
ZWW
ZWW
ZW
ZWW
ZW
ZW

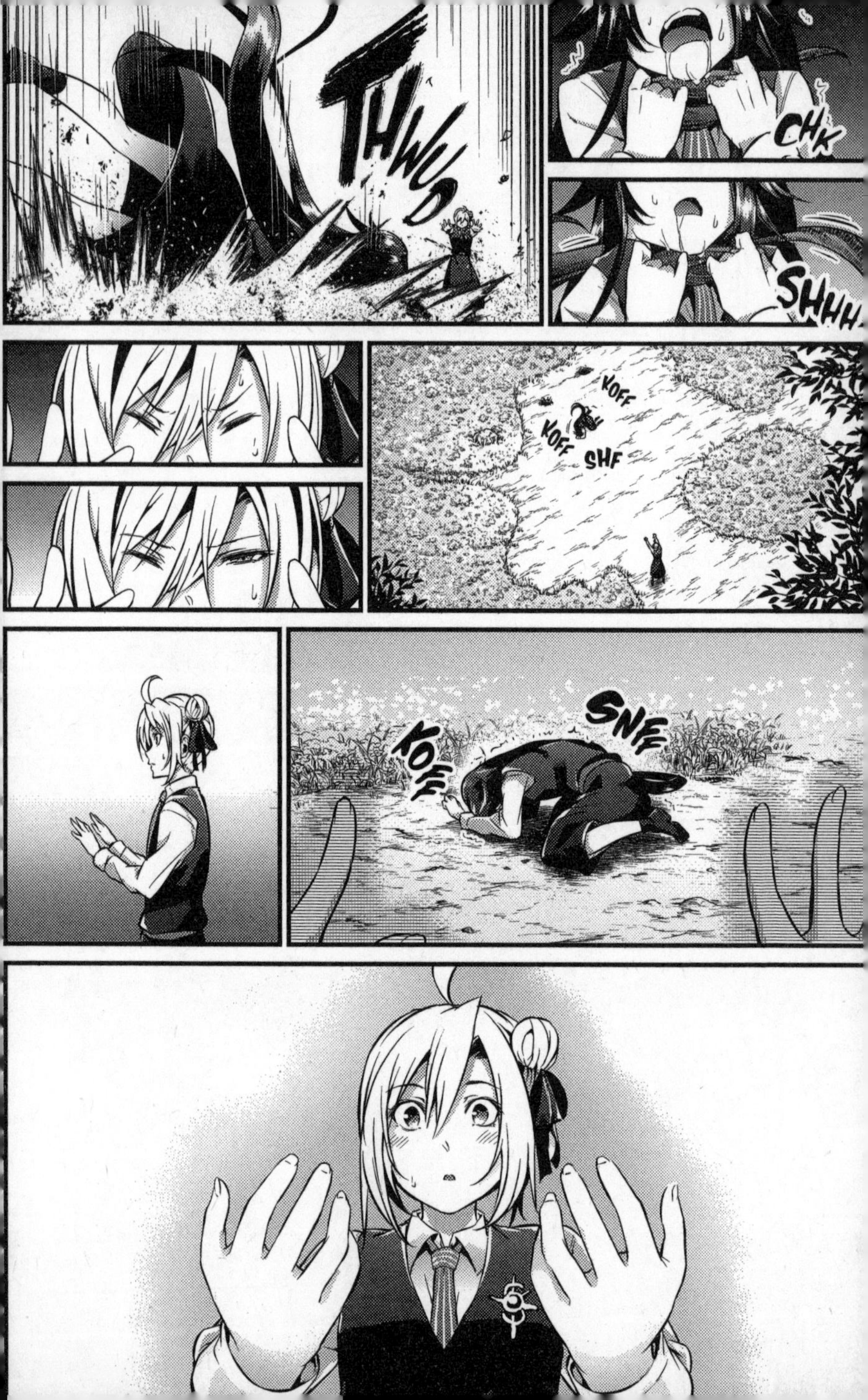
CHK
SHHH
THWUD
KOFF
KOFF
SHF
SNFF
KOFF

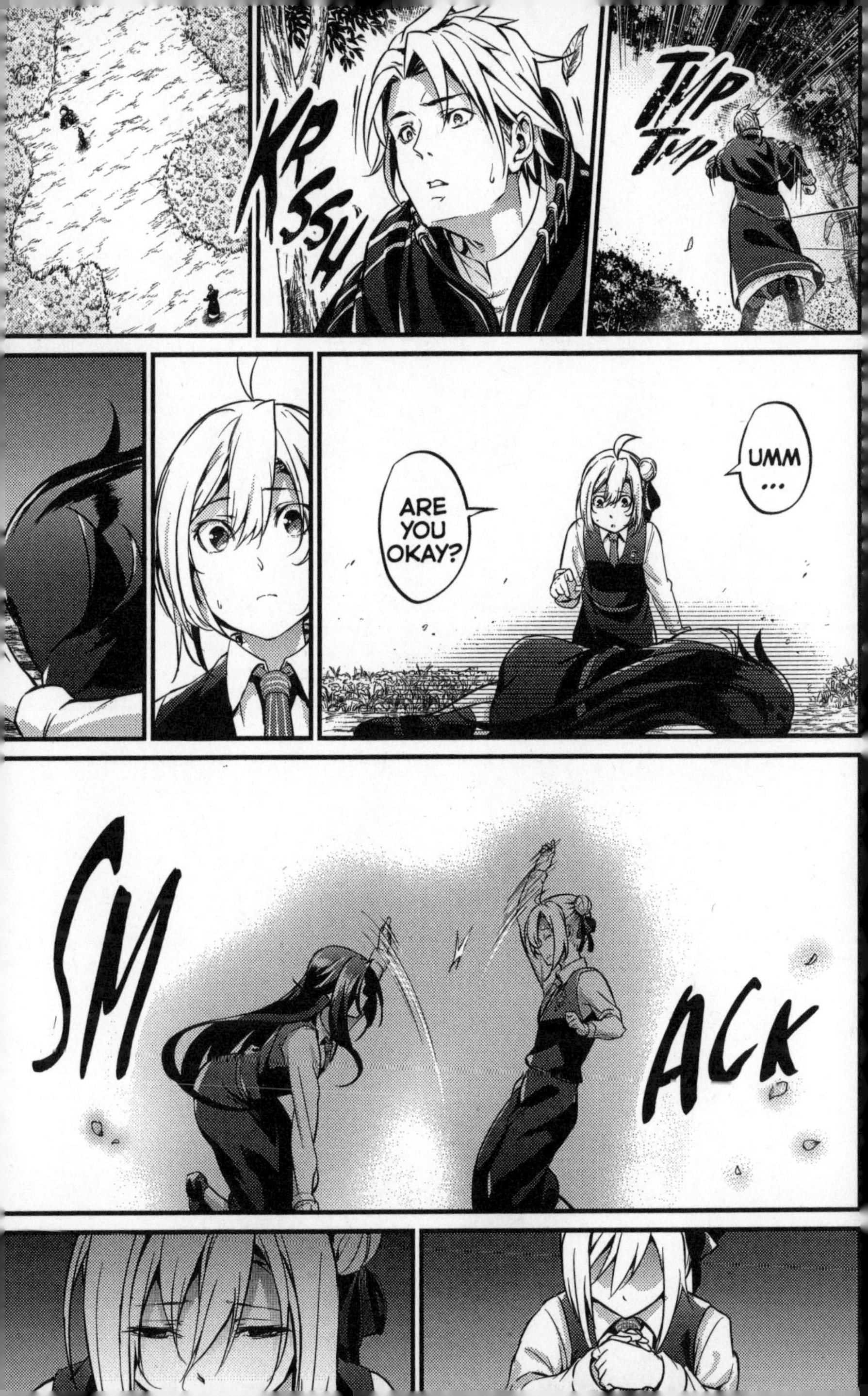
TMP TMP
KRSSH
UMM ...
ARE YOU OKAY?
SMACK

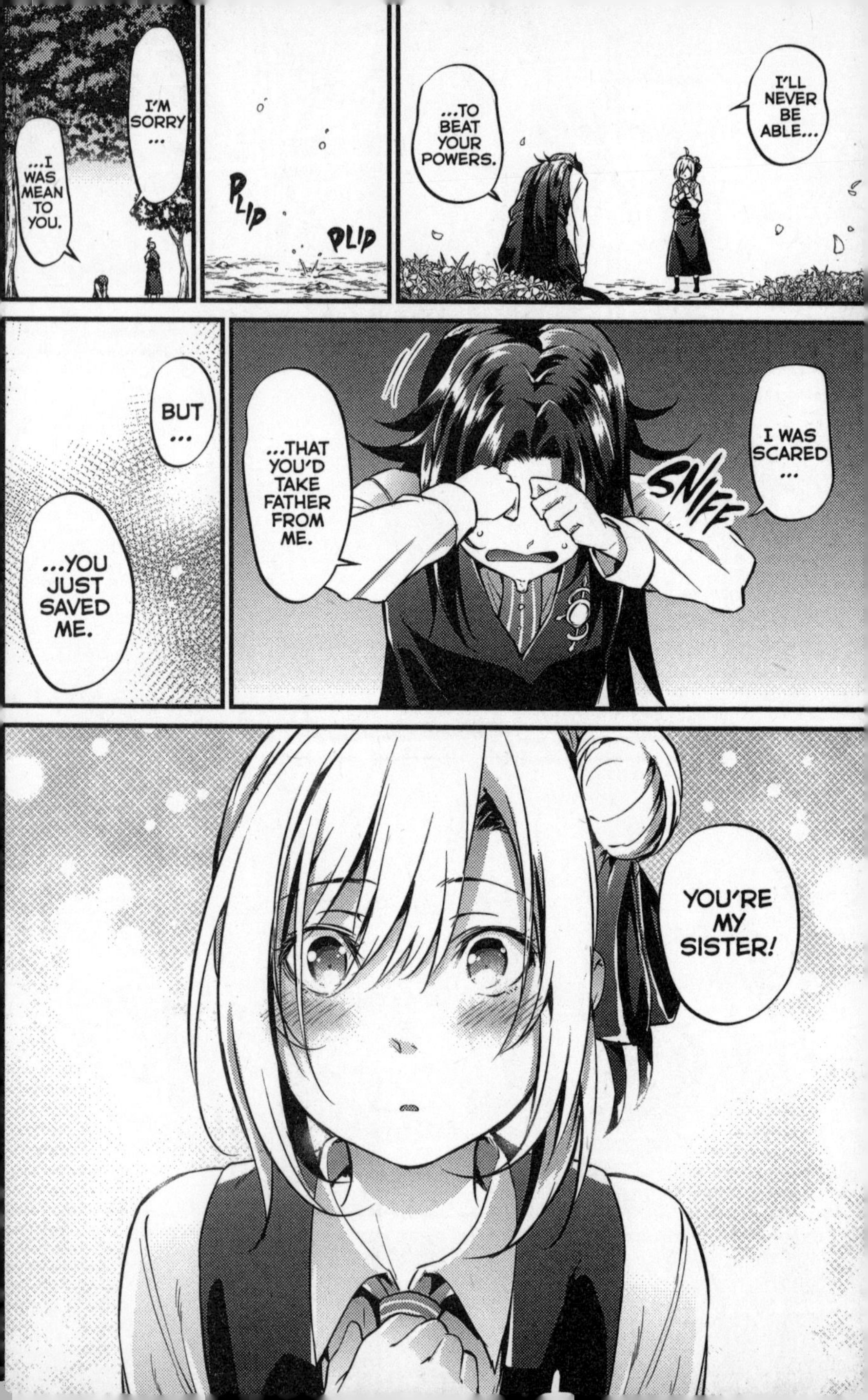
I'LL NEVER BE ABLE...
...TO BEAT YOUR POWERS.
PLIP
PLIP
I'M SORRY...
...I WAS MEAN TO YOU.
I WAS SCARED...
SNIFF
...THAT YOU'D TAKE FATHER FROM ME.
BUT...
...YOU JUST SAVED ME.
YOU'RE MY SISTER!

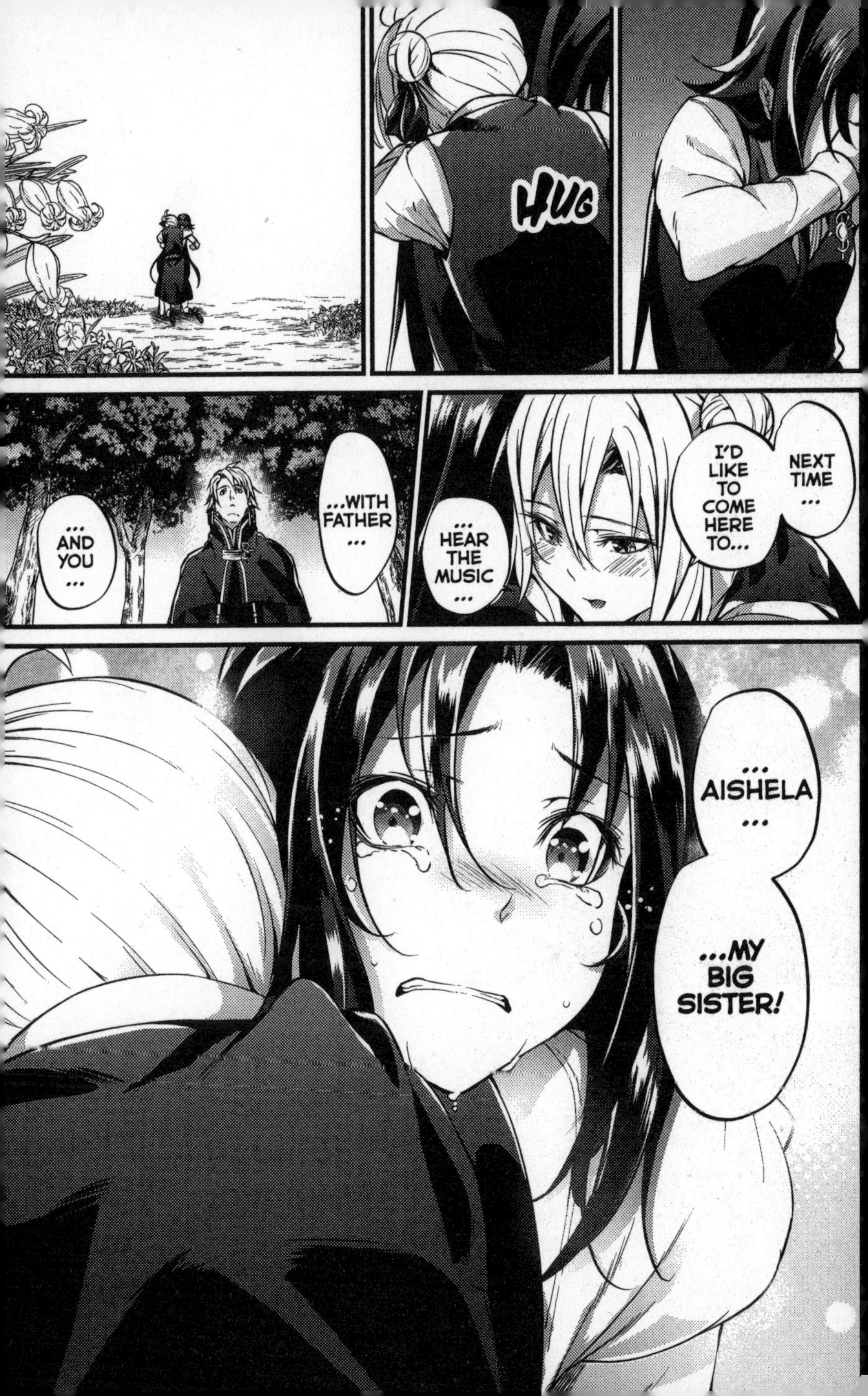
HUG
NEXT TIME ...
I'D LIKE TO COME HERE TO...
... HEAR THE MUSIC ...
...WITH FATHER ...
... AND YOU ...
... AISHELA ...
...MY BIG SISTER!

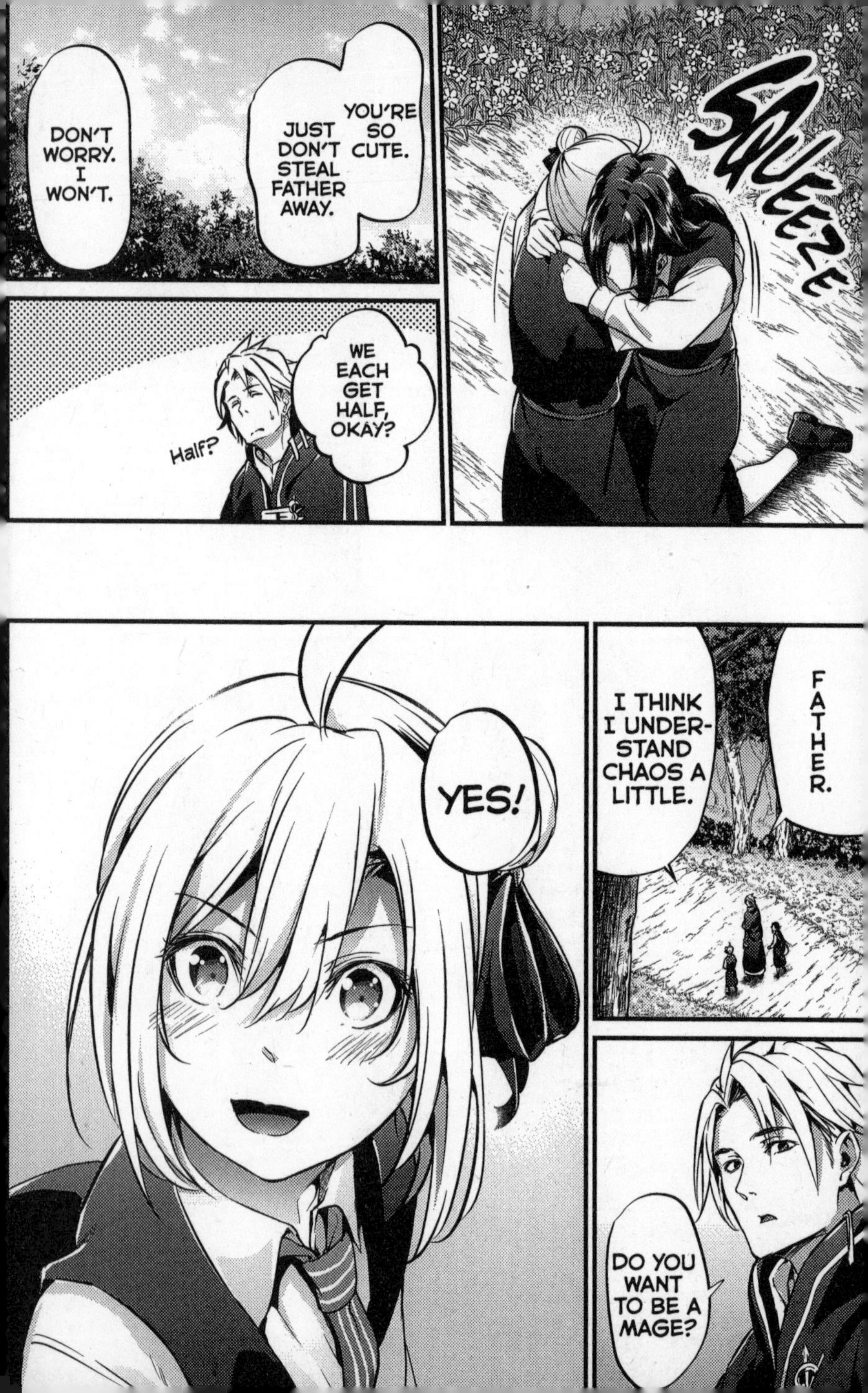
SQUEEZE
YOU'RE SO CUTE. JUST DON'T STEAL FATHER AWAY.
DON'T WORRY. I WON'T.
WE EACH GET HALF, OKAY?
Half?
FATHER.
I THINK I UNDERSTAND CHAOS A LITTLE.
DO YOU WANT TO BE A MAGE?
YES!

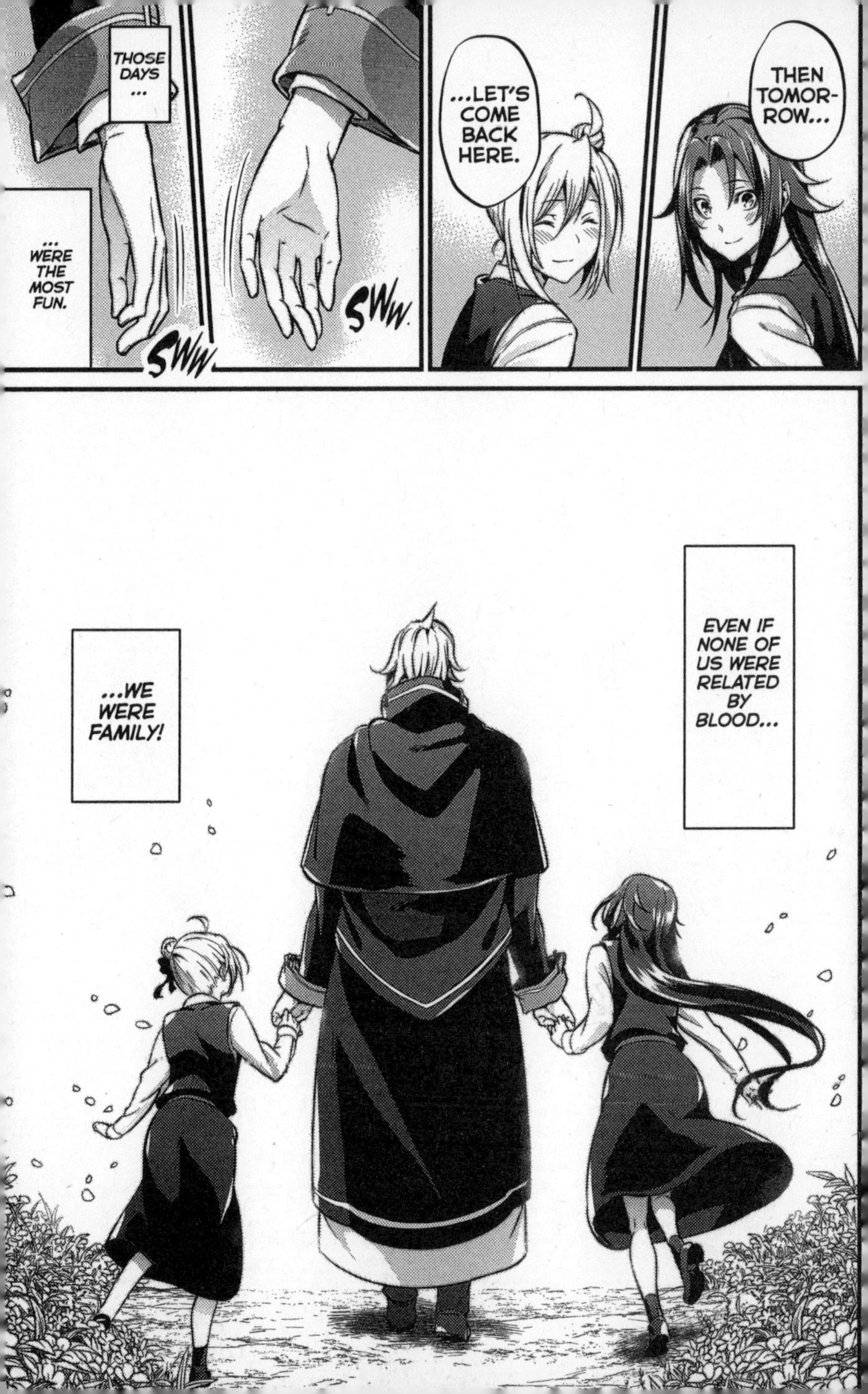
THEN TOMORROW...
...LET'S COME BACK HERE.
THOSE DAYS...
SWW
...WERE THE MOST FUN.
SWW
EVEN IF NONE OF US WERE RELATED BY BLOOD...
...WE WERE FAMILY!

RECORD OF
GRANCREST
WAR

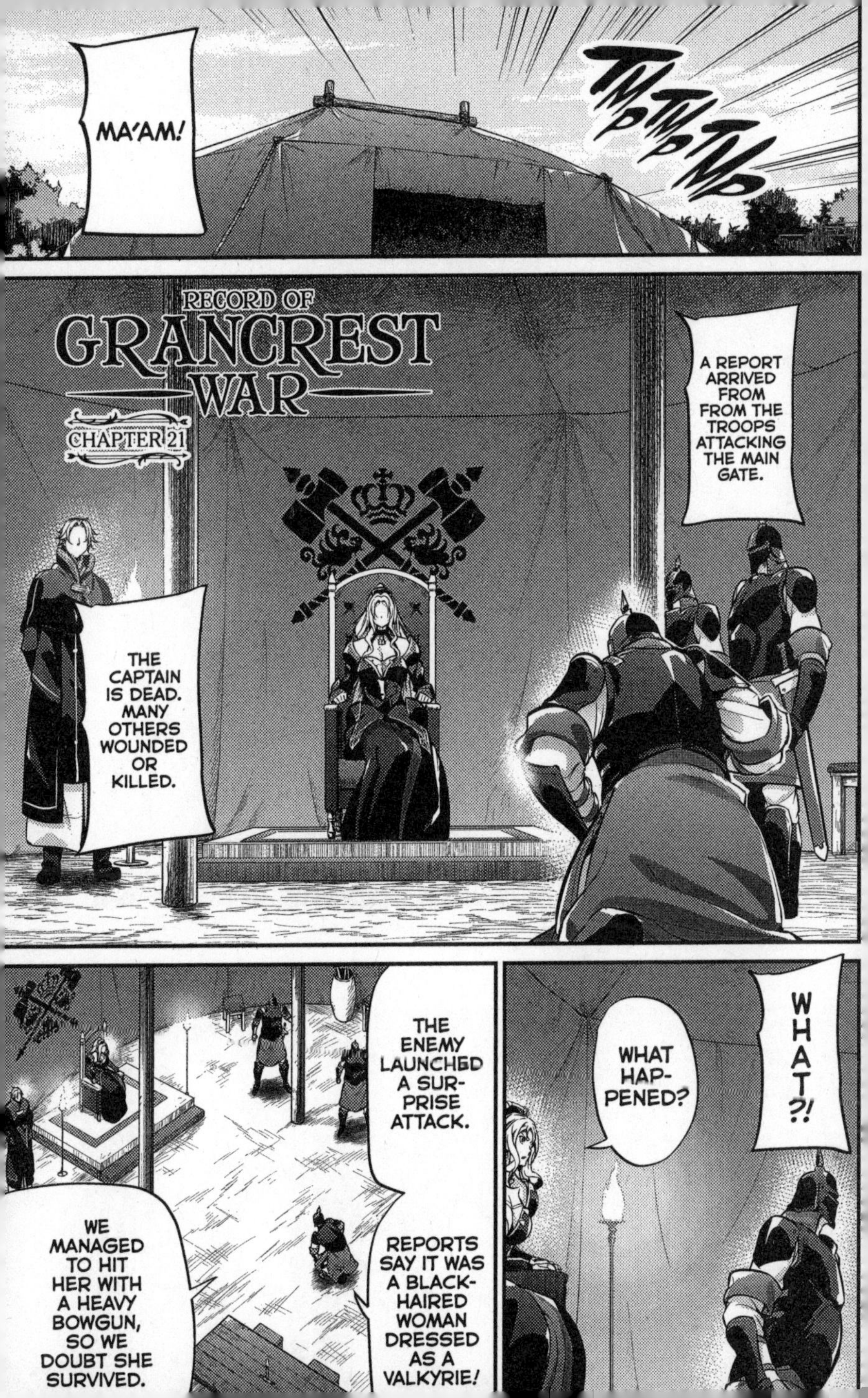
TMP TMP TMP TMP
MA'AM!
RECORD OF GRANCREST WAR
CHAPTER 21
A REPORT ARRIVED FROM FROM THE TROOPS ATTACKING THE MAIN GATE.
THE CAPTAIN IS DEAD. MANY OTHERS WOUNDED OR KILLED.
WHAT?!
WHAT HAPPENED?
THE ENEMY LAUNCHED A SURPRISE ATTACK.
REPORTS SAY IT WAS A BLACK-HAIRED WOMAN DRESSED AS A VALKYRIE!
WE MANAGED TO HIT HER WITH A HEAVY BOWGUN, SO WE DOUBT SHE SURVIVED.

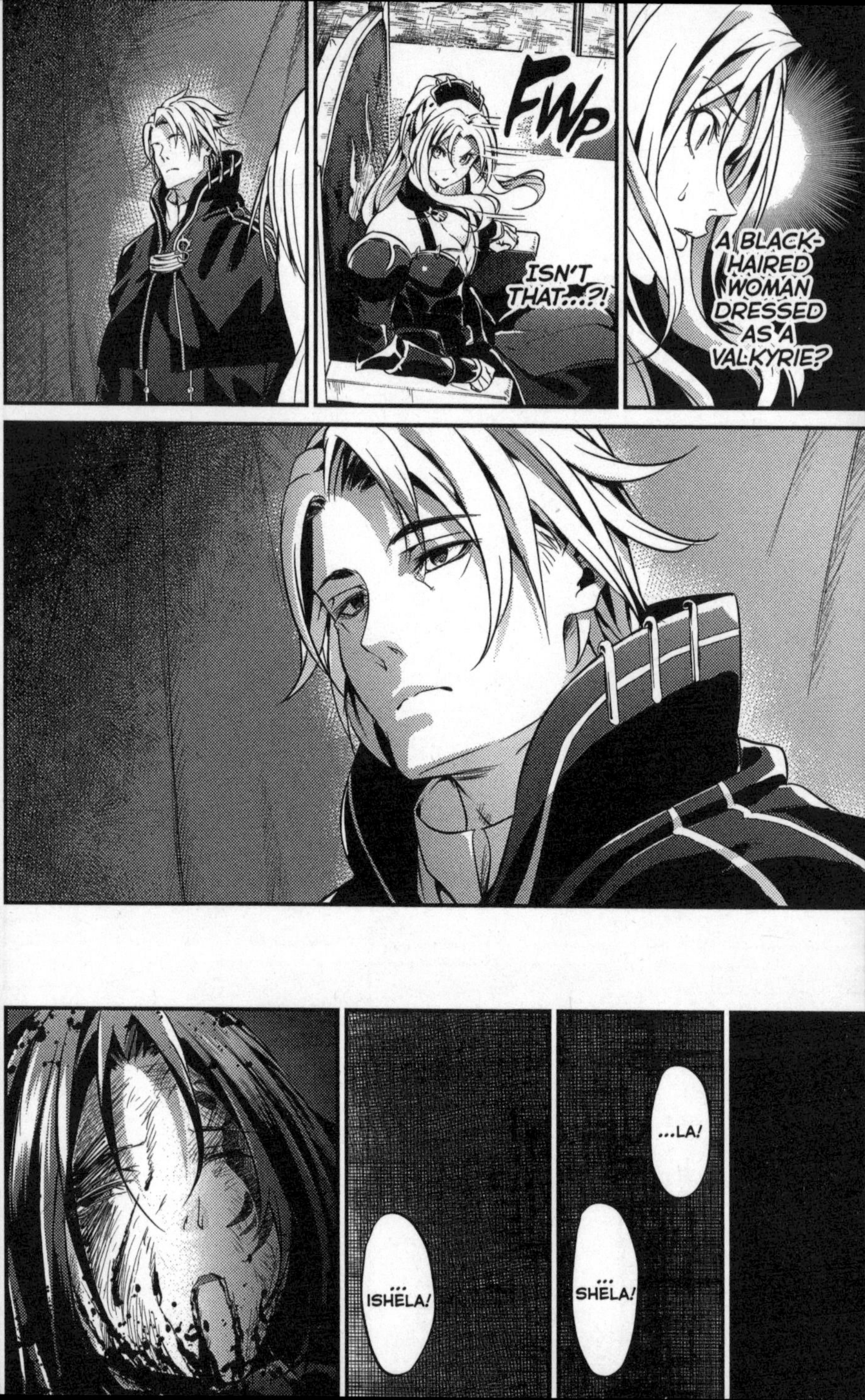
A BLACK-HAIRED WOMAN DRESSED AS A VALKYRIE?
FWP
ISN'T THAT...?!
...LA!
...SHELA!
...ISHELA!

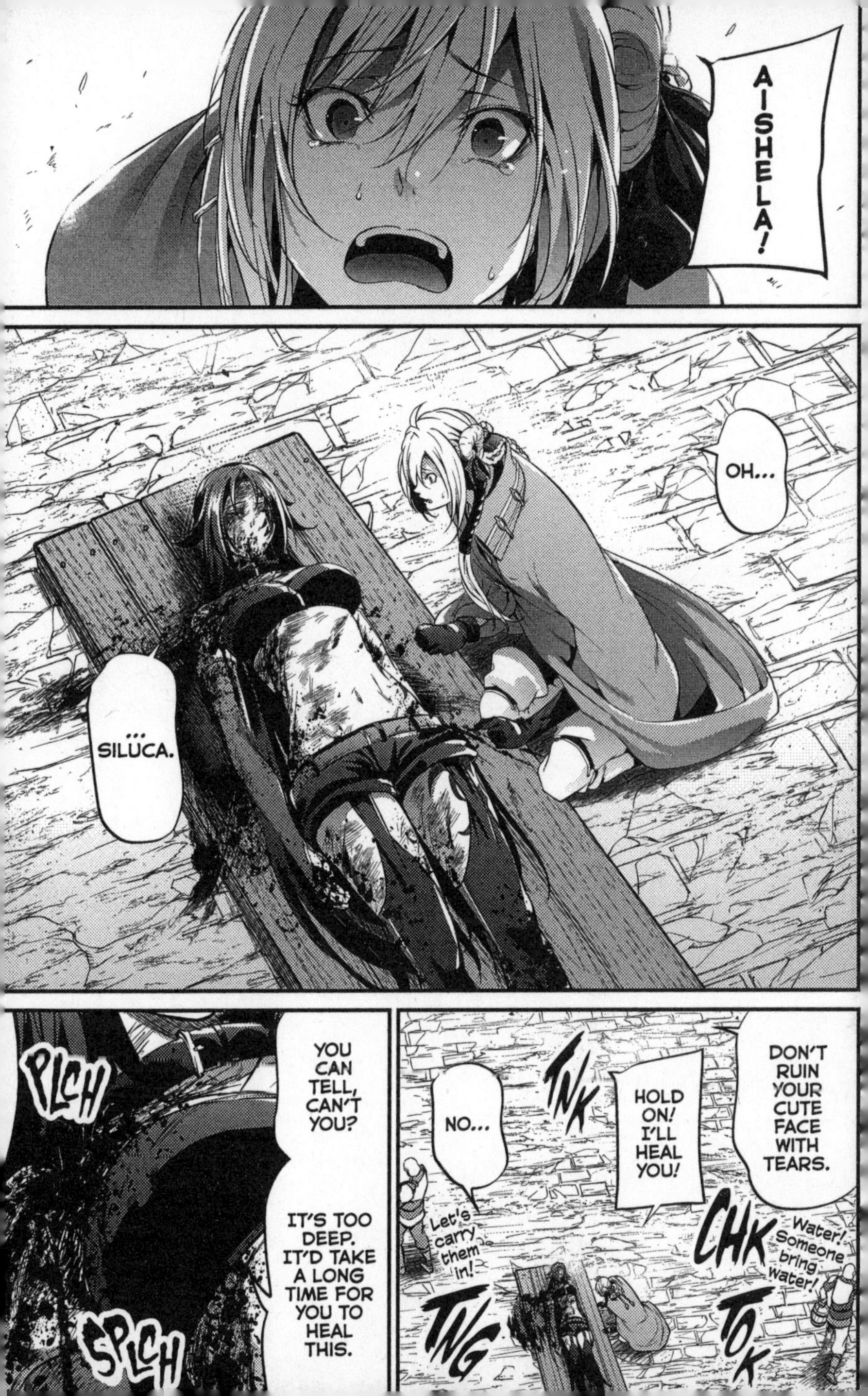
AISHELA!
OH...
... SILUCA.
DON'T RUIN YOUR CUTE FACE WITH TEARS.
TINK
HOLD ON! I'LL HEAL YOU!
NO...
CHK
Water! Someone bring water!
Let's carry them in!
TOK
TNG
YOU CAN TELL, CAN'T YOU?
IT'S TOO DEEP. IT'D TAKE A LONG TIME FOR YOU TO HEAL THIS.
PLCH
SPLCH

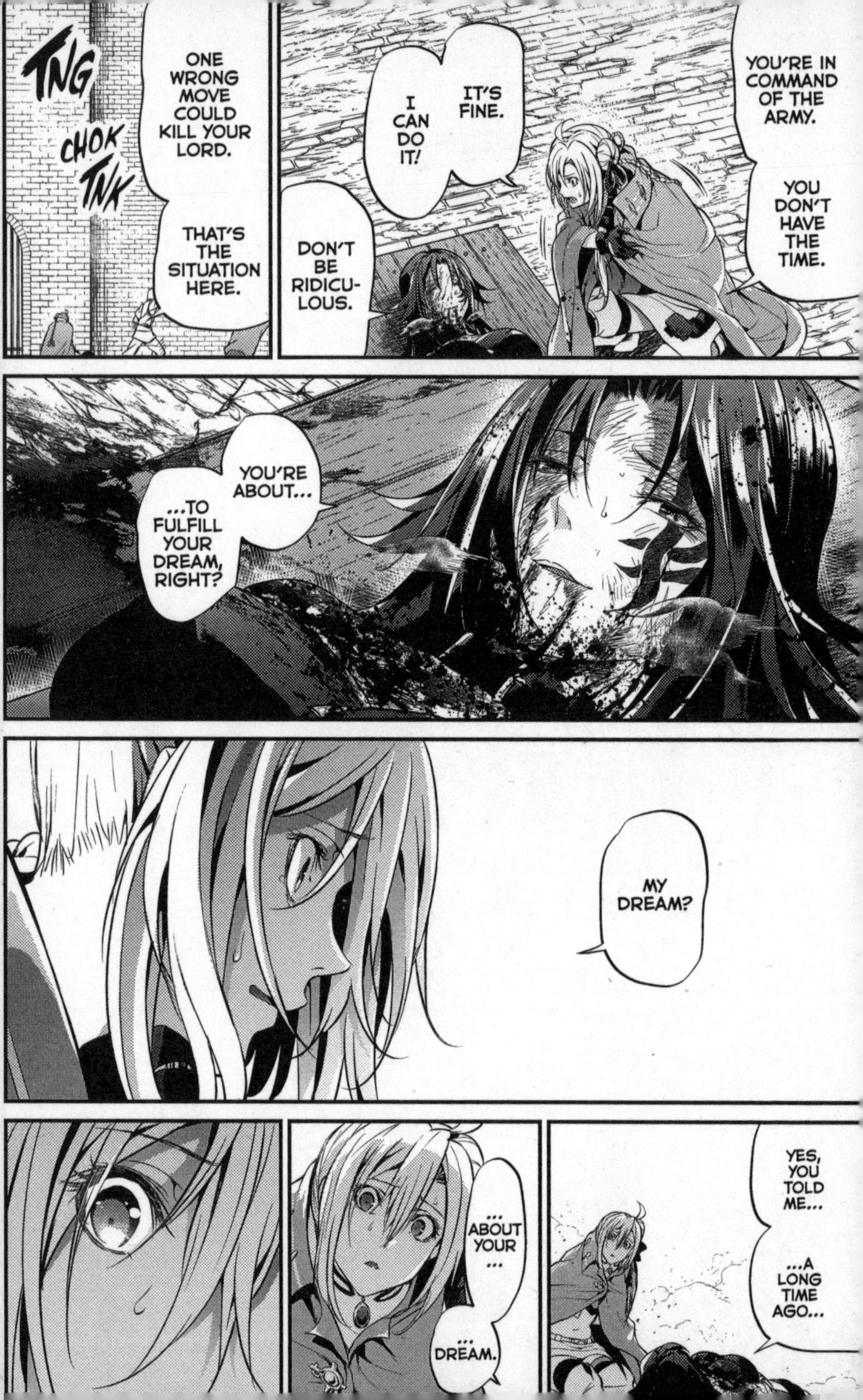
YOU'RE IN COMMAND OF THE ARMY.
YOU DON'T HAVE THE TIME.
IT'S FINE. I CAN DO IT!
DON'T BE RIDICULOUS.
ONE WRONG MOVE COULD KILL YOUR LORD.
THAT'S THE SITUATION HERE.
TNG
CHOK
TNK
YOU'RE ABOUT...
...TO FULFILL YOUR DREAM, RIGHT?
MY DREAM?
YES, YOU TOLD ME...
...A LONG TIME AGO...
...ABOUT YOUR ...
... DREAM.

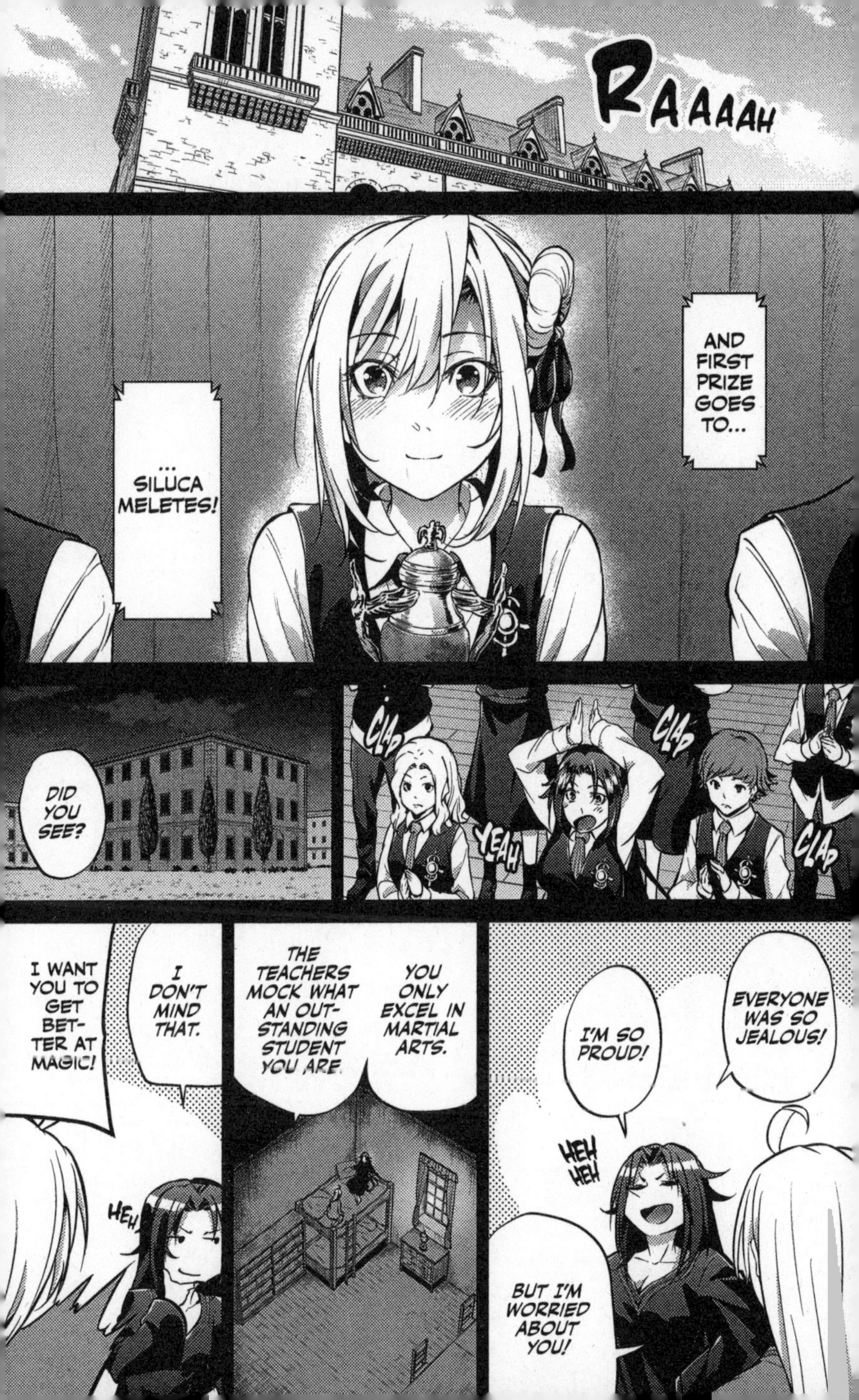
RAAAAH
AND FIRST PRIZE GOES TO...
... SILUCA MELETES!
CLAP
CLAP
CLAP
YEAH
DID YOU SEE?
EVERYONE WAS SO JEALOUS!
I'M SO PROUD!
HEH HEH
BUT I'M WORRIED ABOUT YOU!
YOU ONLY EXCEL IN MARTIAL ARTS.
THE TEACHERS MOCK WHAT AN OUT-STANDING STUDENT YOU ARE.
I DON'T MIND THAT.
I WANT YOU TO GET BET-TER AT MAGIC!
HEH

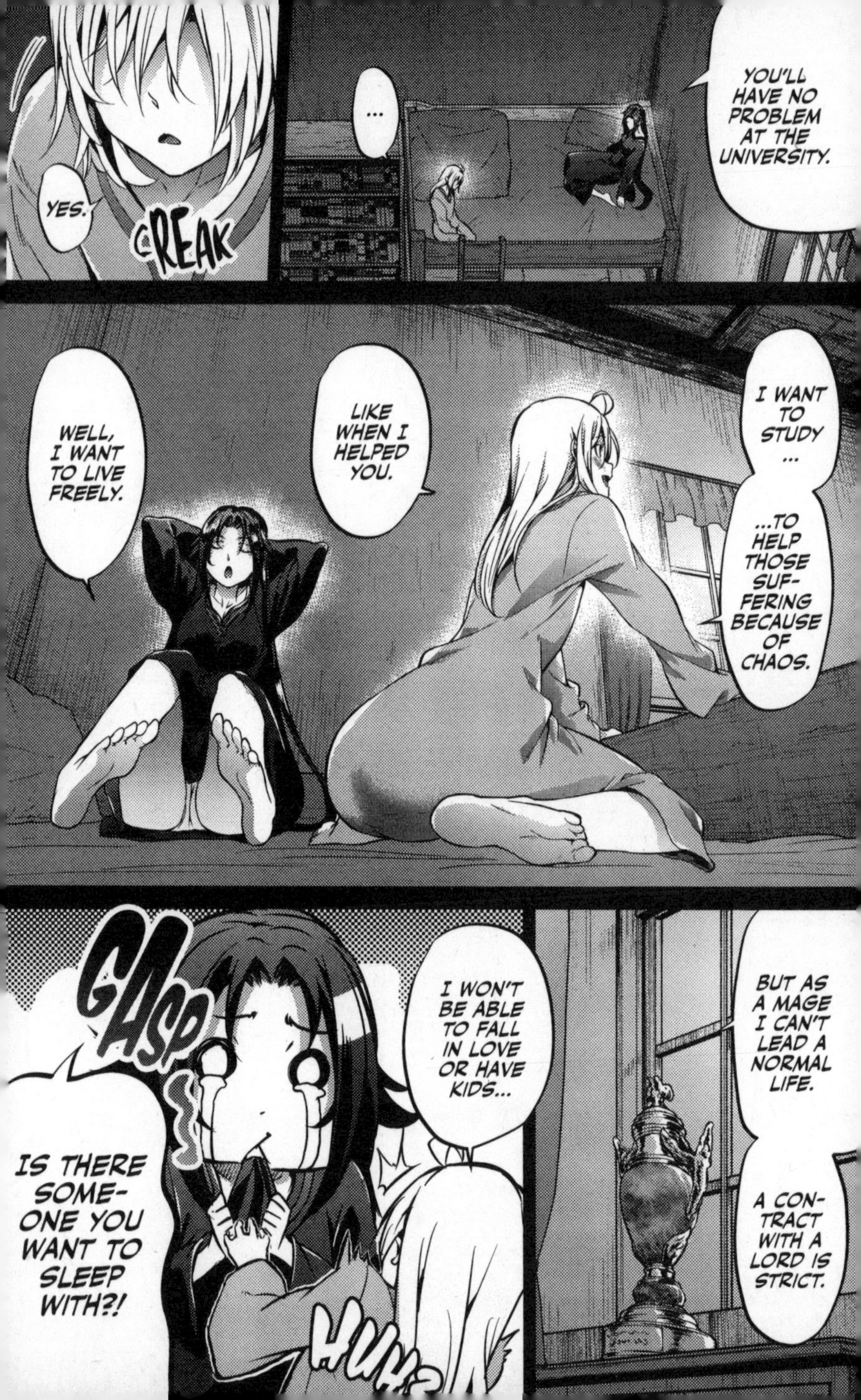
YOU'LL HAVE NO PROBLEM AT THE UNIVERSITY.
...
YES.
CREAK
I WANT TO STUDY ...
...TO HELP THOSE SUF-FERING BECAUSE OF CHAOS.
LIKE WHEN I HELPED YOU.
WELL, I WANT TO LIVE FREELY.
BUT AS A MAGE I CAN'T LEAD A NORMAL LIFE.
A CON-TRACT WITH A LORD IS STRICT.
I WON'T BE ABLE TO FALL IN LOVE OR HAVE KIDS...
GASP
IS THERE SOME-ONE YOU WANT TO SLEEP WITH?!
HUH?

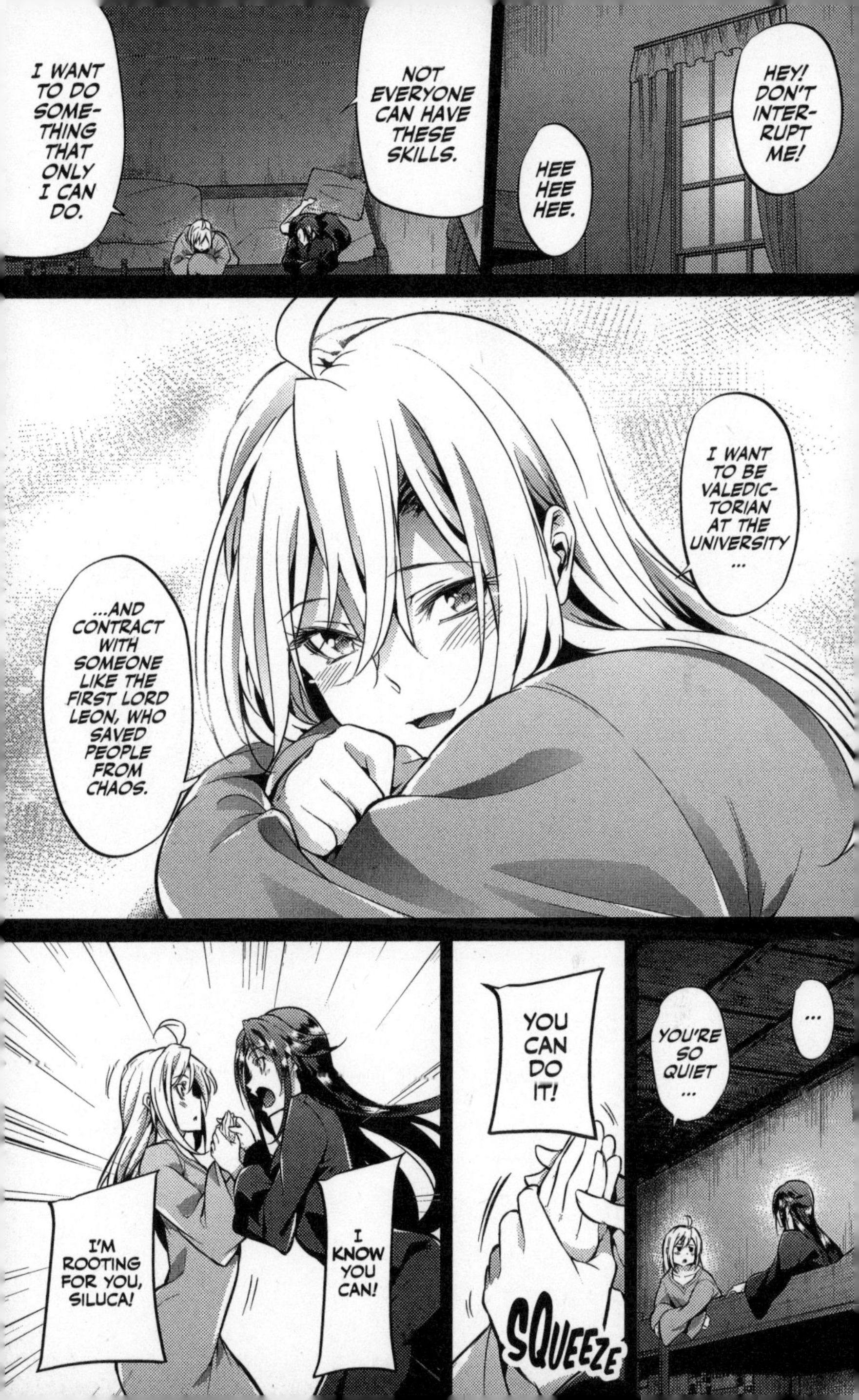
HEY! DON'T INTERRUPT ME!
HEE HEE HEE.
NOT EVERYONE CAN HAVE THESE SKILLS.
I WANT TO DO SOMETHING THAT ONLY I CAN DO.
I WANT TO BE VALEDICTORIAN AT THE UNIVERSITY ...
...AND CONTRACT WITH SOMEONE LIKE THE FIRST LORD LEON, WHO SAVED PEOPLE FROM CHAOS.
...
YOU'RE SO QUIET ...
YOU CAN DO IT!
SQUEEZE
I KNOW YOU CAN!
I'M ROOTING FOR YOU, SILUCA!

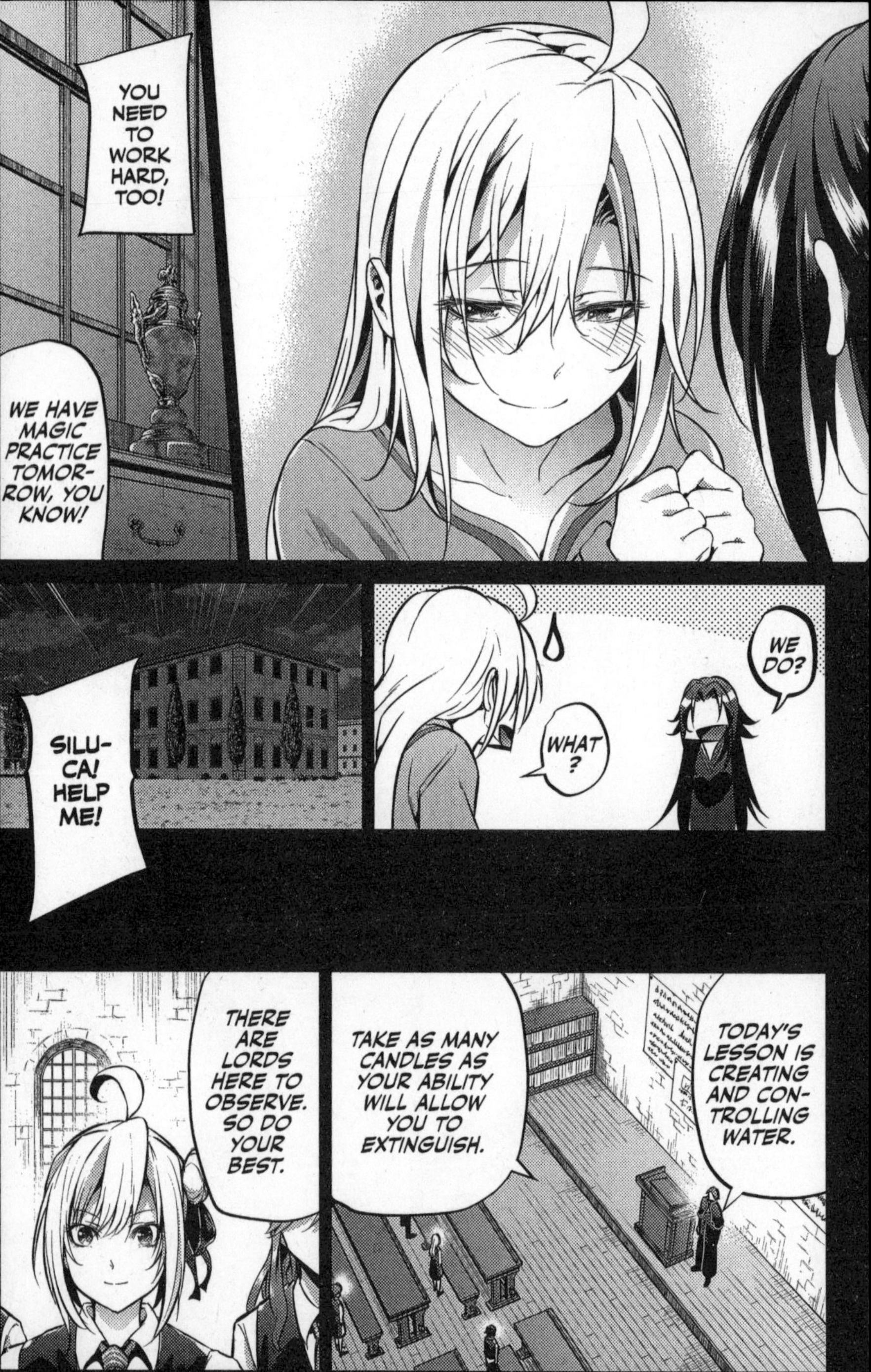
YOU NEED TO WORK HARD, TOO!
WE HAVE MAGIC PRACTICE TOMOR-ROW, YOU KNOW!
WE DO?
WHAT?
SILU-CA! HELP ME!
TODAY'S LESSON IS CREATING AND CON-TROLLING WATER.
TAKE AS MANY CANDLES AS YOUR ABILITY WILL ALLOW YOU TO EXTINGUISH.
THERE ARE LORDS HERE TO OBSERVE. SO DO YOUR BEST.

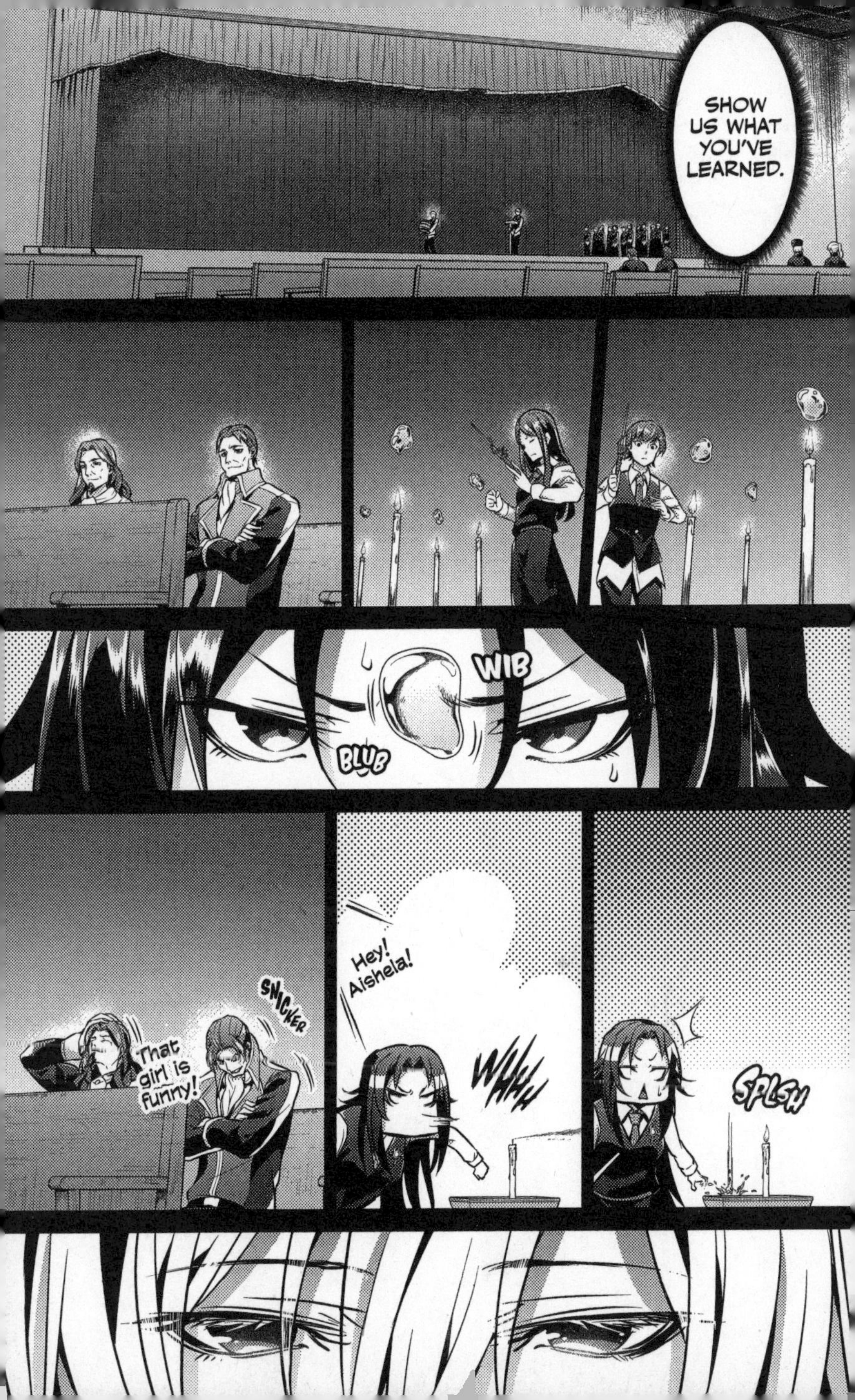
SHOW US WHAT YOU'VE LEARNED.
WIB
BLUB
SPLSH
Hey! Aishela!
SNICKER
That girl is funny!

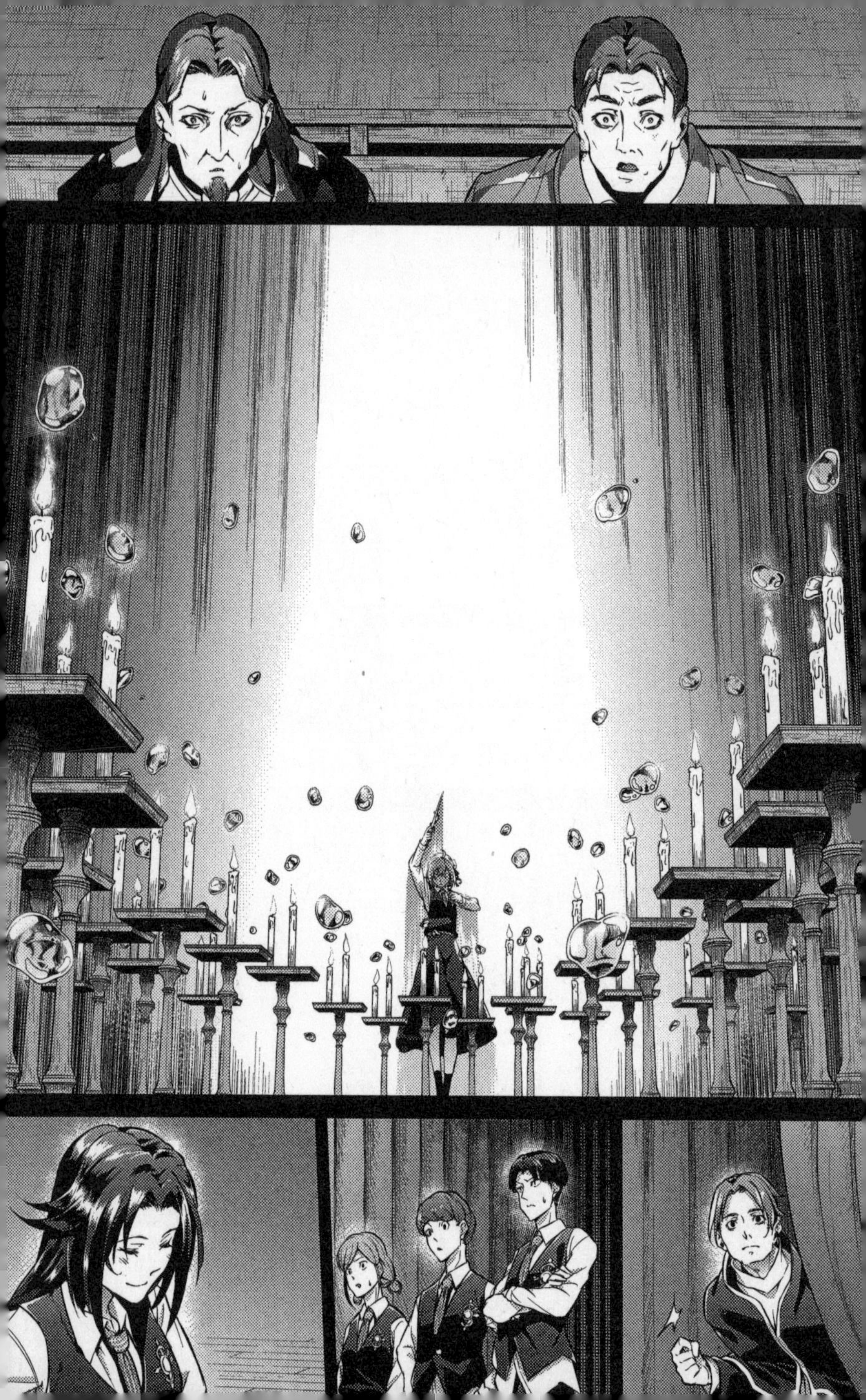

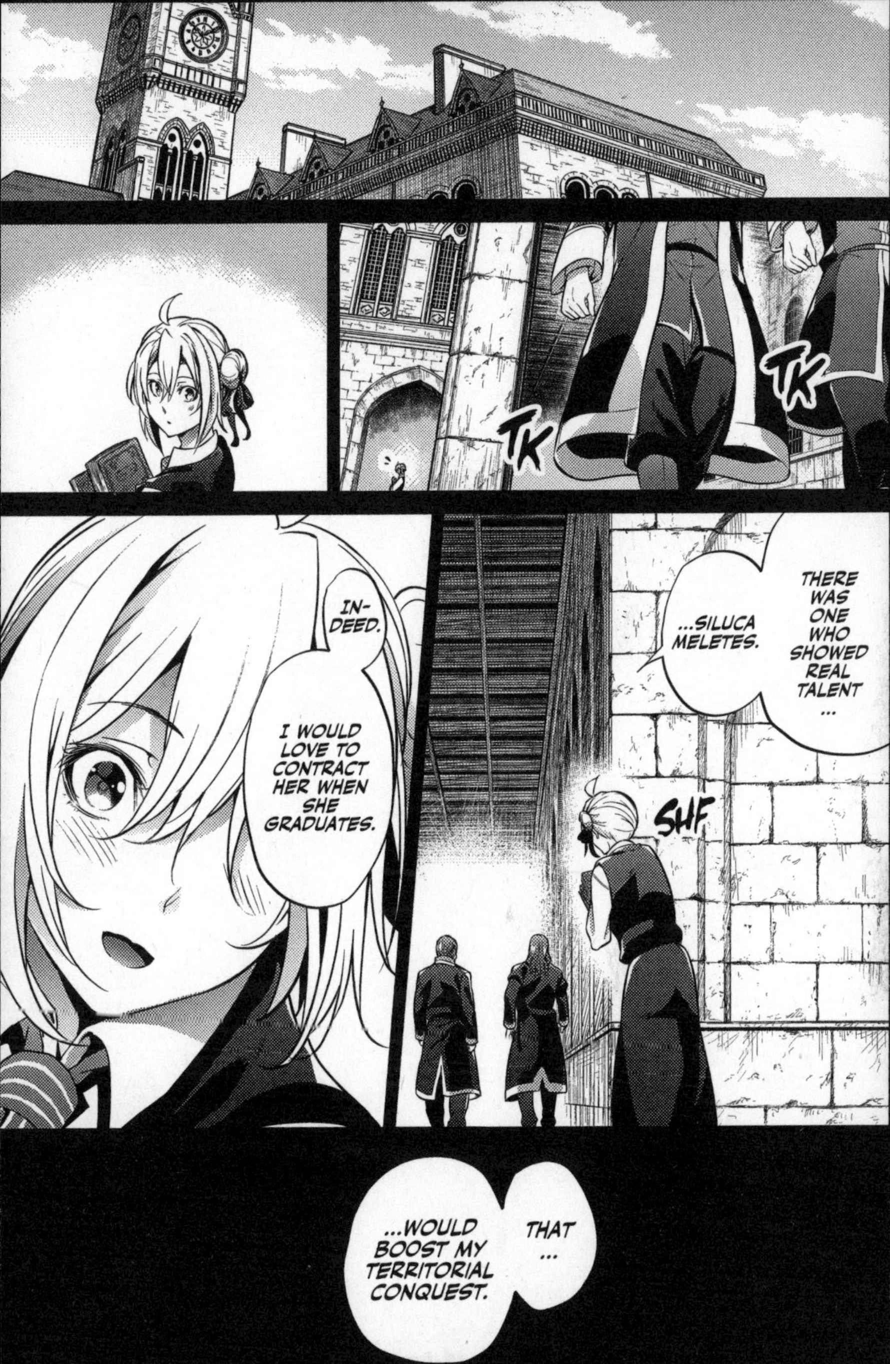
TK
TK
THERE WAS ONE WHO SHOWED REAL TALENT ...
...SILUCA MELETES.
SHF
IN-DEED.
I WOULD LOVE TO CONTRACT HER WHEN SHE GRADUATES.
THAT ...
...WOULD BOOST MY TERRITORIAL CONQUEST.

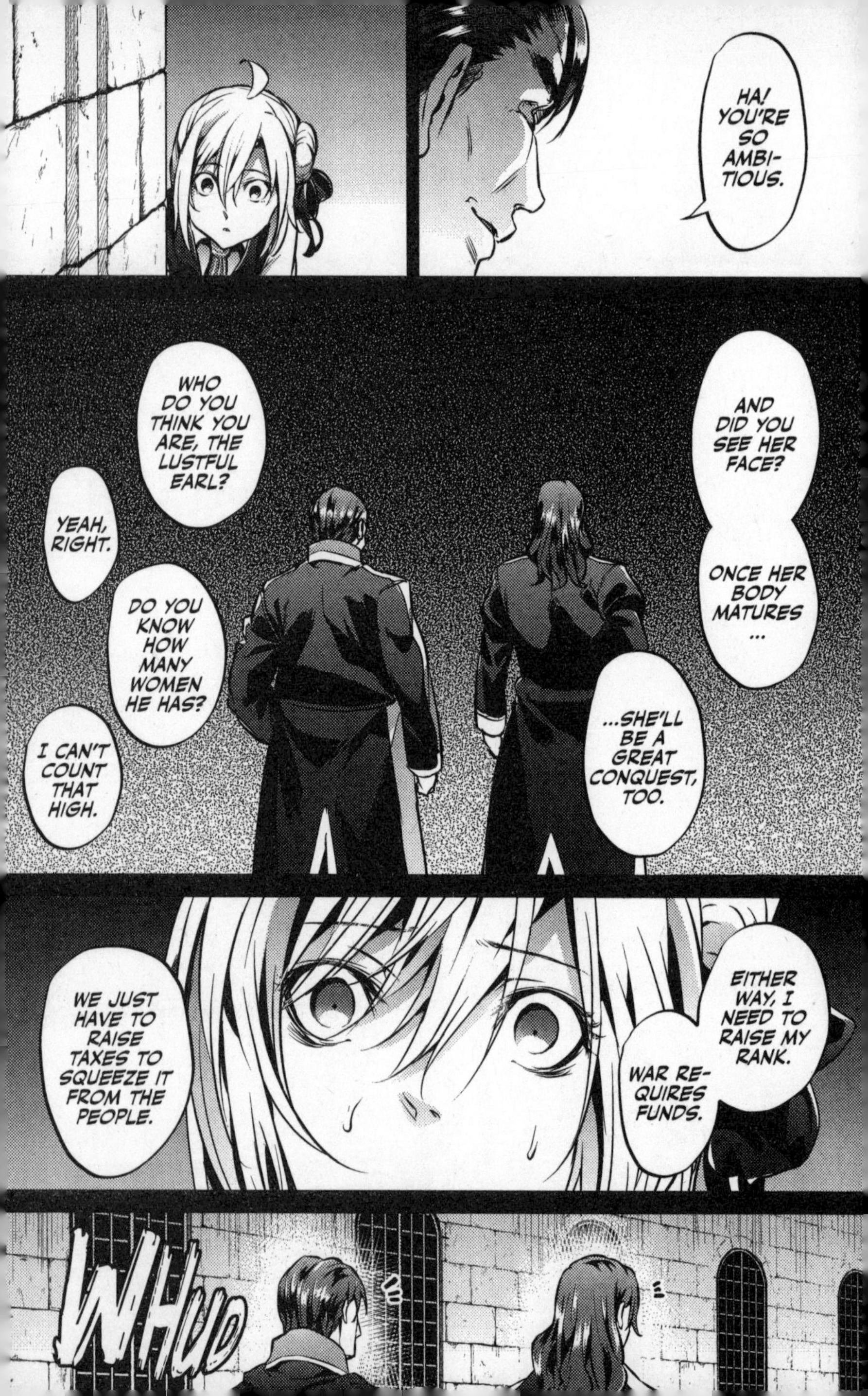
HA! YOU'RE SO AMBITIOUS.
AND DID YOU SEE HER FACE?
ONCE HER BODY MATURES...
...SHE'LL BE A GREAT CONQUEST, TOO.
WHO DO YOU THINK YOU ARE, THE LUSTFUL EARL?
YEAH, RIGHT.
DO YOU KNOW HOW MANY WOMEN HE HAS?
I CAN'T COUNT THAT HIGH.
EITHER WAY, I NEED TO RAISE MY RANK.
WAR REQUIRES FUNDS.
WE JUST HAVE TO RAISE TAXES TO SQUEEZE IT FROM THE PEOPLE.
WHUD

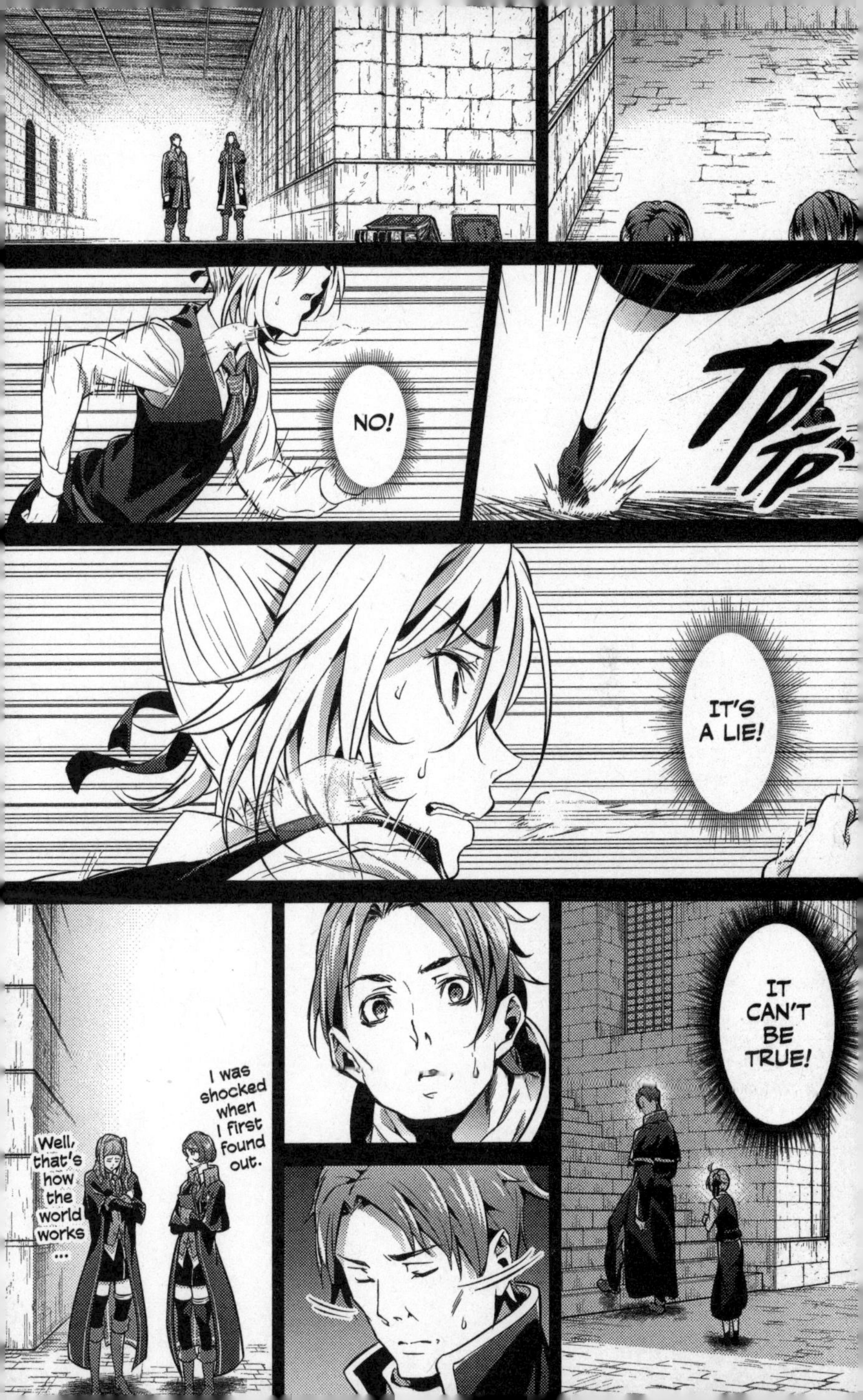
TP TP TP
NO!
IT'S A LIE!
IT CAN'T BE TRUE!
I was shocked when I first found out.
Well, that's how the world works...

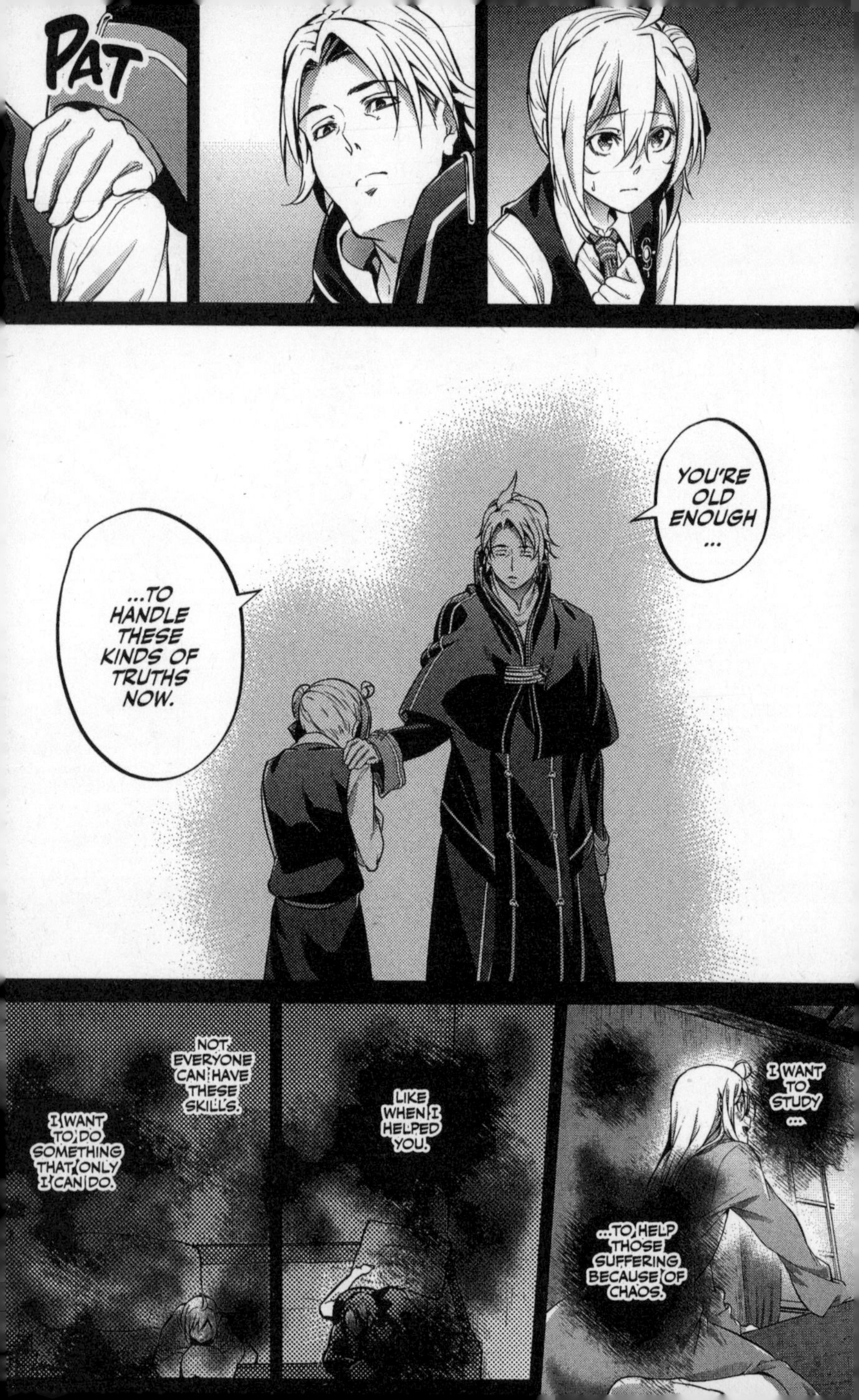
PAT
YOU'RE OLD ENOUGH ...
...TO HANDLE THESE KINDS OF TRUTHS NOW.
I WANT TO STUDY ...
...TO HELP THOSE SUFFERING BECAUSE OF CHAOS.
LIKE WHEN I HELPED YOU.
NOT EVERYONE CAN HAVE THESE SKILLS.
I WANT TO DO SOMETHING THAT ONLY I CAN DO.

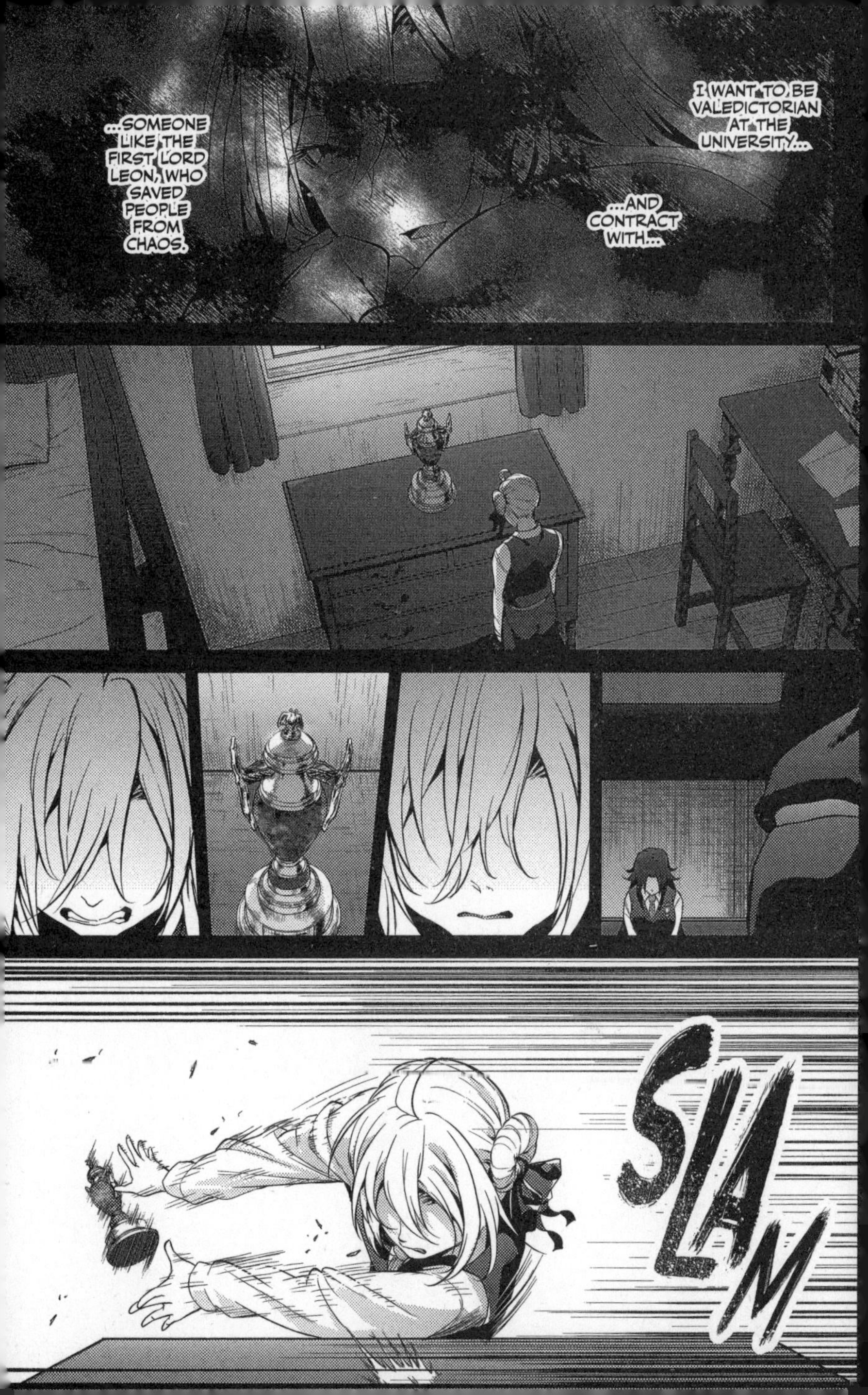
I WANT TO BE VALEDICTORIAN AT THE UNIVERSITY...
...AND CONTRACT WITH...
...SOMEONE LIKE THE FIRST LORD LEON, WHO SAVED PEOPLE FROM CHAOS.
SLAM

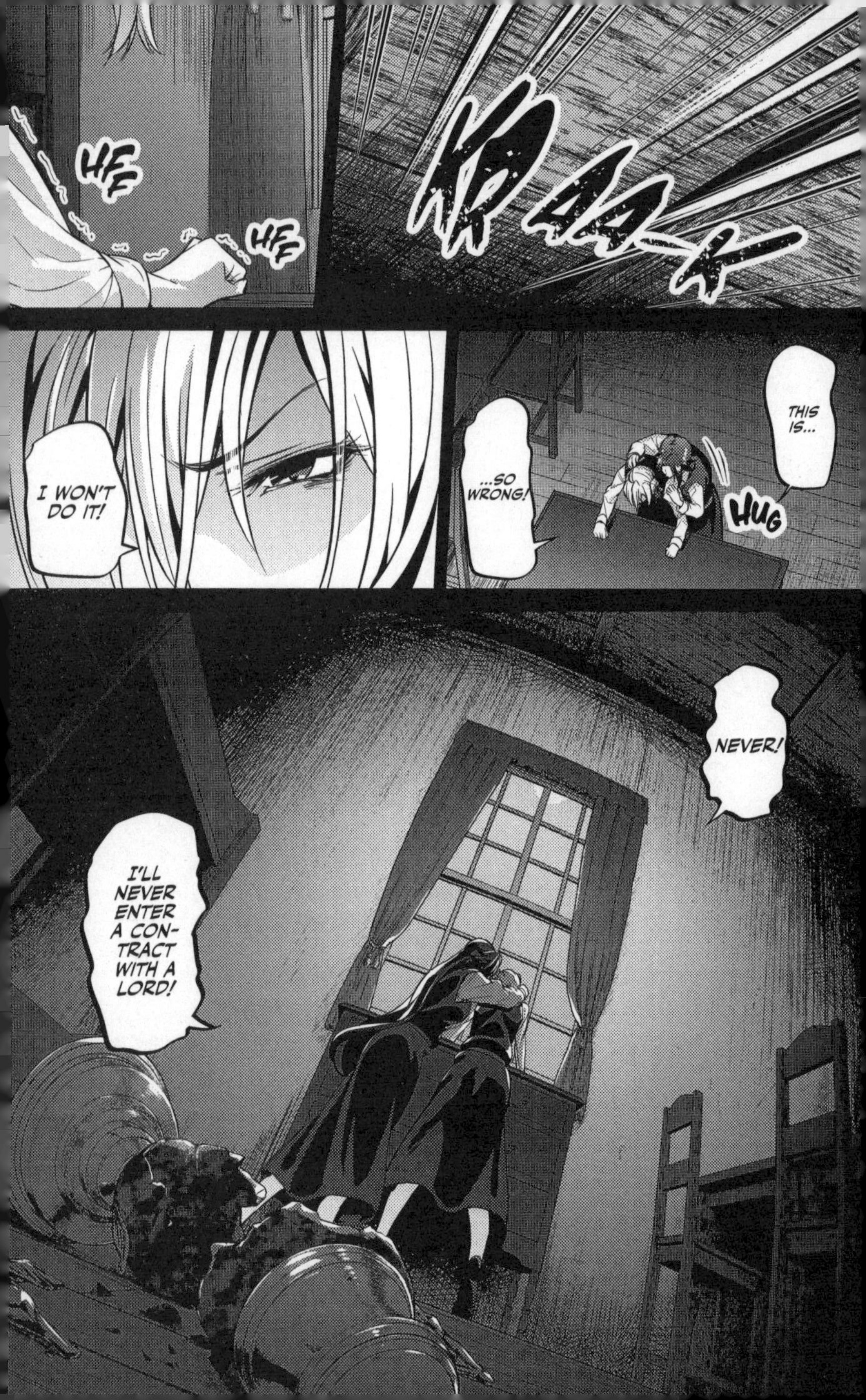
KRAAK
HFF
HFF
THIS IS...
HUG
...SO WRONG!
I WON'T DO IT!
NEVER!
I'LL NEVER ENTER A CONTRACT WITH A LORD!

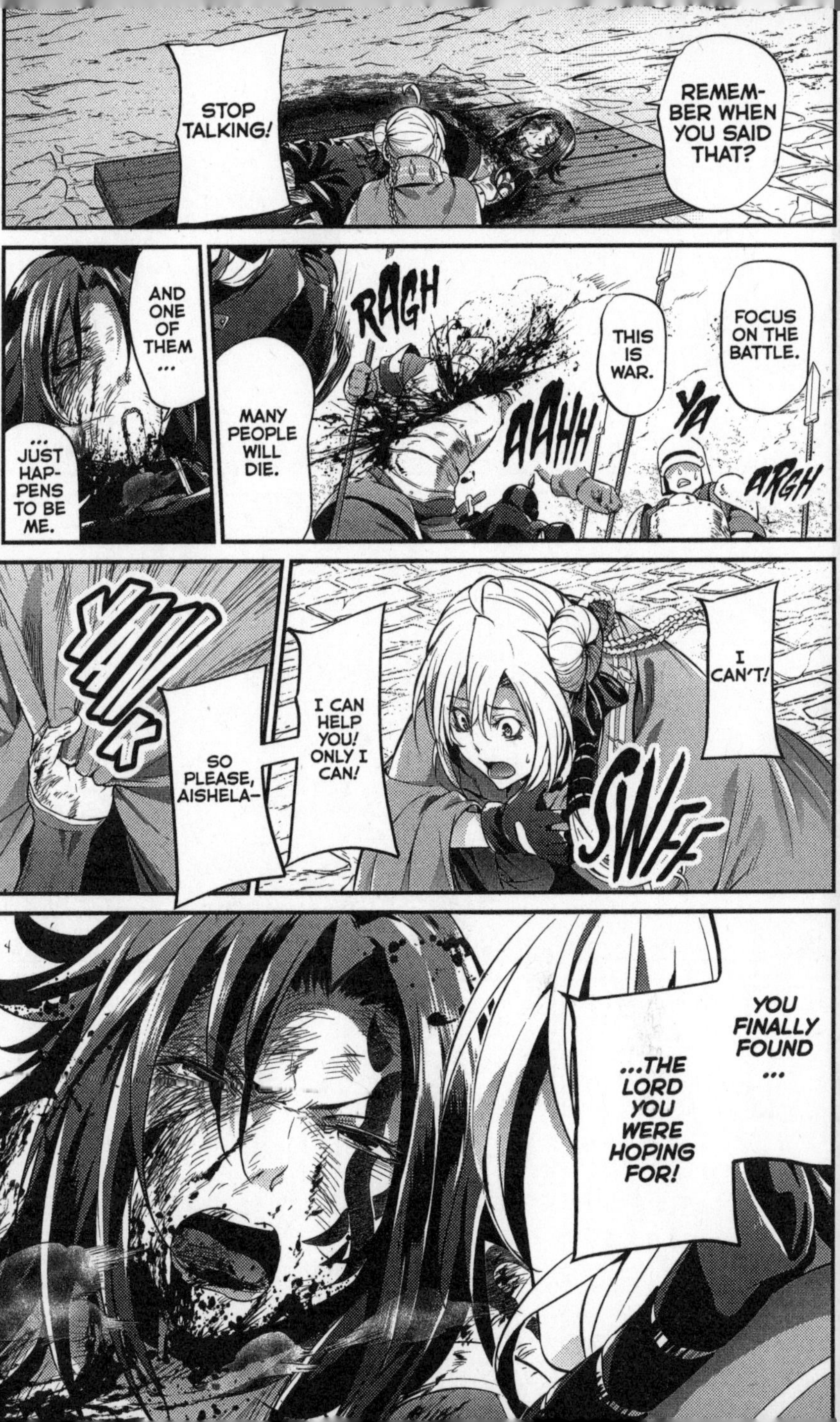
REMEMBER WHEN YOU SAID THAT?
STOP TALKING!
FOCUS ON THE BATTLE.
YA
ARGH
THIS IS WAR.
AAHH
RAGH
MANY PEOPLE WILL DIE.
AND ONE OF THEM ...
... JUST HAPPENS TO BE ME.
I CAN'T!
SNFF
I CAN HELP YOU! ONLY I CAN!
SO PLEASE, AISHELA—
YANK
YOU FINALLY FOUND ...
...THE LORD YOU WERE HOPING FOR!

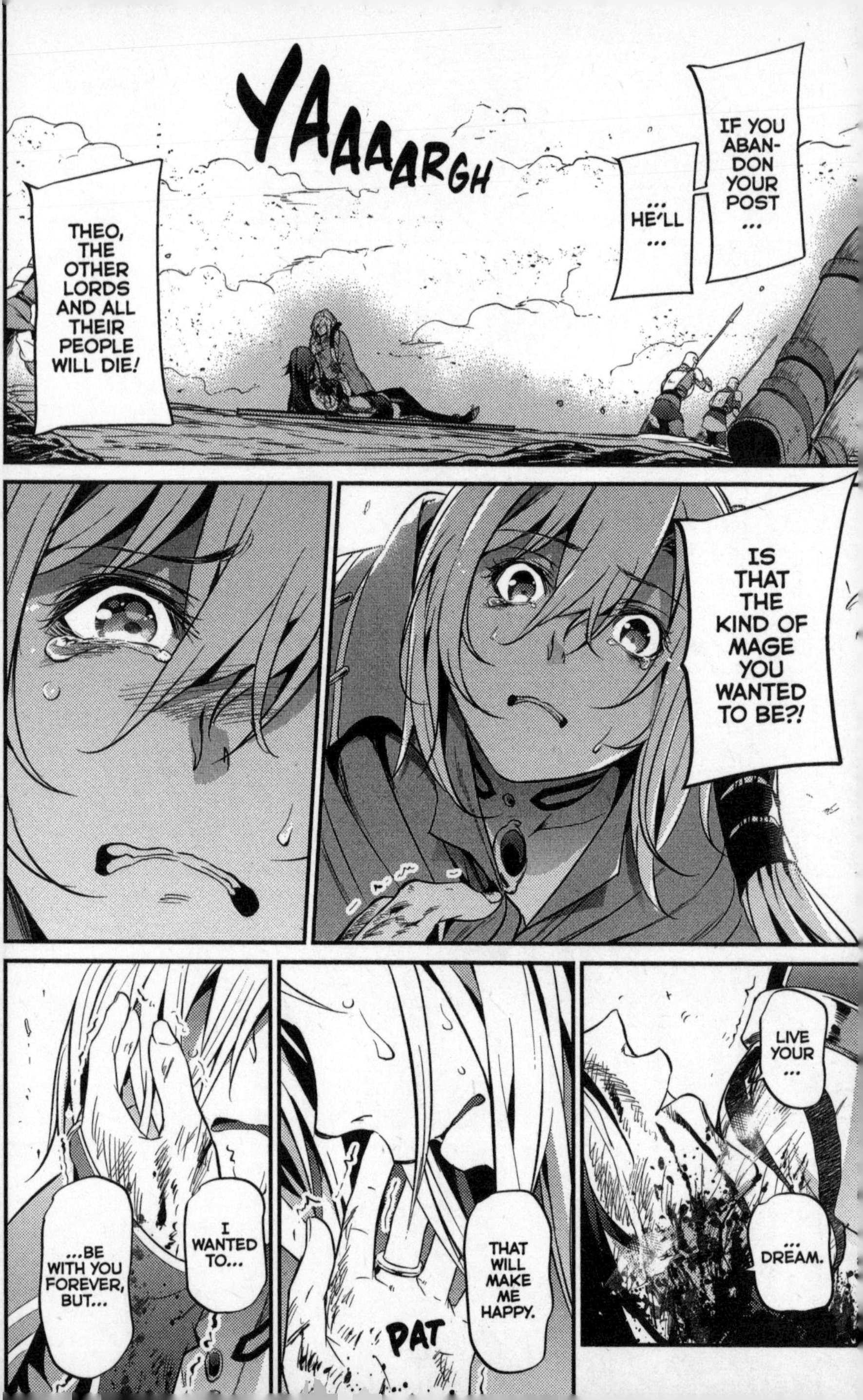
IF YOU ABAN-DON YOUR POST ...
... HE'LL ...
YAAAARGH
THEO, THE OTHER LORDS AND ALL THEIR PEOPLE WILL DIE!
IS THAT THE KIND OF MAGE YOU WANTED TO BE?!
LIVE YOUR ...
... DREAM.
THAT WILL MAKE ME HAPPY.
PAT
I WANTED TO...
...BE WITH YOU FOREVER, BUT...

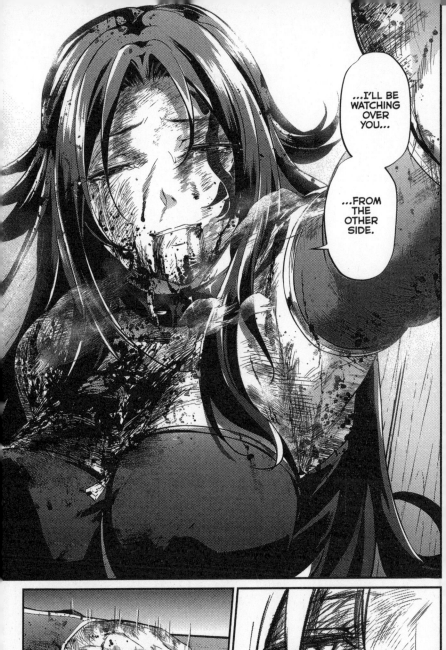

...I'LL BE WATCHING OVER YOU...

...FROM THE OTHER SIDE.

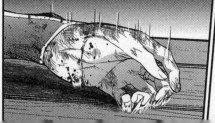

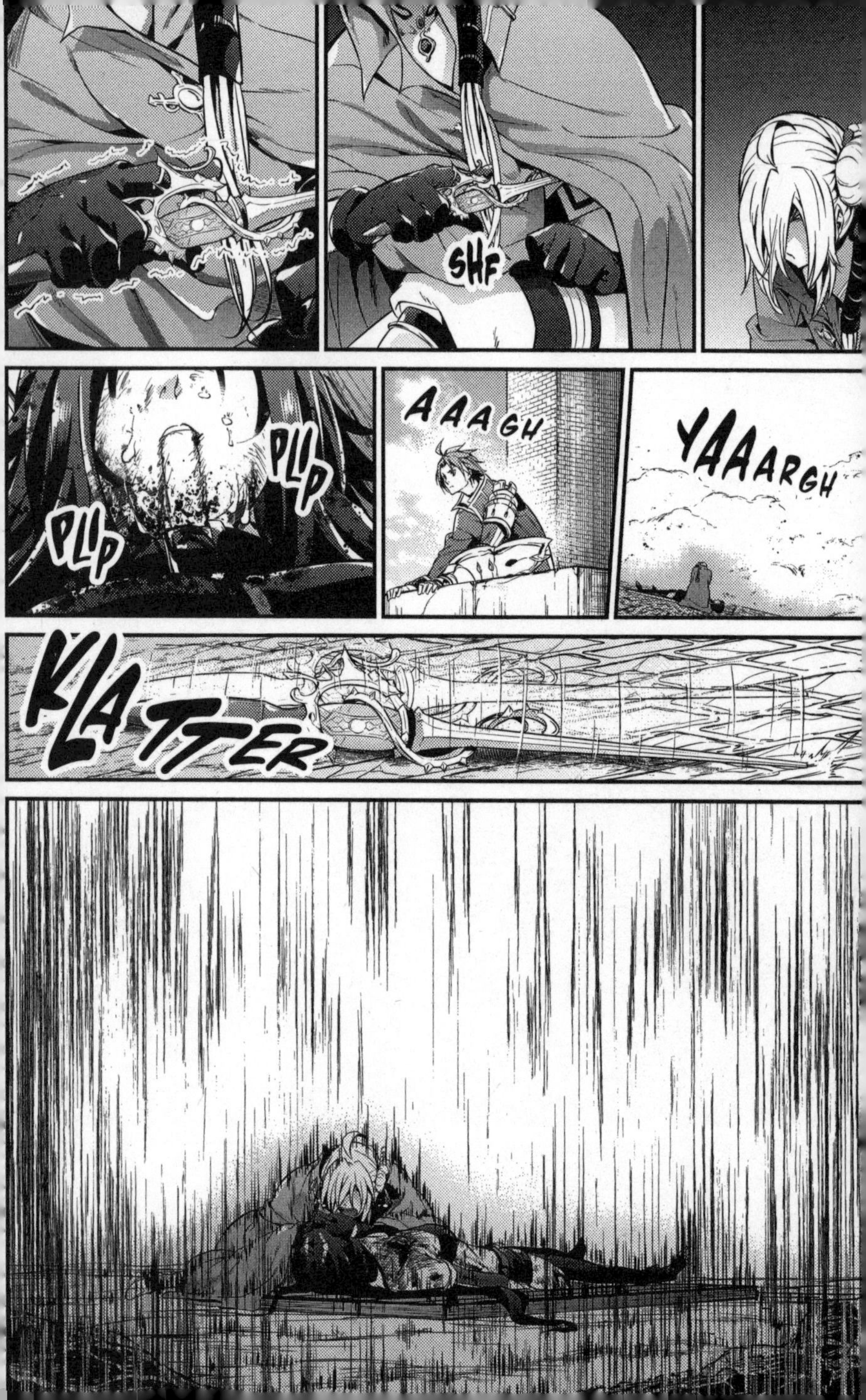
SHF
YAAARGH
AAAGH
PLIP
PLIP
KLATTER

RECORD OF
GRANCREST
WAR

RECORD OF
GRANCREST
WAR

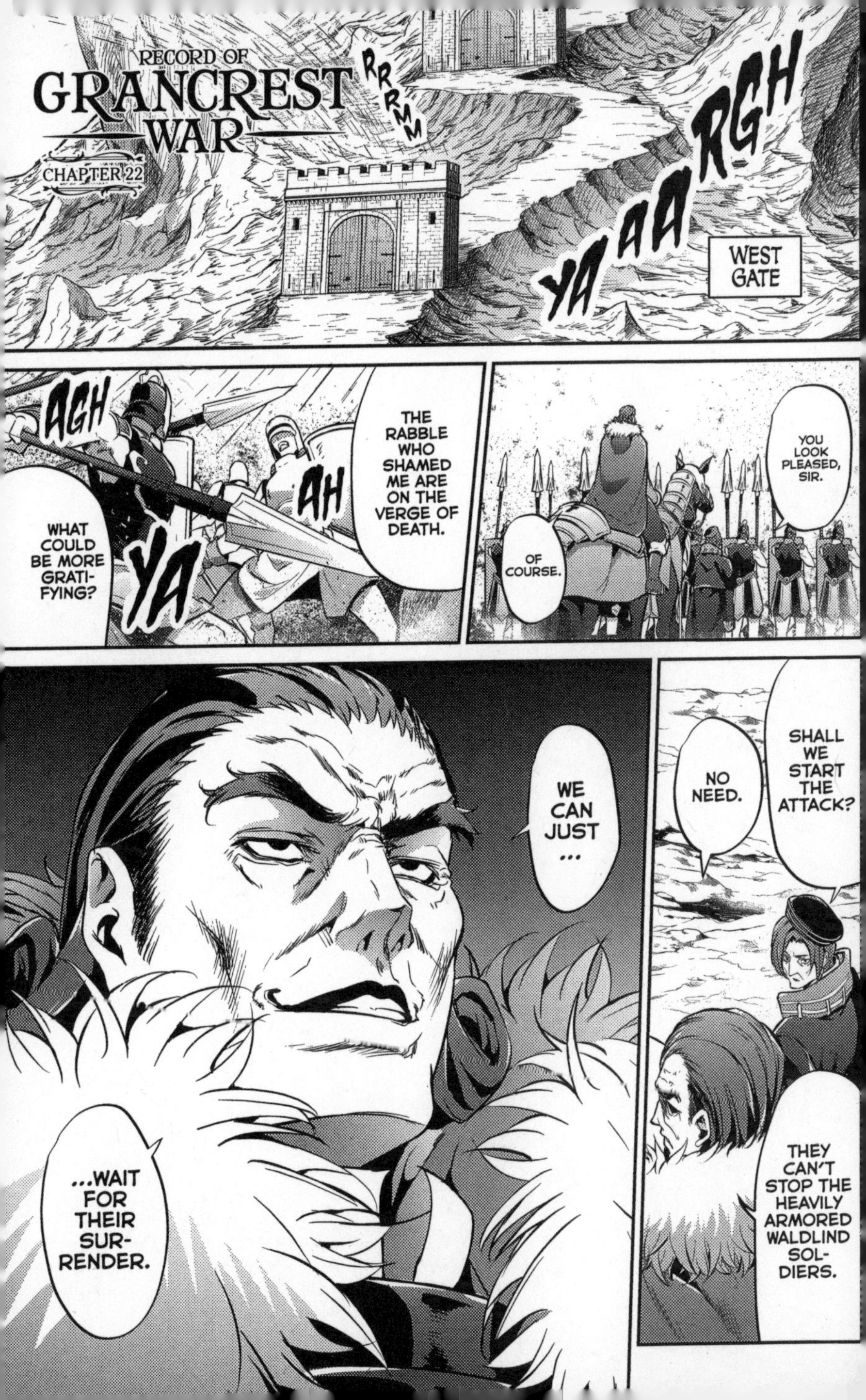
RECORD OF GRANCREST WAR
CHAPTER 22
RRRRMM
YAAAARGH
WEST GATE
YOU LOOK PLEASED, SIR.
OF COURSE.
THE RABBLE WHO SHAMED ME ARE ON THE VERGE OF DEATH.
AH
AGH
YA
WHAT COULD BE MORE GRATI-FYING?
SHALL WE START THE ATTACK?
NO NEED.
THEY CAN'T STOP THE HEAVILY ARMORED WALDLIND SOL-DIERS.
WE CAN JUST...
...WAIT FOR THEIR SUR-RENDER.

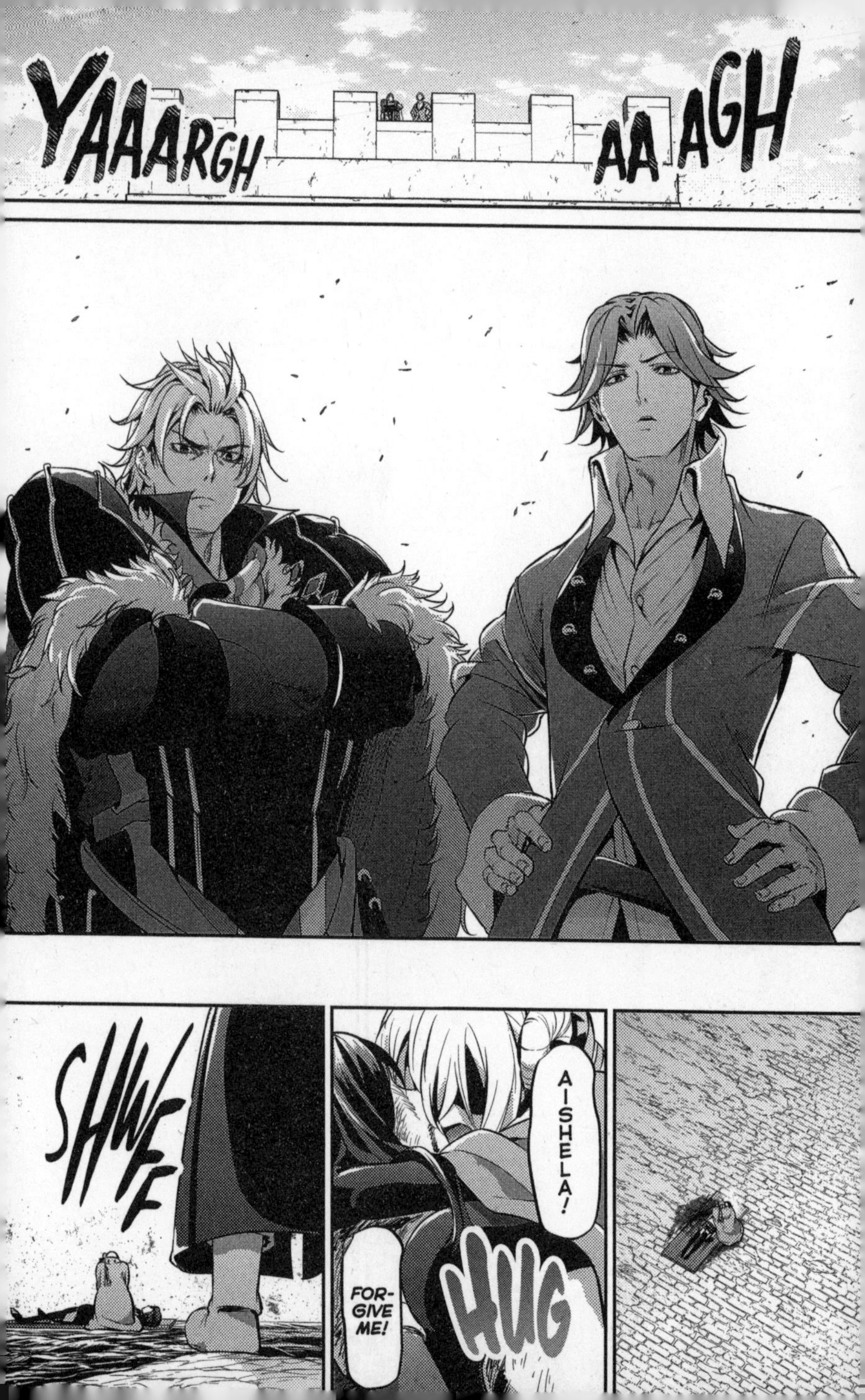
AA AGH
YAAARGH
AISHELA!
HUG
FOR-GIVE ME!
SHUFF

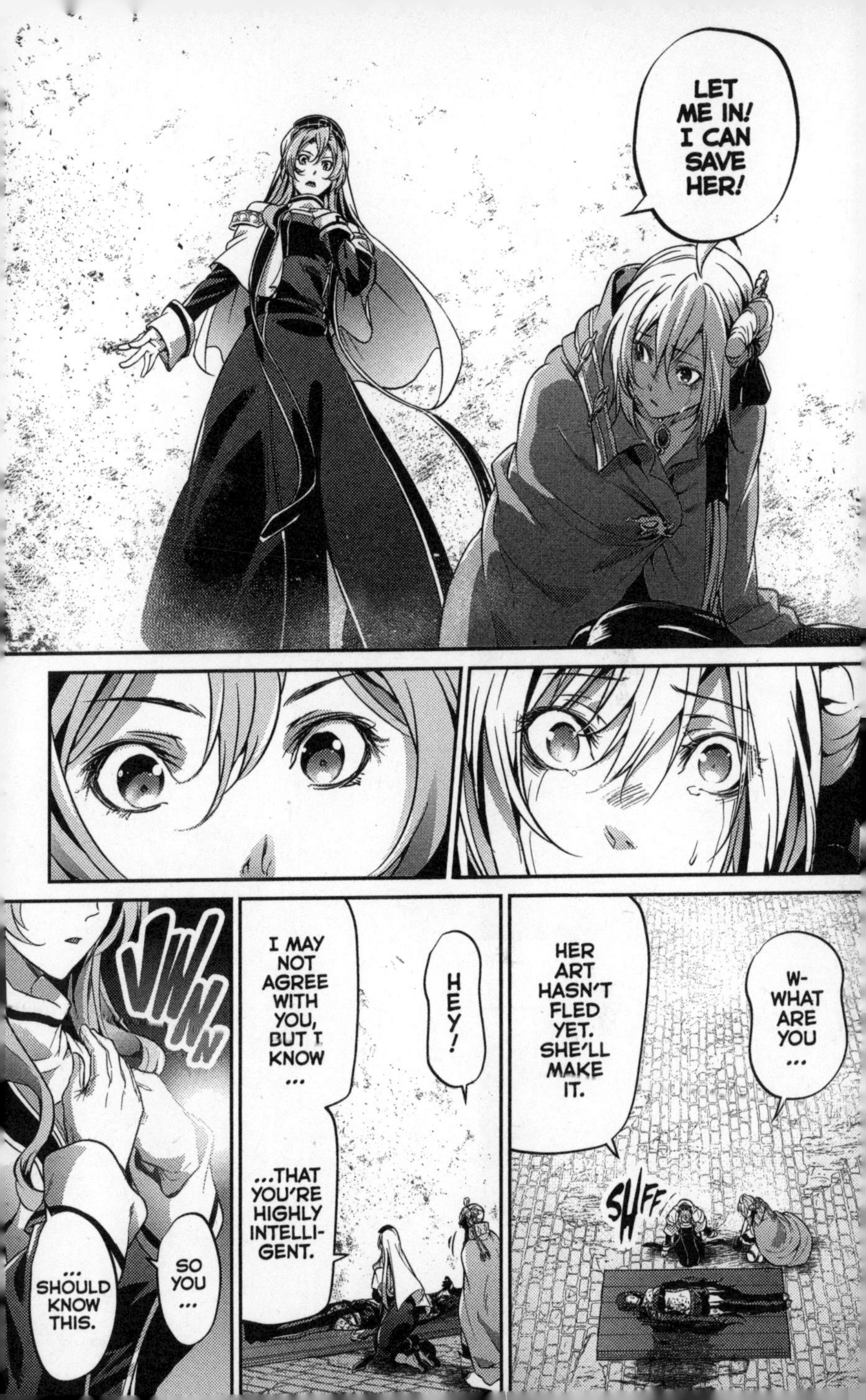
LET ME IN! I CAN SAVE HER!
W-WHAT ARE YOU ...
HER ART HASN'T FLED YET. SHE'LL MAKE IT.
SHFF
HEY!
I MAY NOT AGREE WITH YOU, BUT I KNOW ...
...THAT YOU'RE HIGHLY INTELLIGENT.
VWNN
SO YOU ...
... SHOULD KNOW THIS.

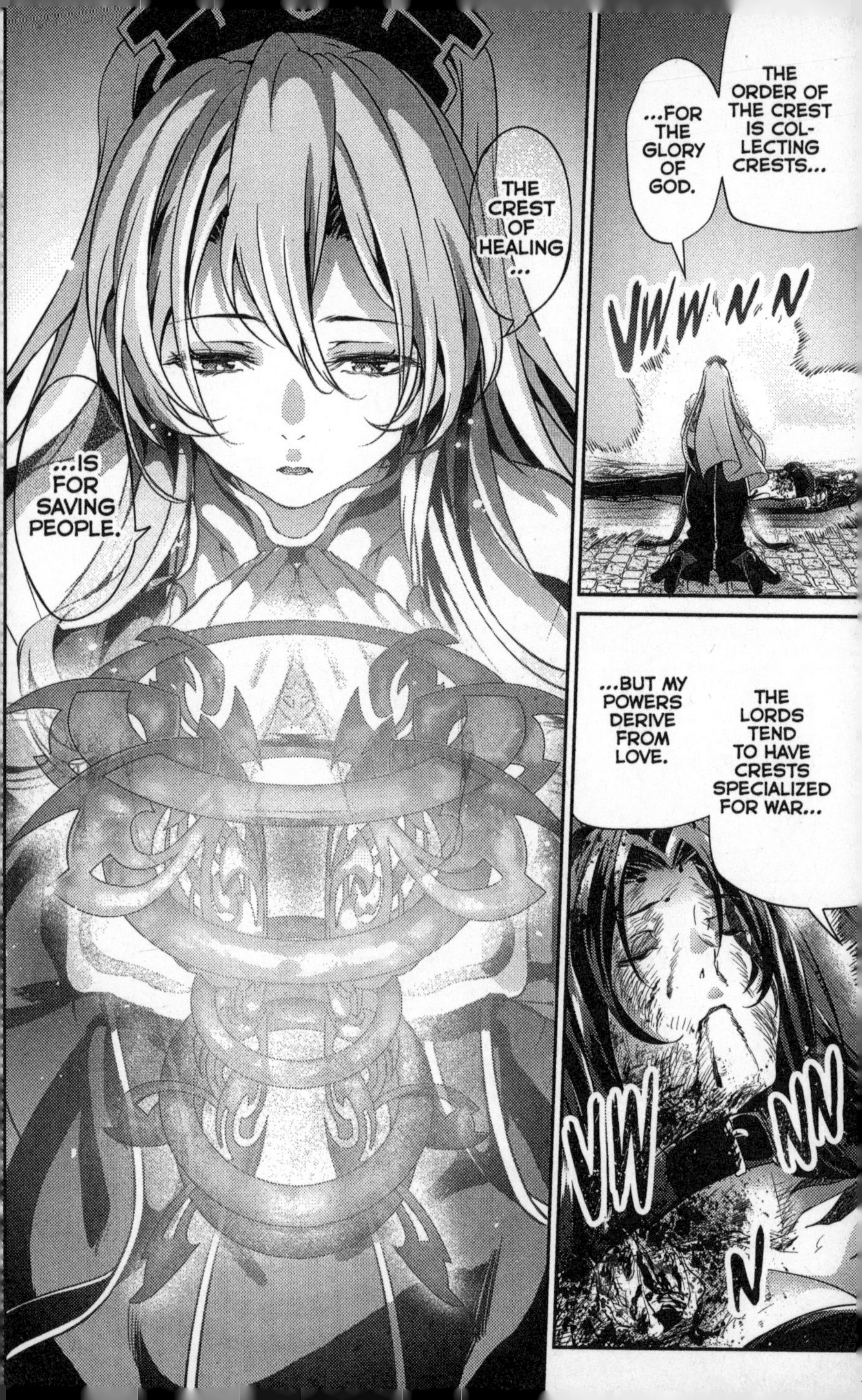
THE ORDER OF THE CREST IS COL-LECTING CRESTS...
...FOR THE GLORY OF GOD.
VWWNNN
THE LORDS TEND TO HAVE CRESTS SPECIALIZED FOR WAR...
...BUT MY POWERS DERIVE FROM LOVE.
VWNNN
THE CREST OF HEALING...
...IS FOR SAVING PEOPLE.

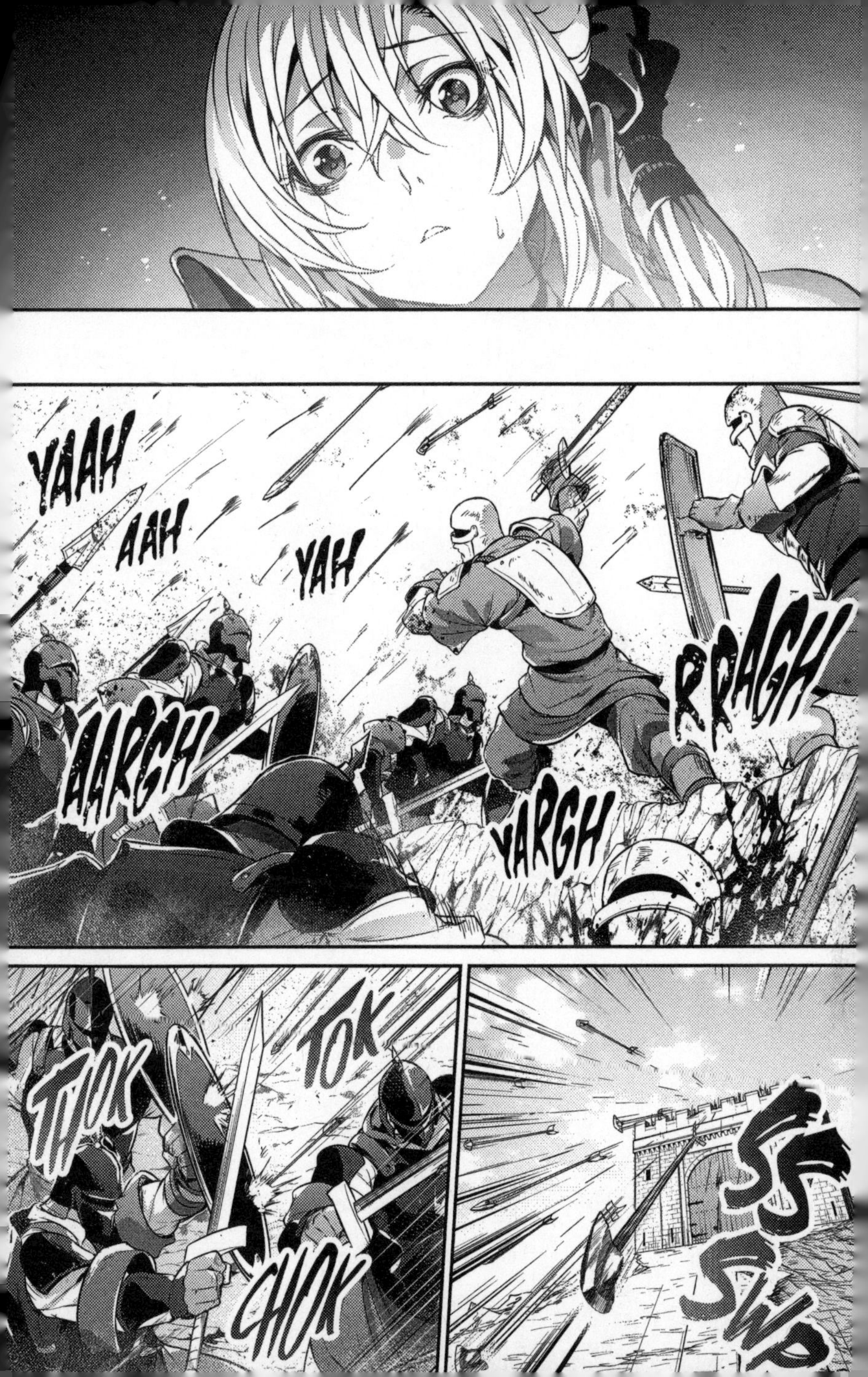
RRAGH
YAH
YAAH
AAH
YARGH
AARGH
SSSWP
TOK
THOK
CHOK

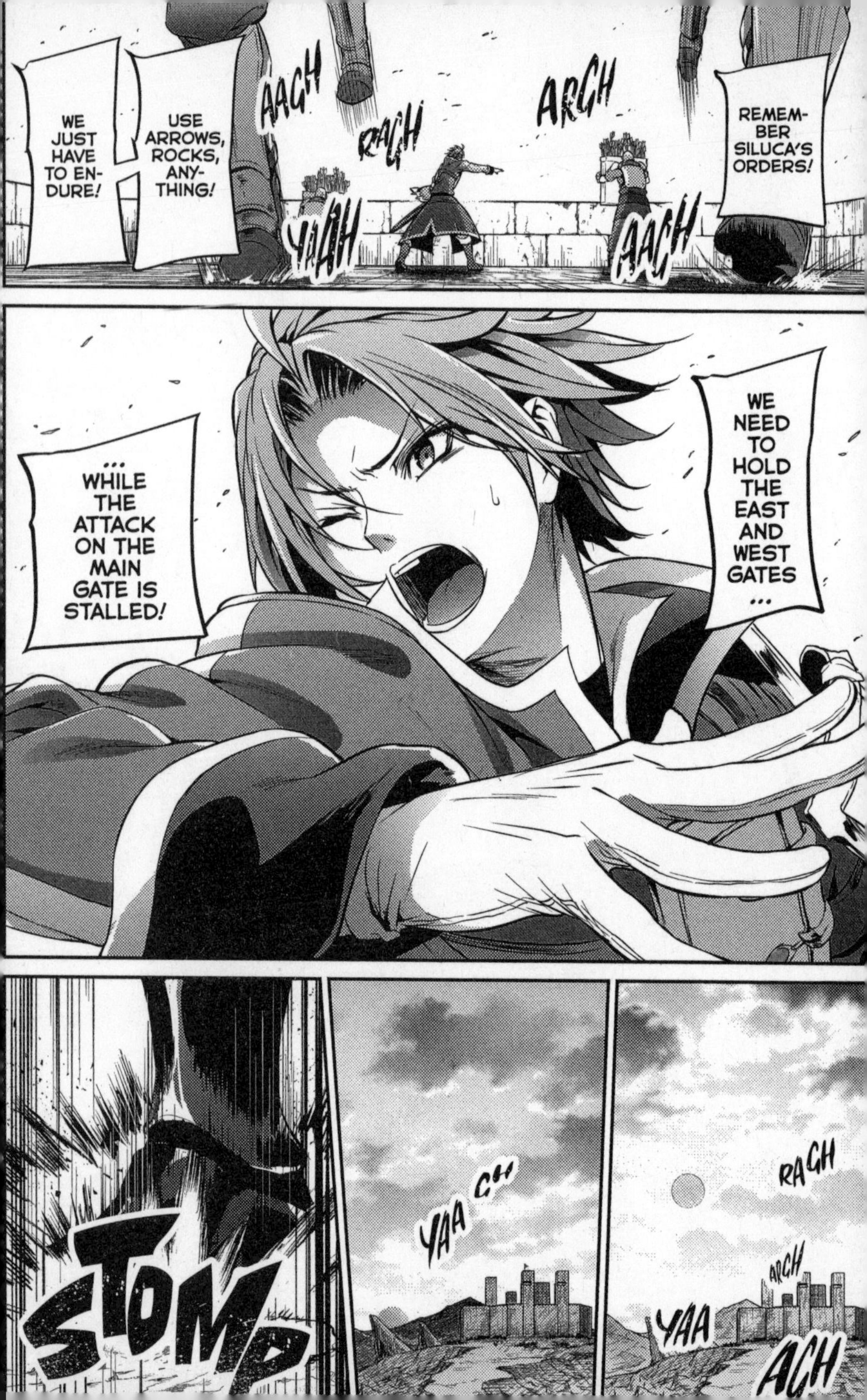
REMEMBER SILUCA'S ORDERS!
AACH
ARCH
RAGH
AAGH
YAAH
USE ARROWS, ROCKS, ANYTHING!
WE JUST HAVE TO ENDURE!
WE NEED TO HOLD THE EAST AND WEST GATES...
...WHILE THE ATTACK ON THE MAIN GATE IS STALLED!
RAGH
ARCH
YAA
ACH
YAA CH
STOMP

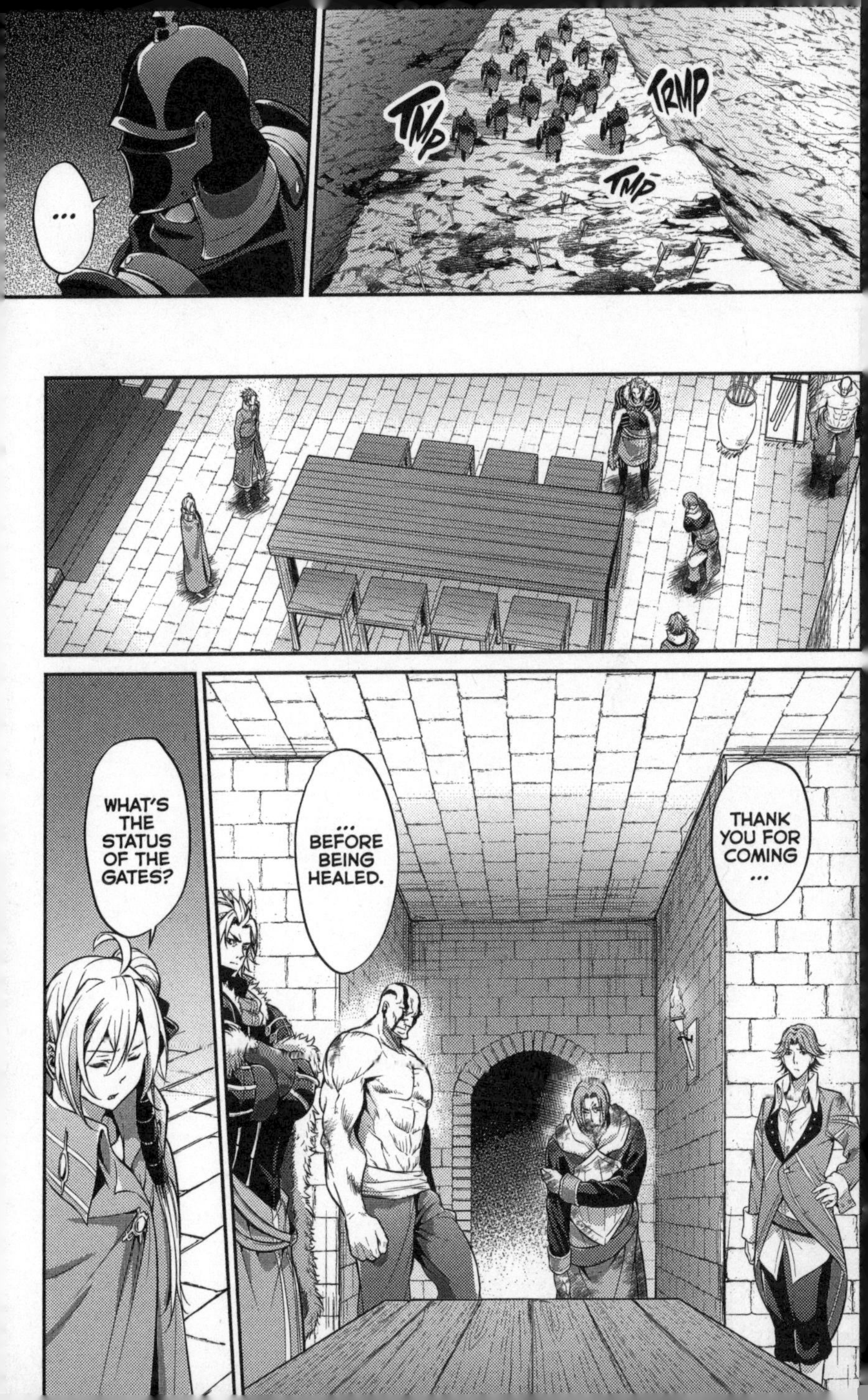
TRMP
TMP
TMP
...
THANK YOU FOR COMING ...
... BEFORE BEING HEALED.
WHAT'S THE STATUS OF THE GATES?

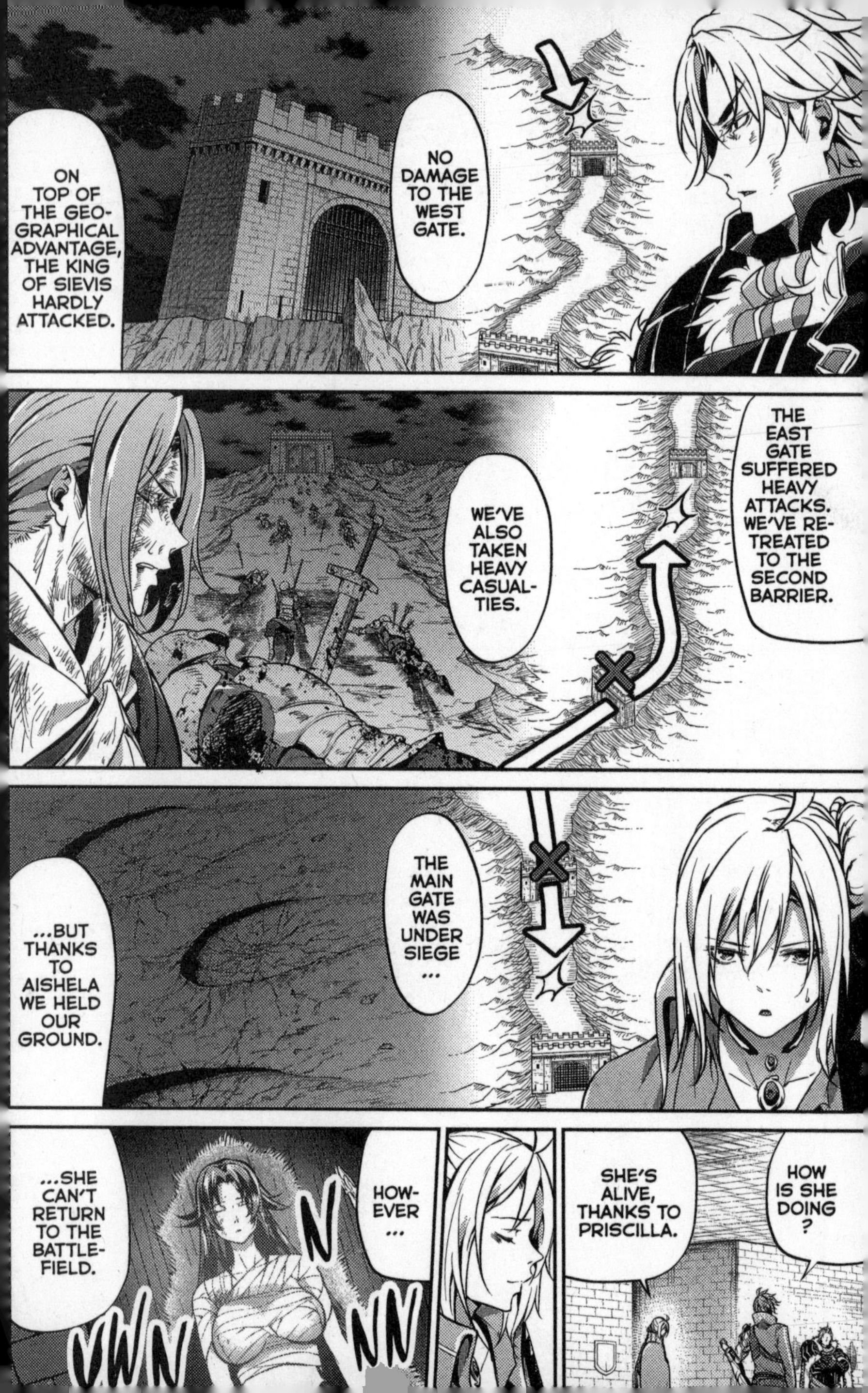
NO DAMAGE TO THE WEST GATE.
ON TOP OF THE GEOGRAPHICAL ADVANTAGE, THE KING OF SIEVIS HARDLY ATTACKED.
THE EAST GATE SUFFERED HEAVY ATTACKS. WE'VE RETREATED TO THE SECOND BARRIER.
WE'VE ALSO TAKEN HEAVY CASUALTIES.
THE MAIN GATE WAS UNDER SIEGE...
...BUT THANKS TO AISHELA WE HELD OUR GROUND.
HOW IS SHE DOING?
SHE'S ALIVE, THANKS TO PRISCILLA.
HOWEVER...
...SHE CAN'T RETURN TO THE BATTLEFIELD.
VWN
N
NN

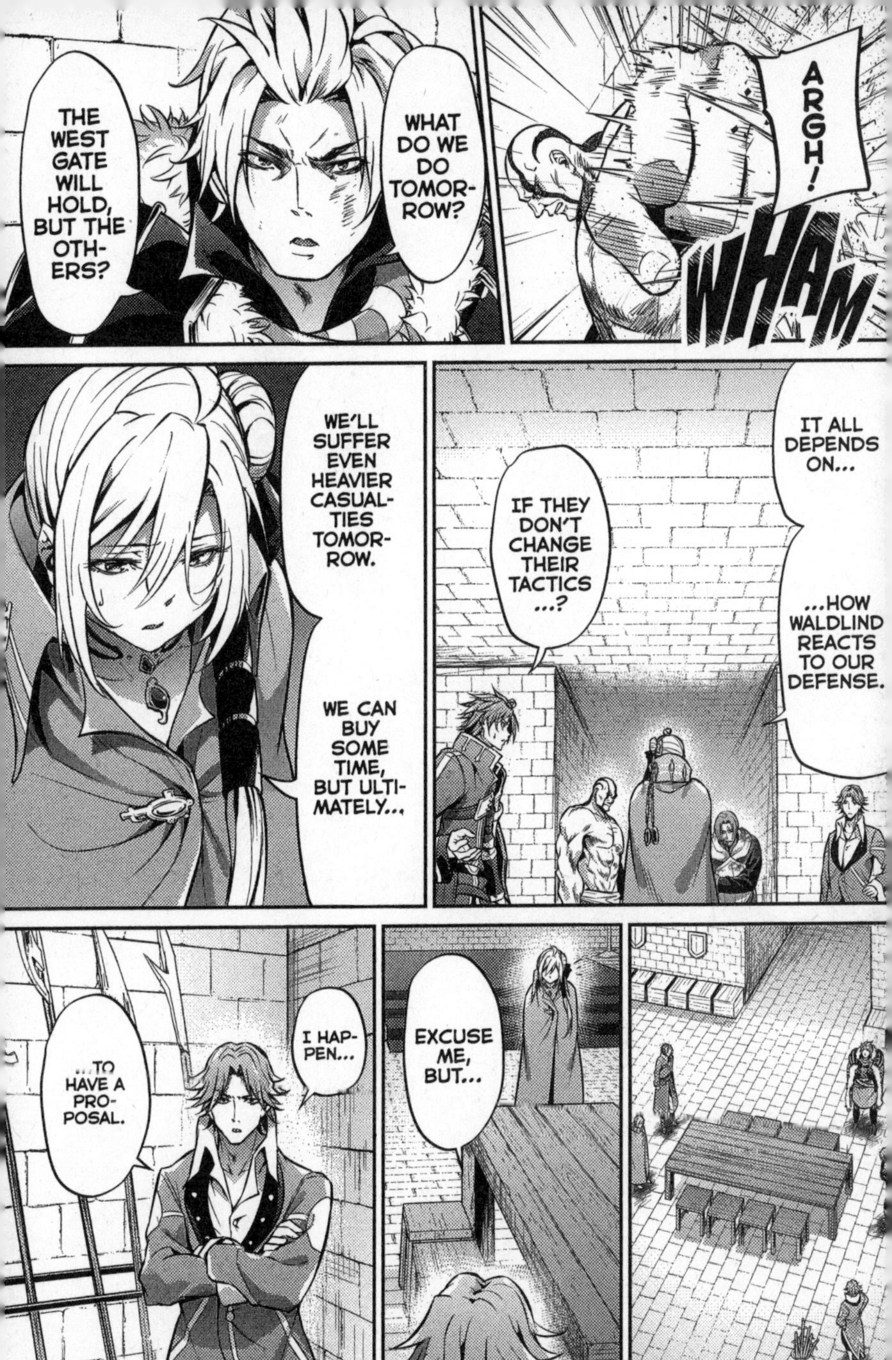
ARGH!
WHAM
WHAT DO WE DO TOMORROW?
THE WEST GATE WILL HOLD, BUT THE OTHERS?
IT ALL DEPENDS ON...
IF THEY DON'T CHANGE THEIR TACTICS...?
...HOW WALDLIND REACTS TO OUR DEFENSE.
WE'LL SUFFER EVEN HEAVIER CASUALTIES TOMORROW.
WE CAN BUY SOME TIME, BUT ULTIMATELY...
EXCUSE ME, BUT...
I HAPPEN...
...TO HAVE A PROPOSAL.

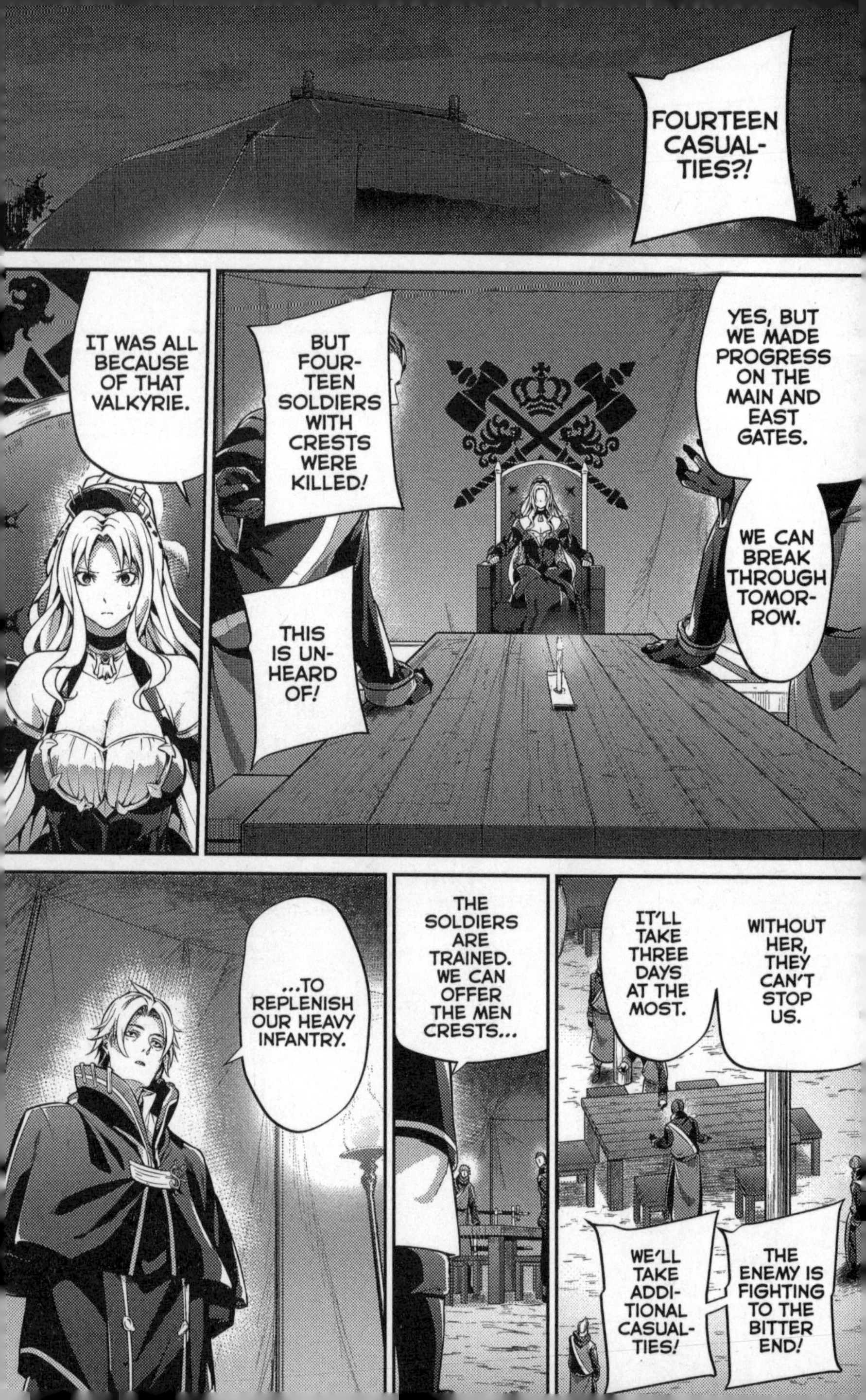
FOURTEEN CASUALTIES?!
YES, BUT WE MADE PROGRESS ON THE MAIN AND EAST GATES.
WE CAN BREAK THROUGH TOMORROW.
BUT FOURTEEN SOLDIERS WITH CRESTS WERE KILLED!
THIS IS UNHEARD OF!
IT WAS ALL BECAUSE OF THAT VALKYRIE.
WITHOUT HER, THEY CAN'T STOP US.
IT'LL TAKE THREE DAYS AT THE MOST.
THE ENEMY IS FIGHTING TO THE BITTER END!
WE'LL TAKE ADDITIONAL CASUALTIES!
THE SOLDIERS ARE TRAINED. WE CAN OFFER THE MEN CRESTS...
...TO REPLENISH OUR HEAVY INFANTRY.

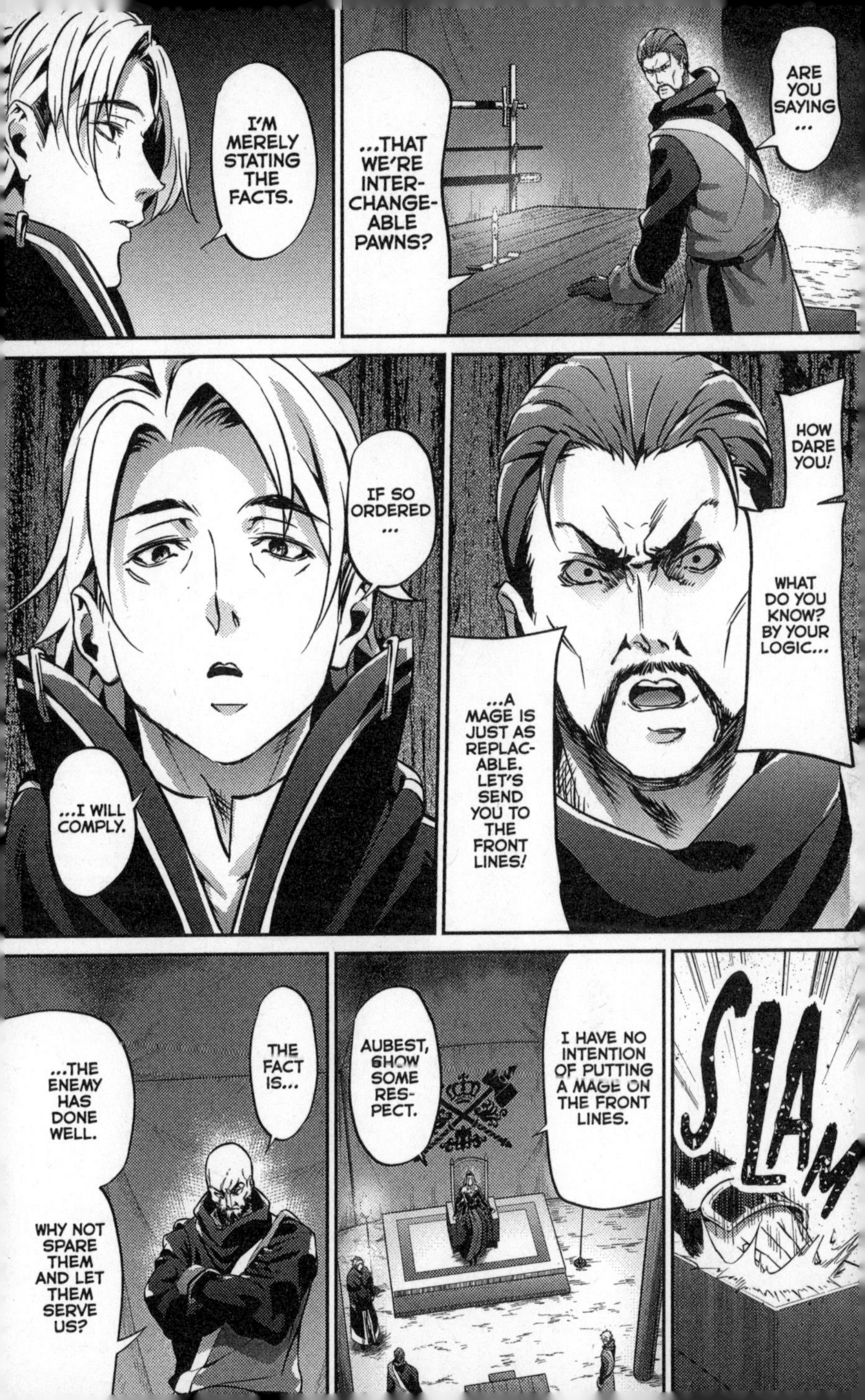
ARE YOU SAYING...
...THAT WE'RE INTERCHANGE-ABLE PAWNS?
I'M MERELY STATING THE FACTS.
HOW DARE YOU!
WHAT DO YOU KNOW? BY YOUR LOGIC...
...A MAGE IS JUST AS REPLAC-ABLE. LET'S SEND YOU TO THE FRONT LINES!
IF SO ORDERED...
...I WILL COMPLY.
SLAM
I HAVE NO INTENTION OF PUTTING A MAGE ON THE FRONT LINES.
AUBEST, SHOW SOME RES-PECT.
THE FACT IS...
...THE ENEMY HAS DONE WELL.
WHY NOT SPARE THEM AND LET THEM SERVE US?

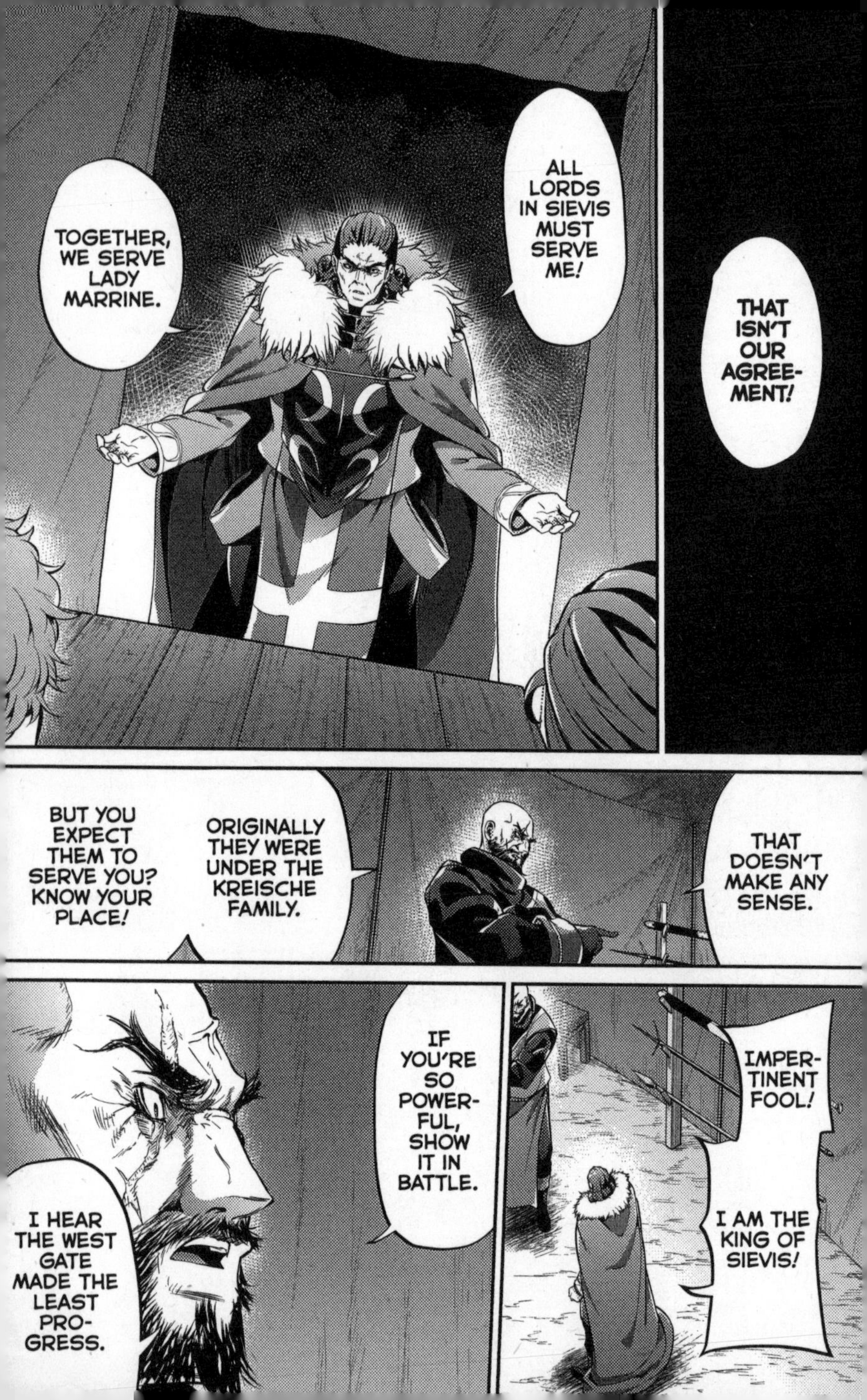
THAT ISN'T OUR AGREEMENT!
ALL LORDS IN SIEVIS MUST SERVE ME!
TOGETHER, WE SERVE LADY MARRINE.
THAT DOESN'T MAKE ANY SENSE.
ORIGINALLY THEY WERE UNDER THE KREISCHE FAMILY.
BUT YOU EXPECT THEM TO SERVE YOU? KNOW YOUR PLACE!
IMPERTINENT FOOL!
I AM THE KING OF SIEVIS!
IF YOU'RE SO POWERFUL, SHOW IT IN BATTLE.
I HEAR THE WEST GATE MADE THE LEAST PROGRESS.

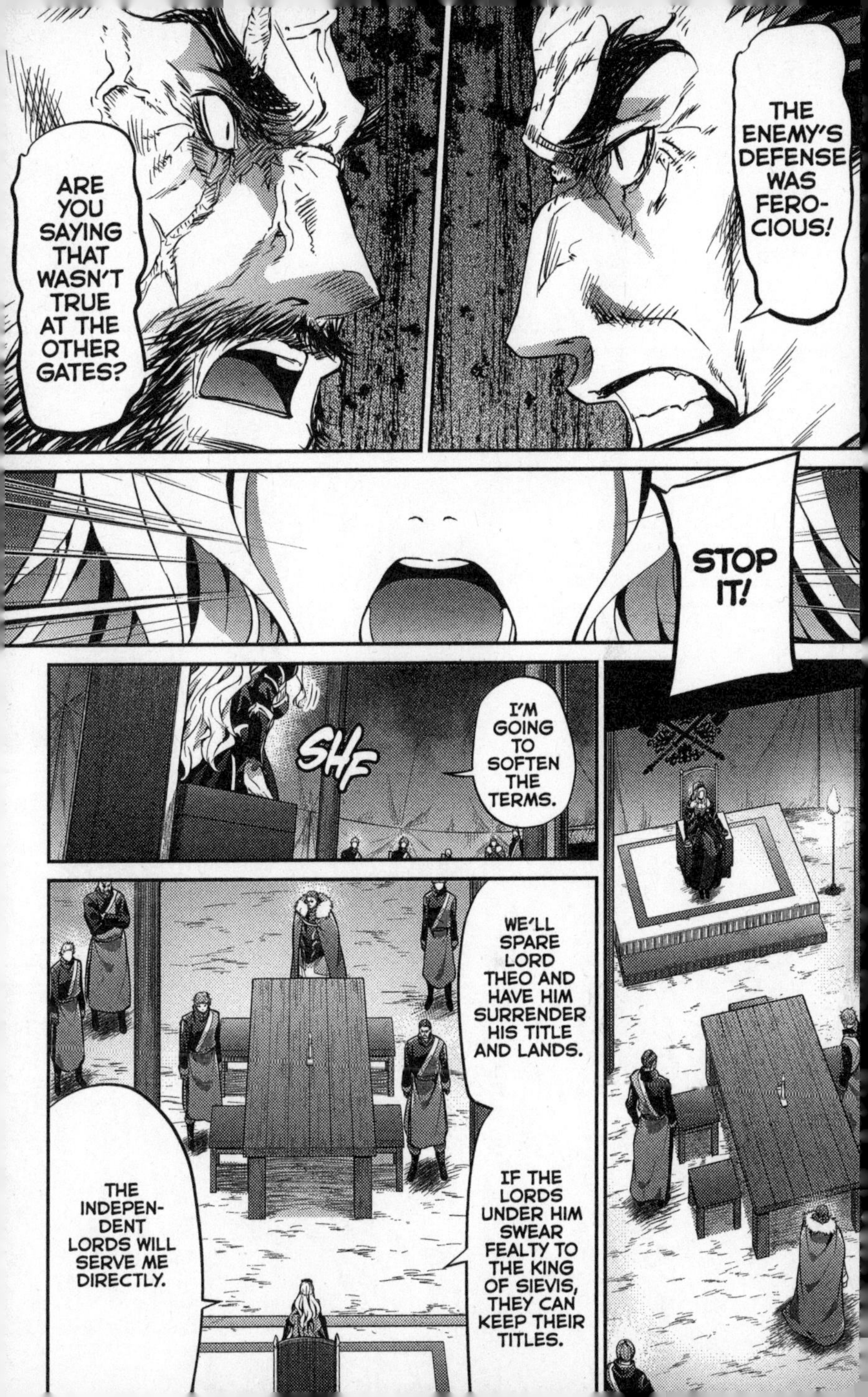
THE ENEMY'S DEFENSE WAS FERO-CIOUS!
ARE YOU SAYING THAT WASN'T TRUE AT THE OTHER GATES?
STOP IT!
SHF
I'M GOING TO SOFTEN THE TERMS.
WE'LL SPARE LORD THEO AND HAVE HIM SURRENDER HIS TITLE AND LANDS.
IF THE LORDS UNDER HIM SWEAR FEALTY TO THE KING OF SIEVIS, THEY CAN KEEP THEIR TITLES.
THE INDEPEN-DENT LORDS WILL SERVE ME DIRECTLY.

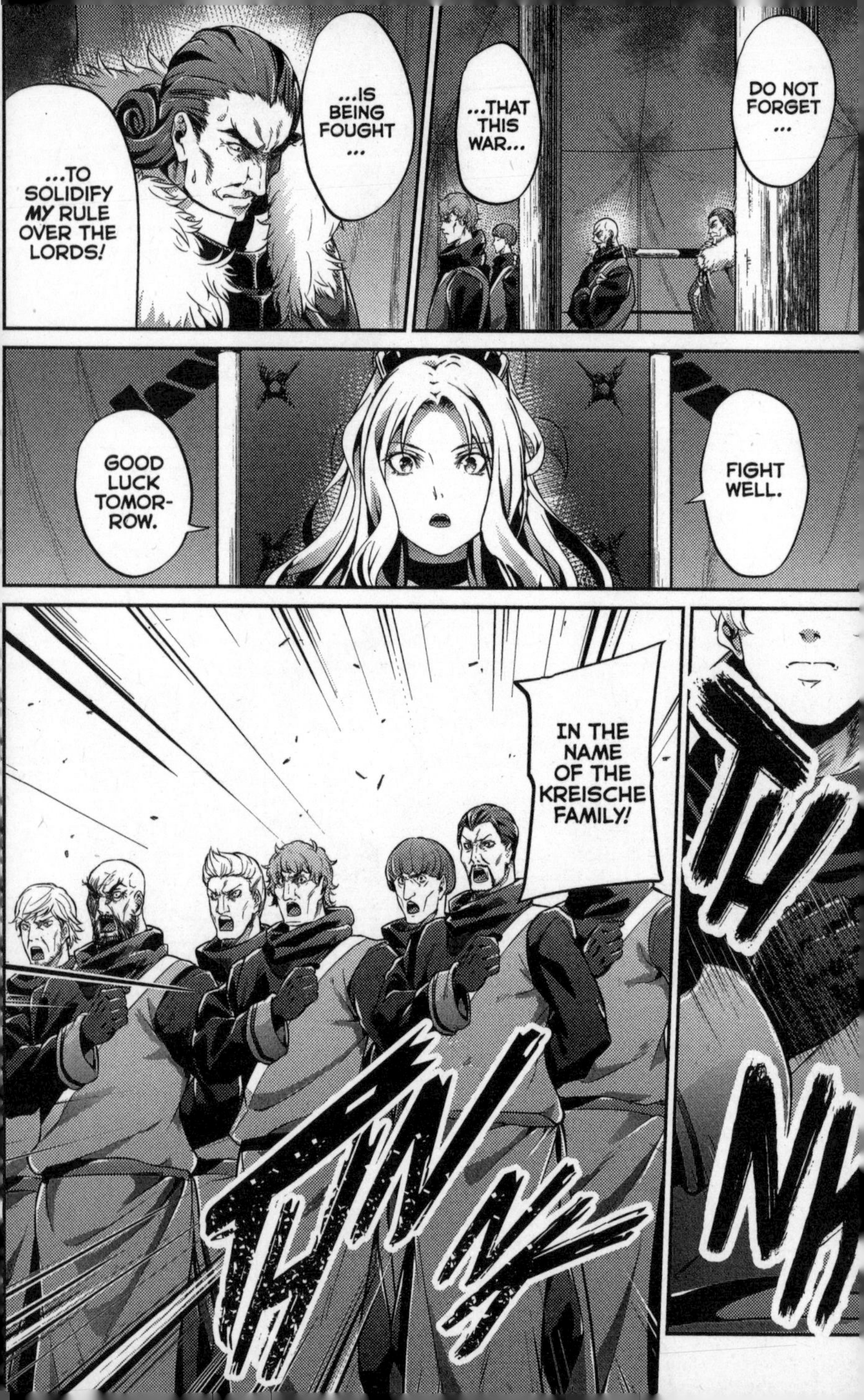
DO NOT FORGET ...
...THAT THIS WAR...
...IS BEING FOUGHT ...
...TO SOLIDIFY MY RULE OVER THE LORDS!
FIGHT WELL.
GOOD LUCK TOMOR-ROW.
IN THE NAME OF THE KREISCHE FAMILY!

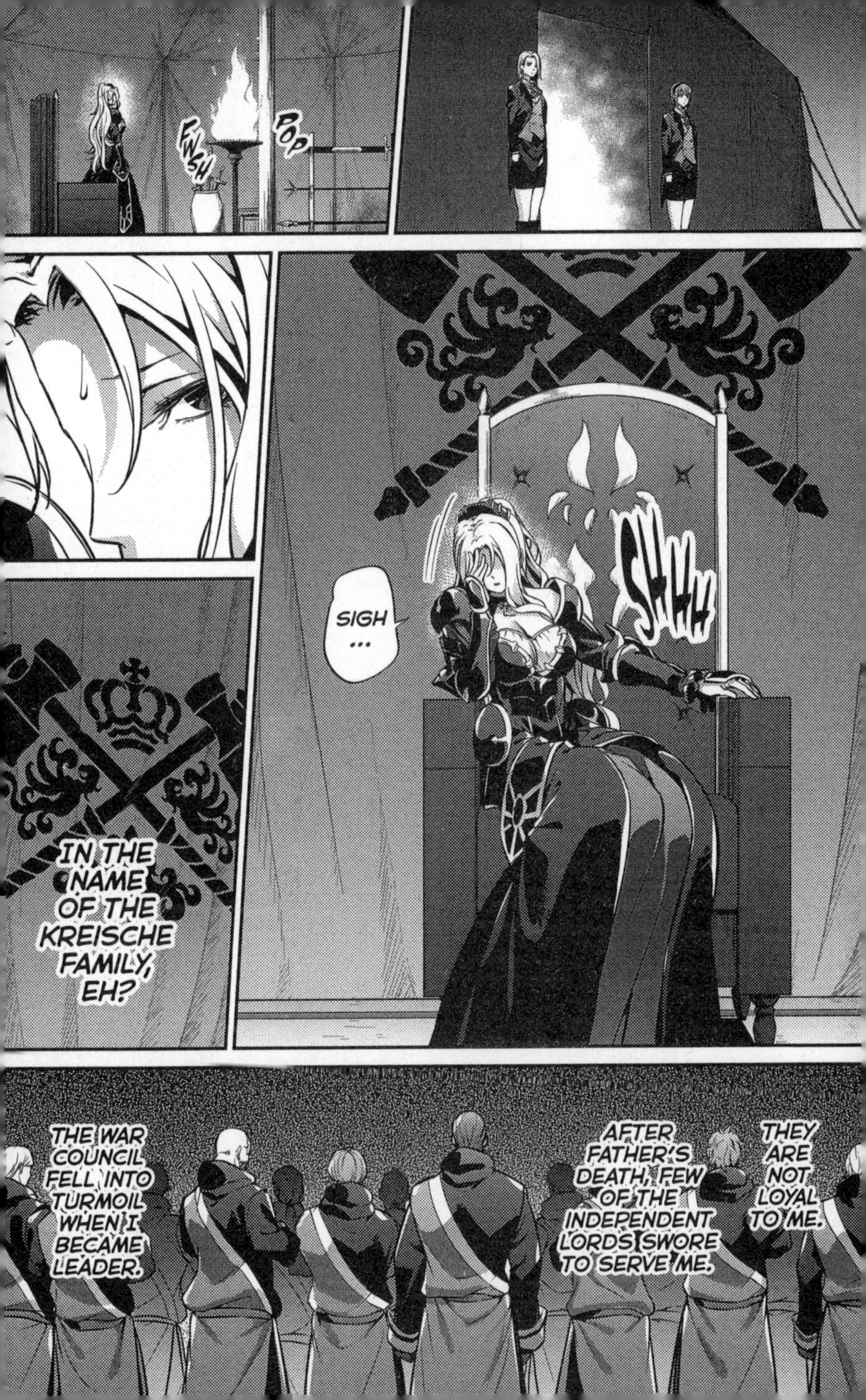
POP
FWSH
SHHH
SIGH...
IN THE NAME OF THE KREISCHE FAMILY, EH?
THEY ARE NOT LOYAL TO ME.
AFTER FATHER'S DEATH, FEW OF THE INDEPENDENT LORDS SWORE TO SERVE ME.
THE WAR COUNCIL FELL INTO TURMOIL WHEN I BECAME LEADER.

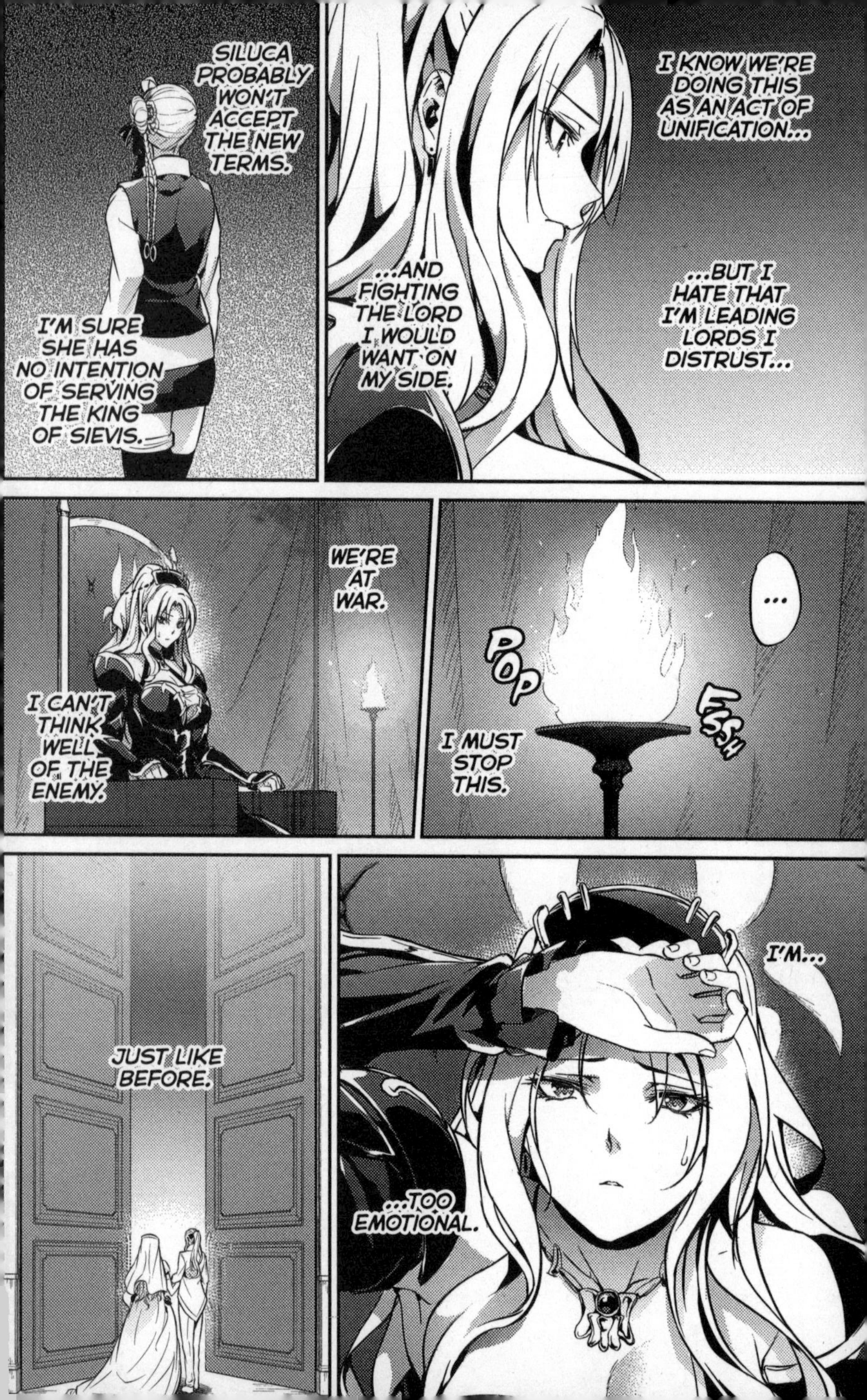
I KNOW WE'RE DOING THIS AS AN ACT OF UNIFICATION...
...BUT I HATE THAT I'M LEADING LORDS I DISTRUST...
...AND FIGHTING THE LORD I WOULD WANT ON MY SIDE.
SILUCA PROBABLY WON'T ACCEPT THE NEW TERMS.
I'M SURE SHE HAS NO INTENTION OF SERVING THE KING OF SIEVIS.
...
POP
FSSH
I MUST STOP THIS.
WE'RE AT WAR.
I CAN'T THINK WELL OF THE ENEMY.
I'M...
...TOO EMOTIONAL.
JUST LIKE BEFORE.

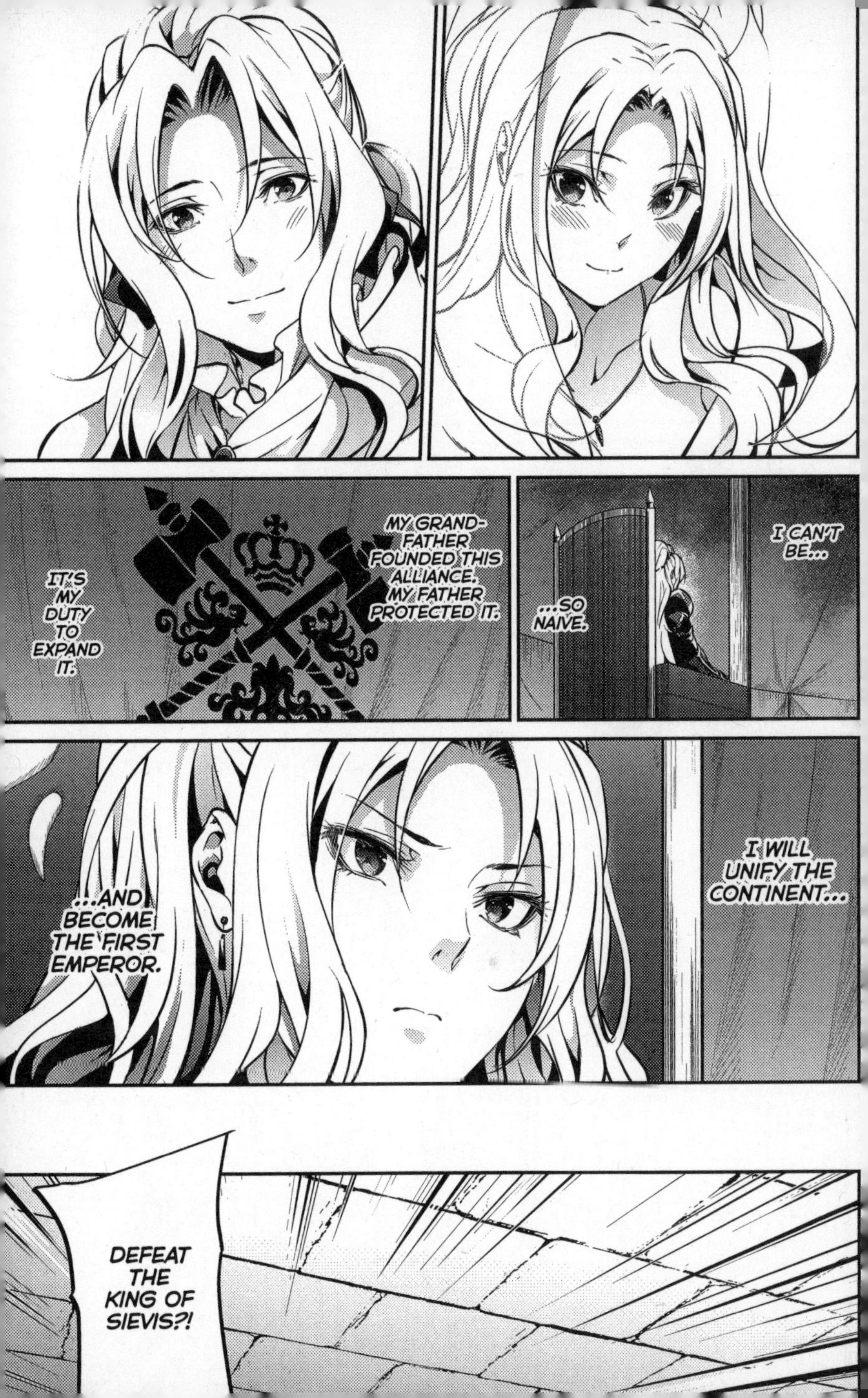
I CAN'T BE...
...SO NAIVE.
MY GRAND-FATHER FOUNDED THIS ALLIANCE. MY FATHER PROTECTED IT.
IT'S MY DUTY TO EXPAND IT.
I WILL UNIFY THE CONTINENT...
...AND BECOME THE FIRST EMPEROR.
DEFEAT THE KING OF SIEVIS?!

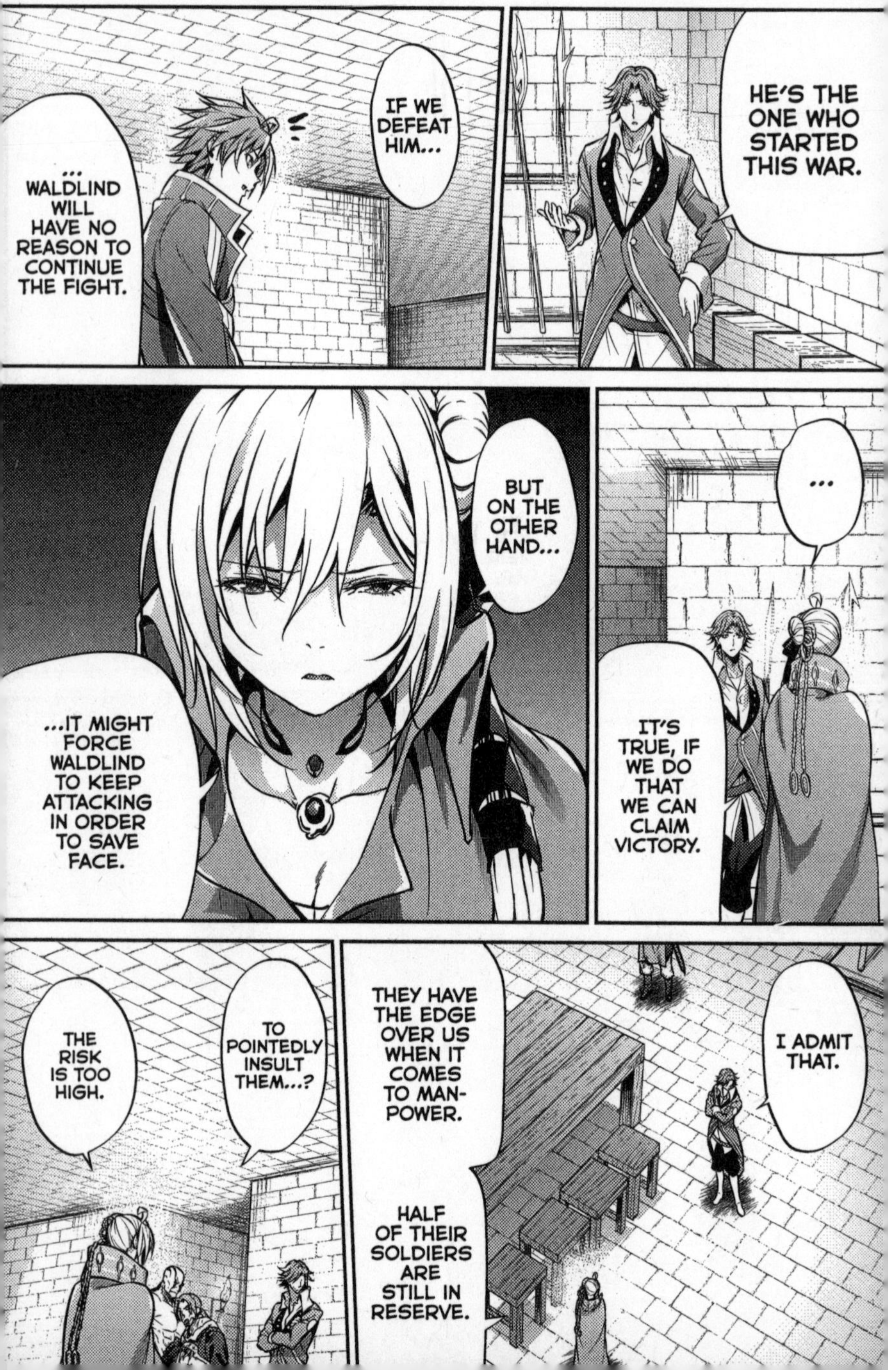
HE'S THE ONE WHO STARTED THIS WAR.
IF WE DEFEAT HIM...
...WALDLIND WILL HAVE NO REASON TO CONTINUE THE FIGHT.
...
IT'S TRUE, IF WE DO THAT WE CAN CLAIM VICTORY.
BUT ON THE OTHER HAND...
...IT MIGHT FORCE WALDLIND TO KEEP ATTACKING IN ORDER TO SAVE FACE.
I ADMIT THAT.
THEY HAVE THE EDGE OVER US WHEN IT COMES TO MAN-POWER.
HALF OF THEIR SOLDIERS ARE STILL IN RESERVE.
TO POINTEDLY INSULT THEM...?
THE RISK IS TOO HIGH.

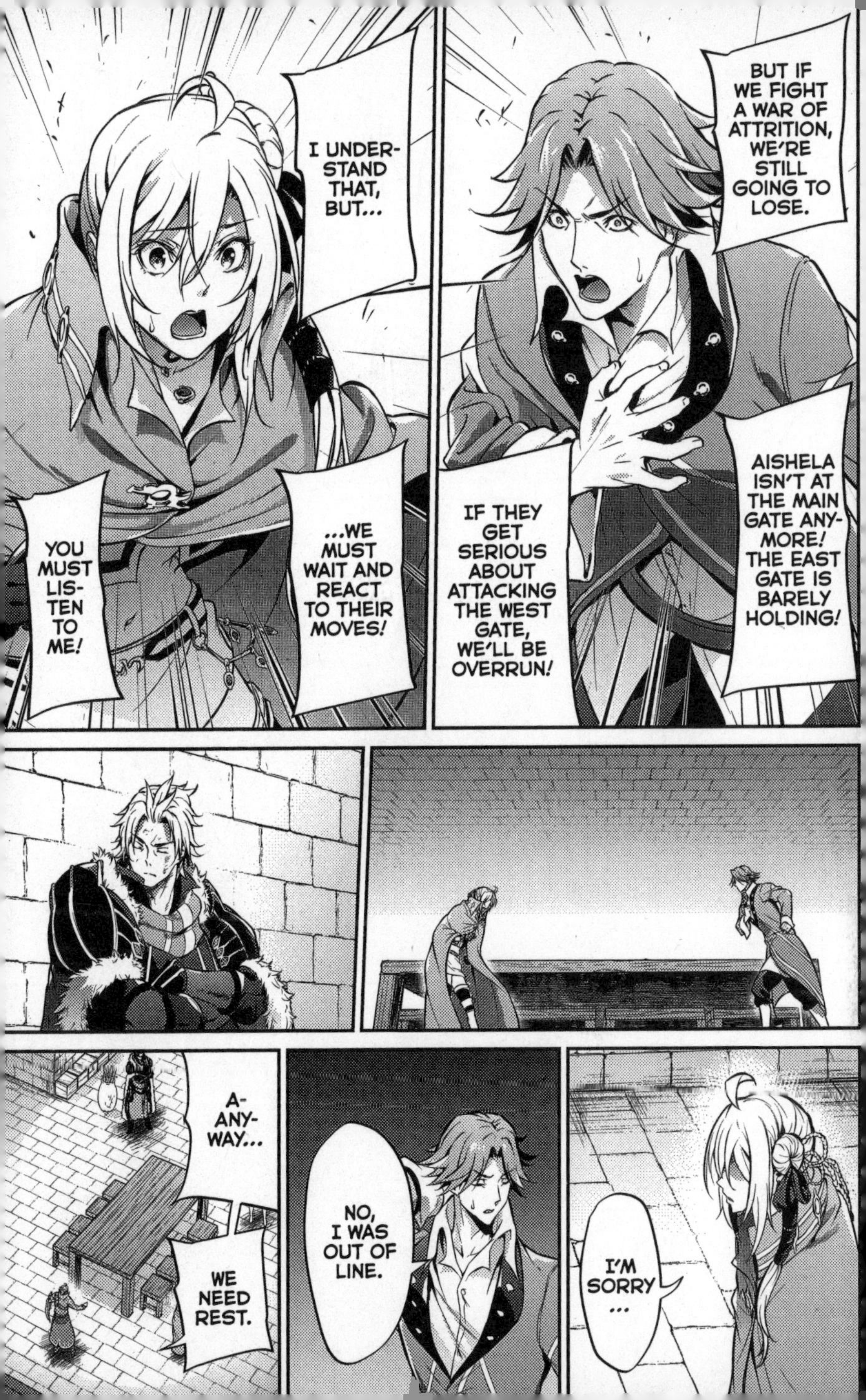
BUT IF WE FIGHT A WAR OF ATTRITION, WE'RE STILL GOING TO LOSE.
AISHELA ISN'T AT THE MAIN GATE ANYMORE! THE EAST GATE IS BARELY HOLDING!
IF THEY GET SERIOUS ABOUT ATTACKING THE WEST GATE, WE'LL BE OVERRUN!
I UNDERSTAND THAT, BUT...
...WE MUST WAIT AND REACT TO THEIR MOVES!
YOU MUST LISTEN TO ME!
I'M SORRY...
NO, I WAS OUT OF LINE.
A-ANYWAY...
WE NEED REST.

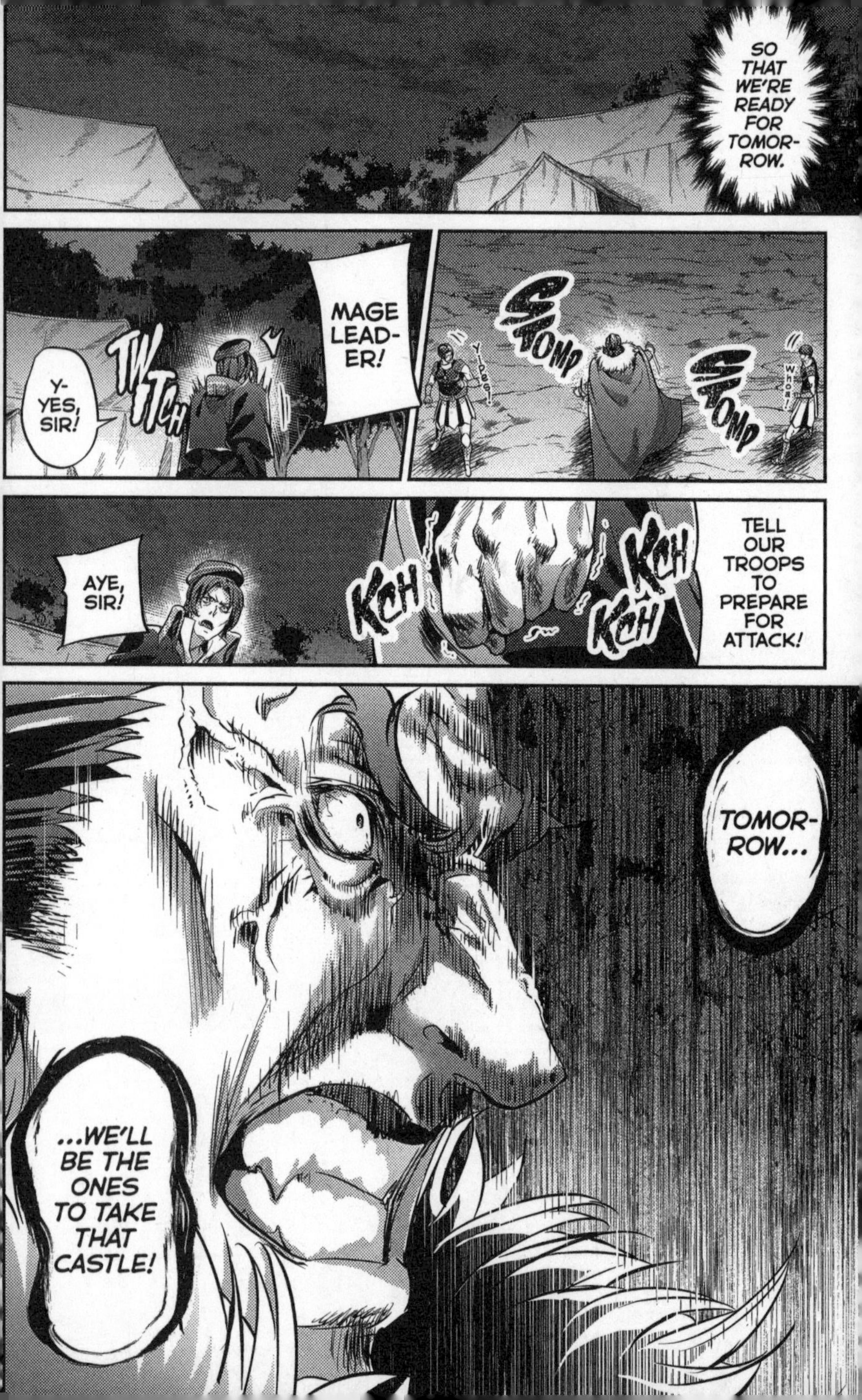
SO THAT WE'RE READY FOR TOMOR-ROW.
STOMP
Whoa!
STOMP
Yipes!
MAGE LEADER!
TWITCH
Y-YES, SIR!
TELL OUR TROOPS TO PREPARE FOR ATTACK!
KCH
KCH
KCH
KCH
AYE, SIR!
TOMOR-ROW...
...WE'LL BE THE ONES TO TAKE THAT CASTLE!

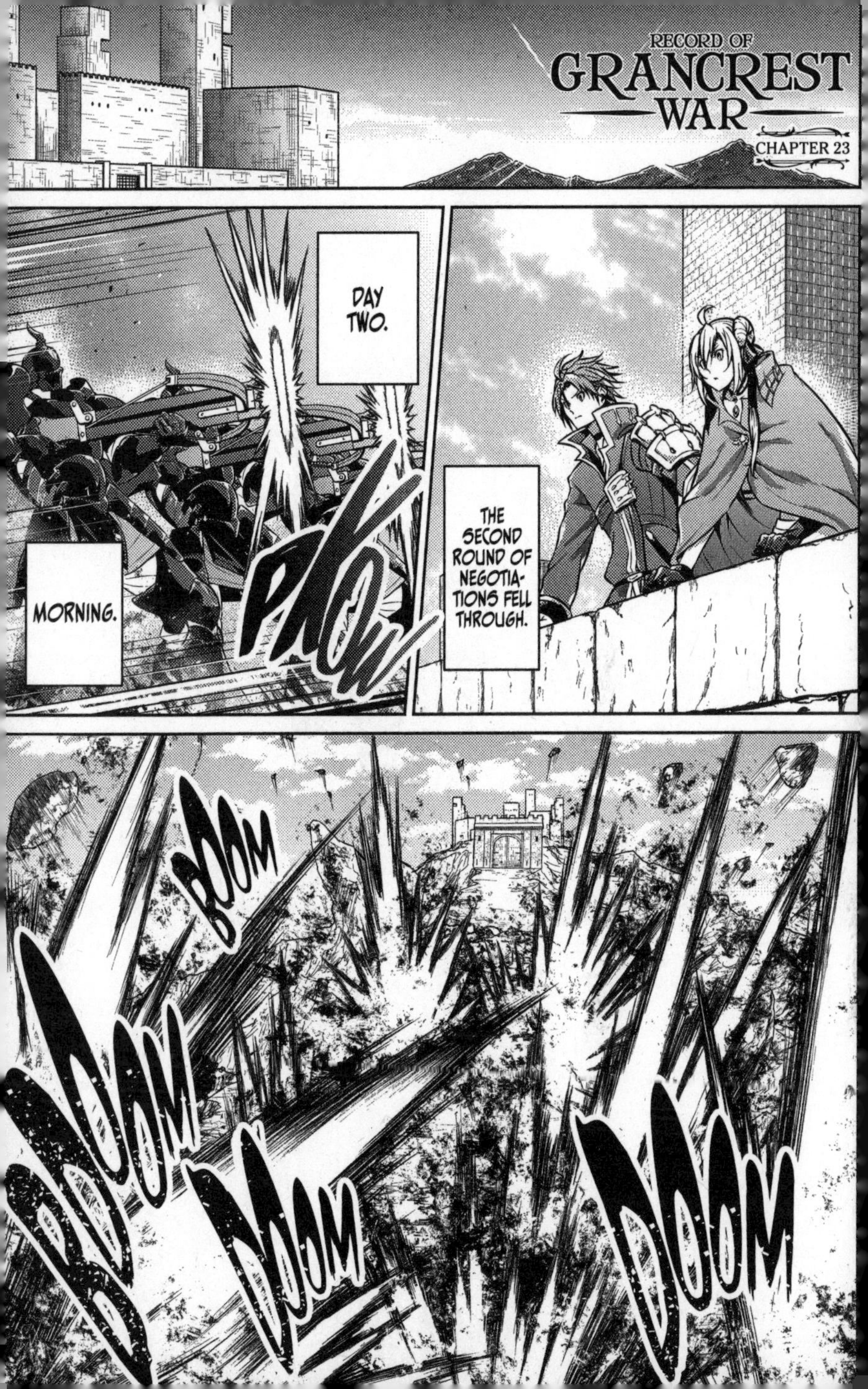
RECORD OF
GRANCREST
WAR
CHAPTER 23
THE SECOND ROUND OF NEGOTIATIONS FELL THROUGH.
DAY TWO.
MORNING.
PHOW
BOOM
BOOM
BOOM
BOOM
BOOM

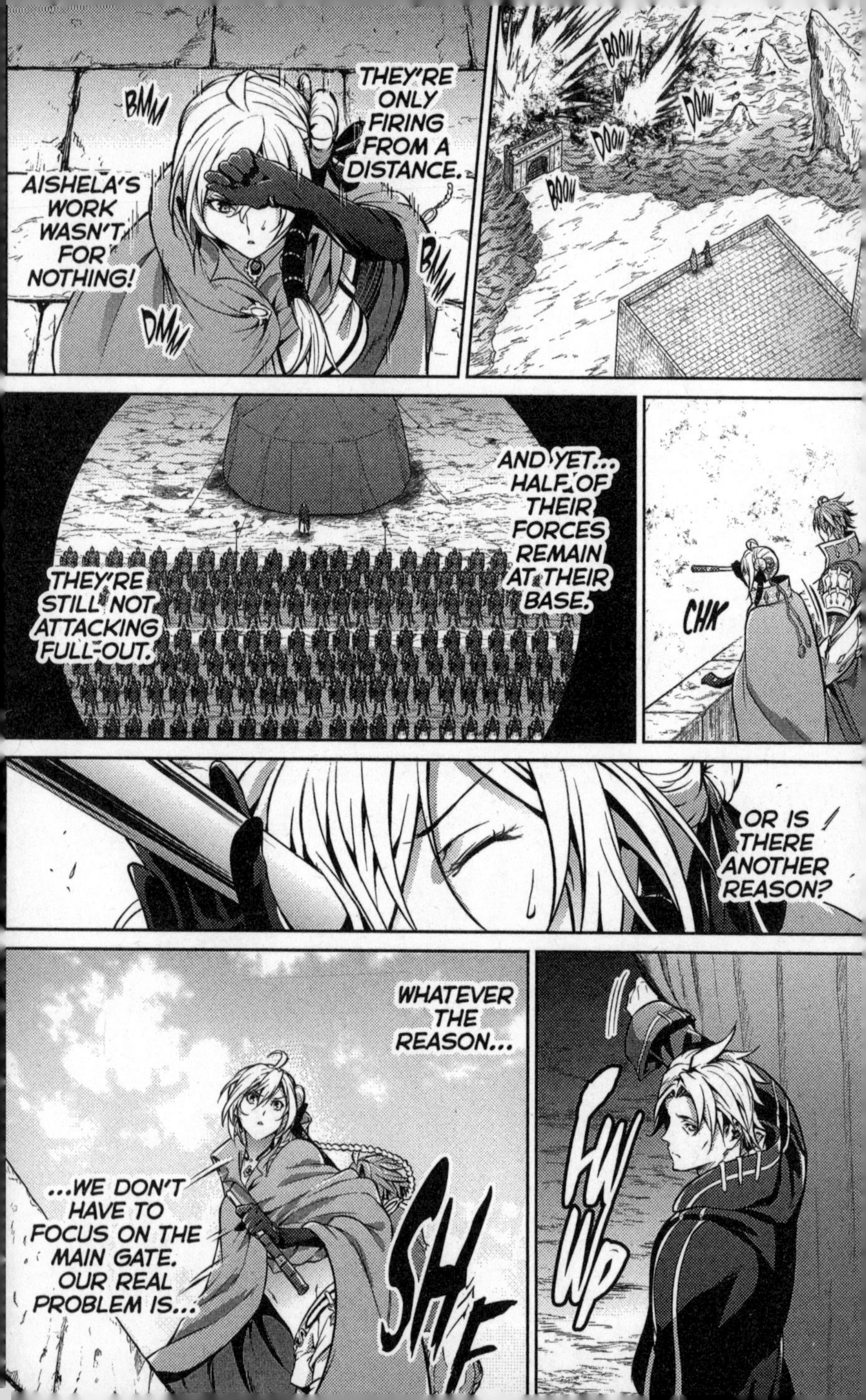
BOOM
DOOM
DOOM
BOOM
THEY'RE ONLY FIRING FROM A DISTANCE.
BMM
AISHELA'S WORK WASN'T FOR NOTHING!
BMM
DMM
CHK
AND YET... HALF OF THEIR FORCES REMAIN AT THEIR BASE.
THEY'RE STILL NOT ATTACKING FULL-OUT.
OR IS THERE ANOTHER REASON?
HWUP
WHATEVER THE REASON...
...WE DON'T HAVE TO FOCUS ON THE MAIN GATE. OUR REAL PROBLEM IS...
SHF

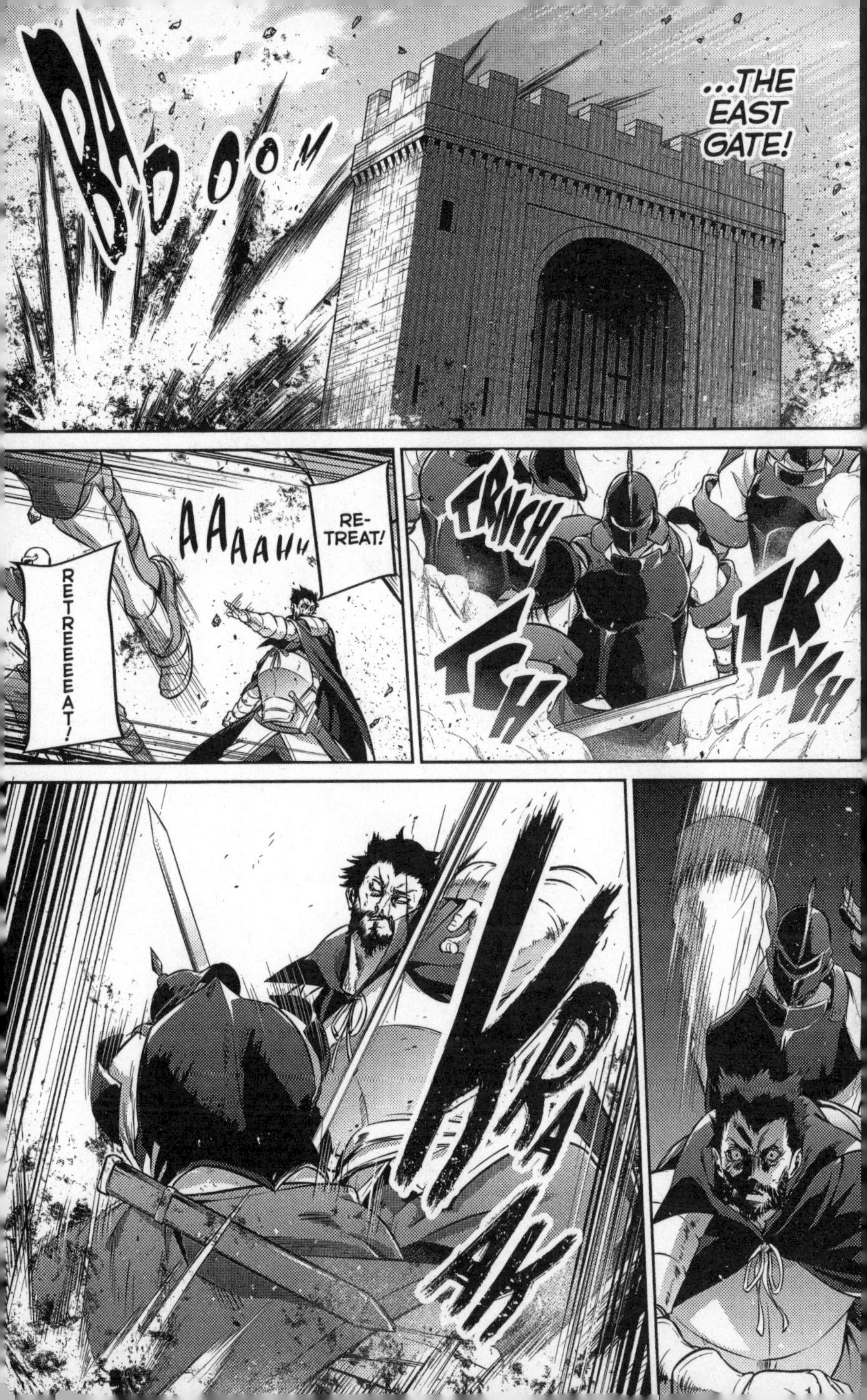
BADOOM
...THE EAST GATE!
TRNCH
TCH
TRNCH
RE-TREAT!
AAAAHH
RETREEEEAT!
KRAAK

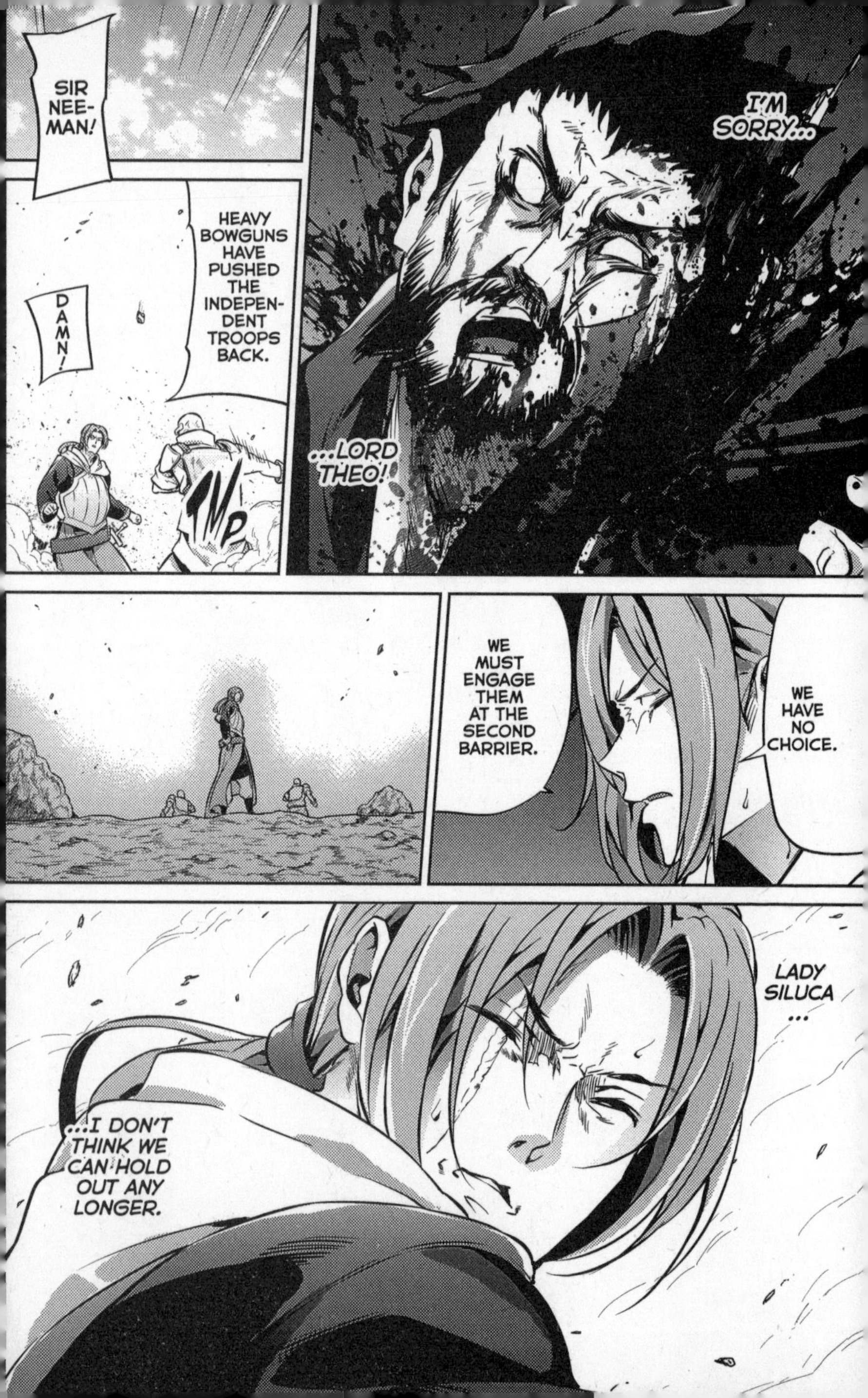
I'M SORRY...
...LORD THEO!
SIR NEE-MAN!
HEAVY BOWGUNS HAVE PUSHED THE INDEPENDENT TROOPS BACK.
DAMN!
WE HAVE NO CHOICE.
WE MUST ENGAGE THEM AT THE SECOND BARRIER.
LADY SILUCA...
...I DON'T THINK WE CAN HOLD OUT ANY LONGER.

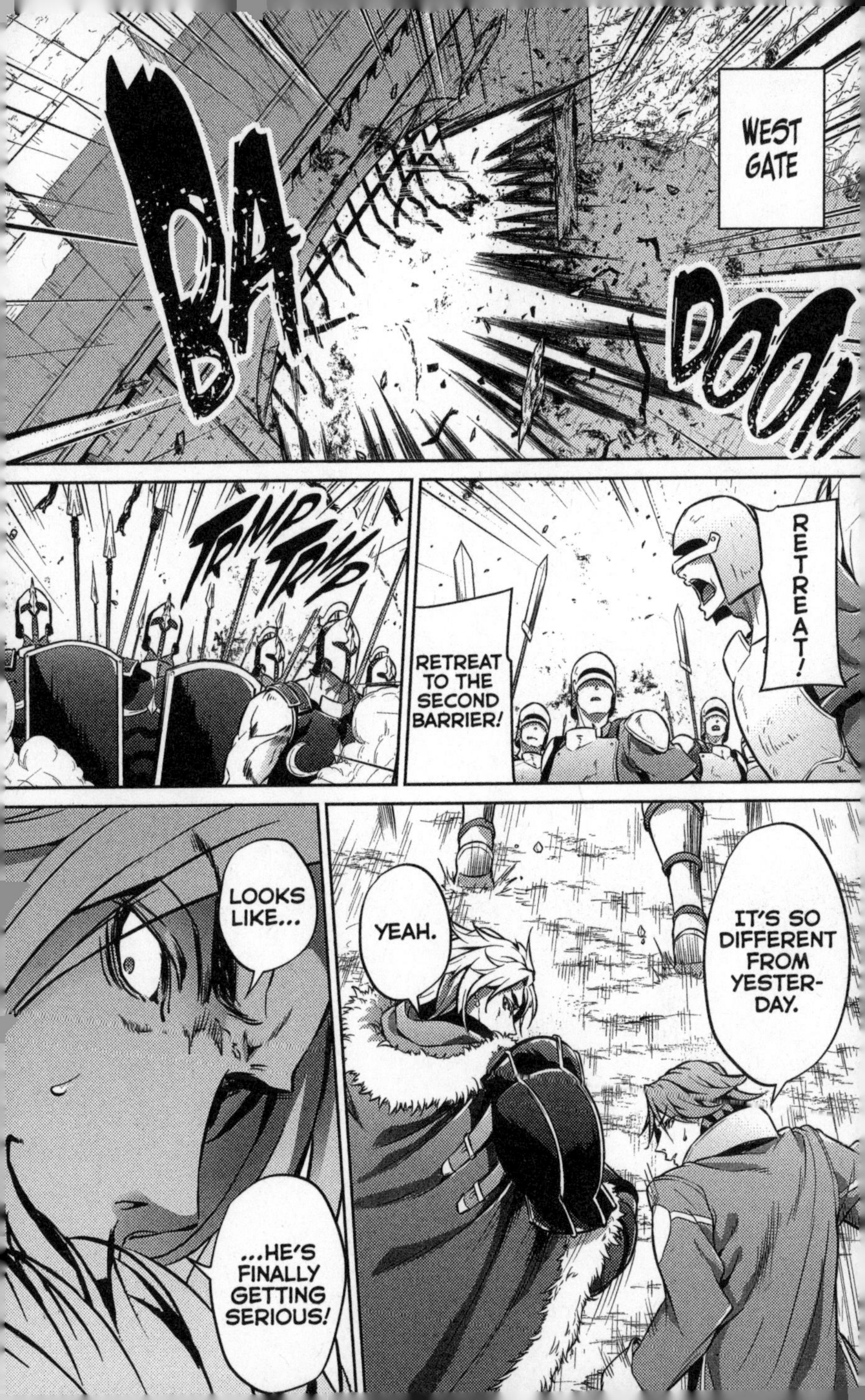
WEST GATE
BA
DOOM
RETREAT!
RETREAT TO THE SECOND BARRIER!
TRMP TRMP
IT'S SO DIFFERENT FROM YESTERDAY.
YEAH.
LOOKS LIKE...
...HE'S FINALLY GETTING SERIOUS!

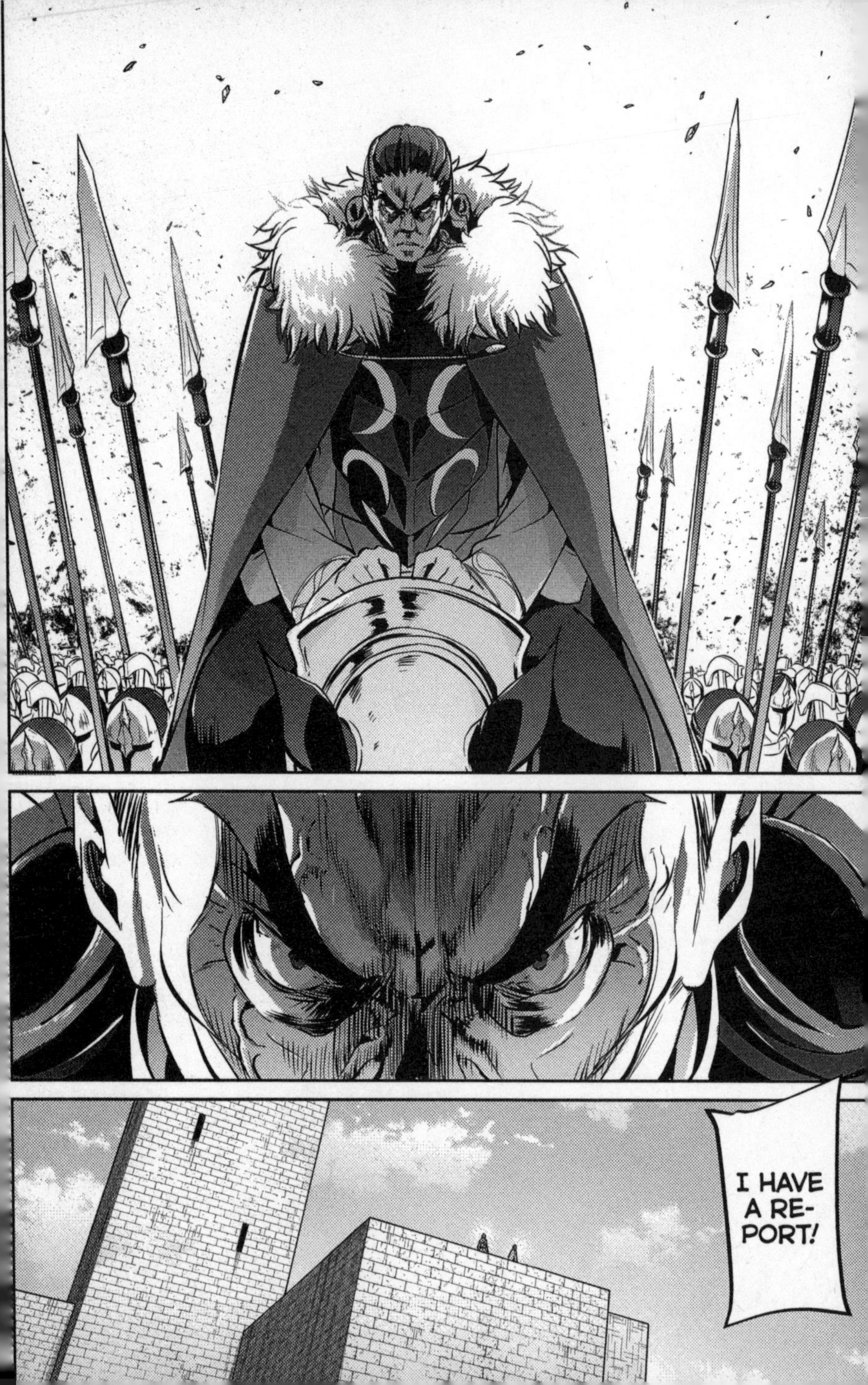
I HAVE A RE-PORT!

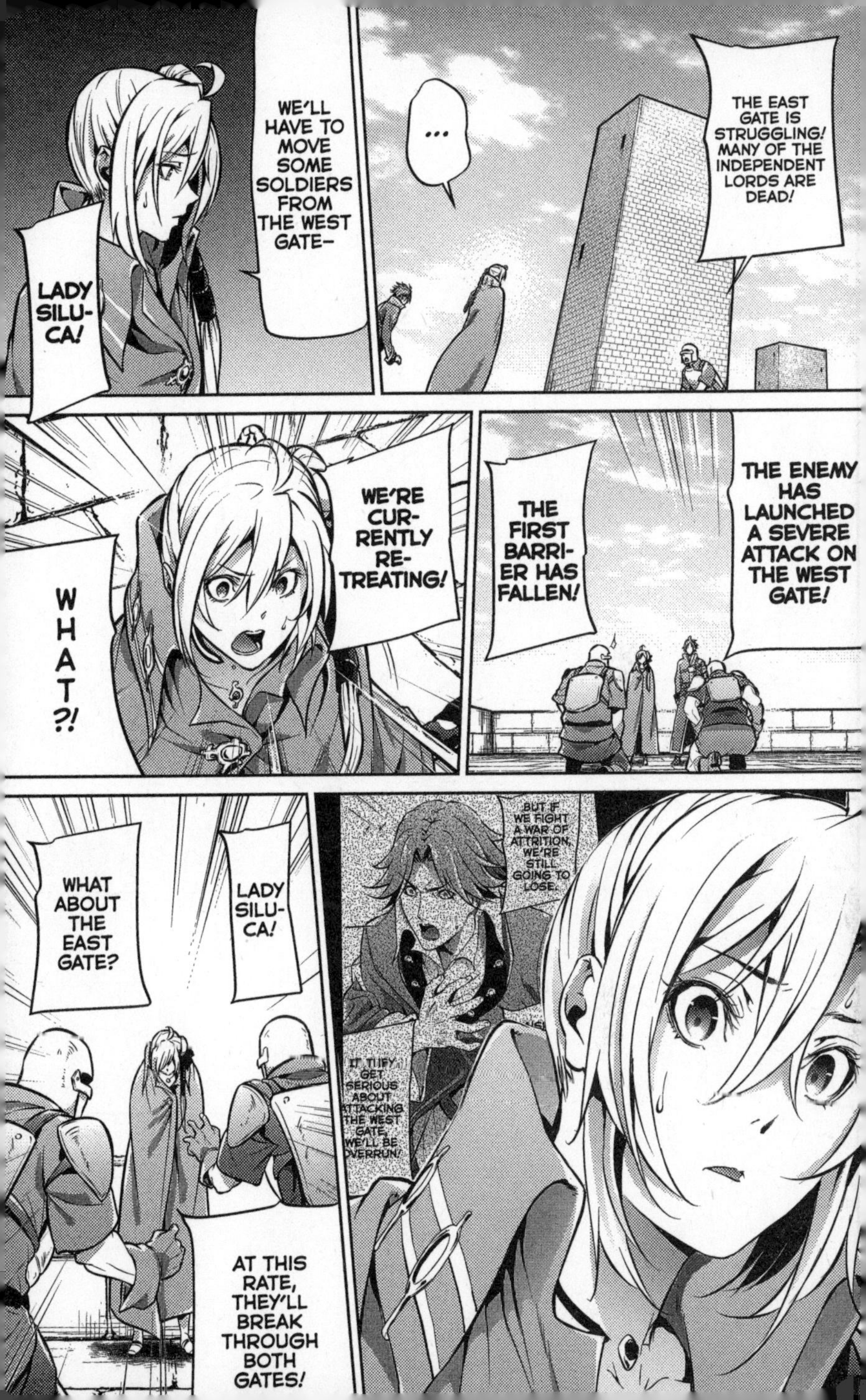
THE EAST GATE IS STRUGGLING! MANY OF THE INDEPENDENT LORDS ARE DEAD!
...
WE'LL HAVE TO MOVE SOME SOLDIERS FROM THE WEST GATE–
LADY SILUCA!
THE ENEMY HAS LAUNCHED A SEVERE ATTACK ON THE WEST GATE!
THE FIRST BARRIER HAS FALLEN!
WE'RE CURRENTLY RETREATING!
WHAT?!
BUT IF WE FIGHT A WAR OF ATTRITION, WE'RE STILL GOING TO LOSE.
IF THEY GET SERIOUS ABOUT ATTACKING THE WEST GATE, WE'LL BE OVERRUN!
LADY SILUCA!
WHAT ABOUT THE EAST GATE?
AT THIS RATE, THEY'LL BREAK THROUGH BOTH GATES!

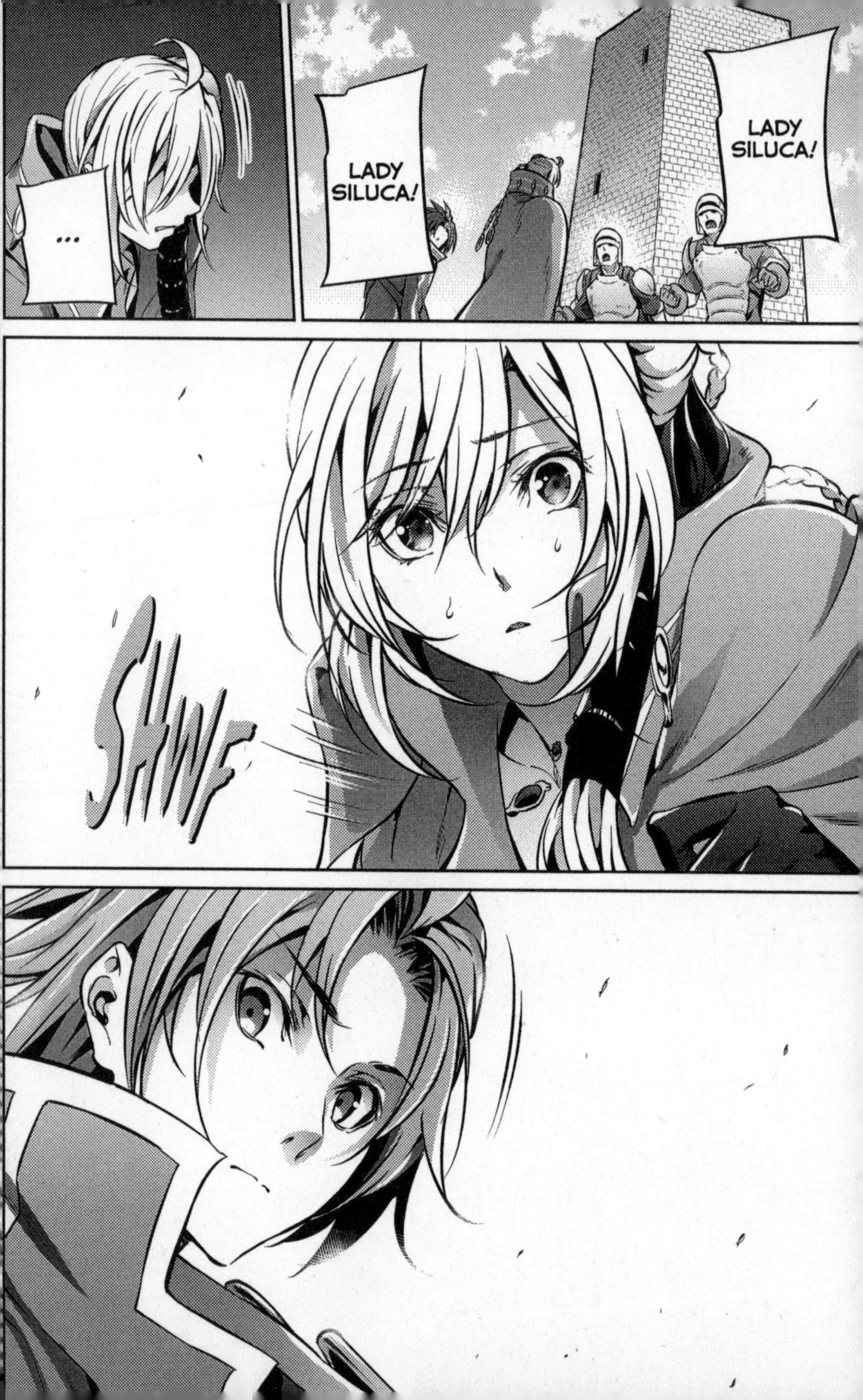
LADY SILUCA!
LADY SILUCA!
...
SHWF

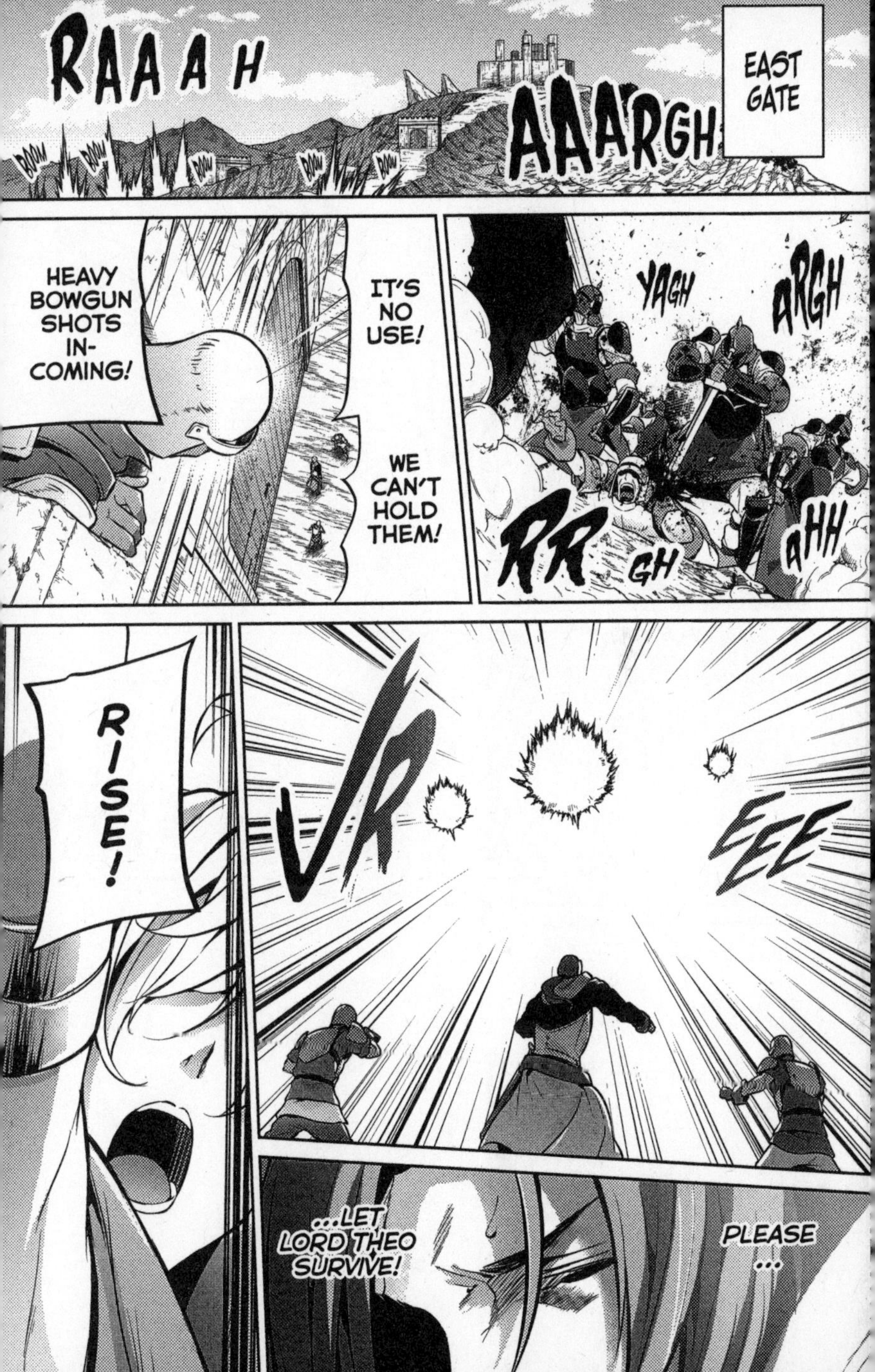
EAST GATE
AAARGH
RAAAH
BOOM
BOOM
BOOM
BOOM
BOOM
YAGH
ARGH
RRGH
AHH
IT'S NO USE!
HEAVY BOWGUN SHOTS IN-COMING!
WE CAN'T HOLD THEM!
VREEE
PLEASE...
...LET LORD THEO SURVIVE!
RISE!

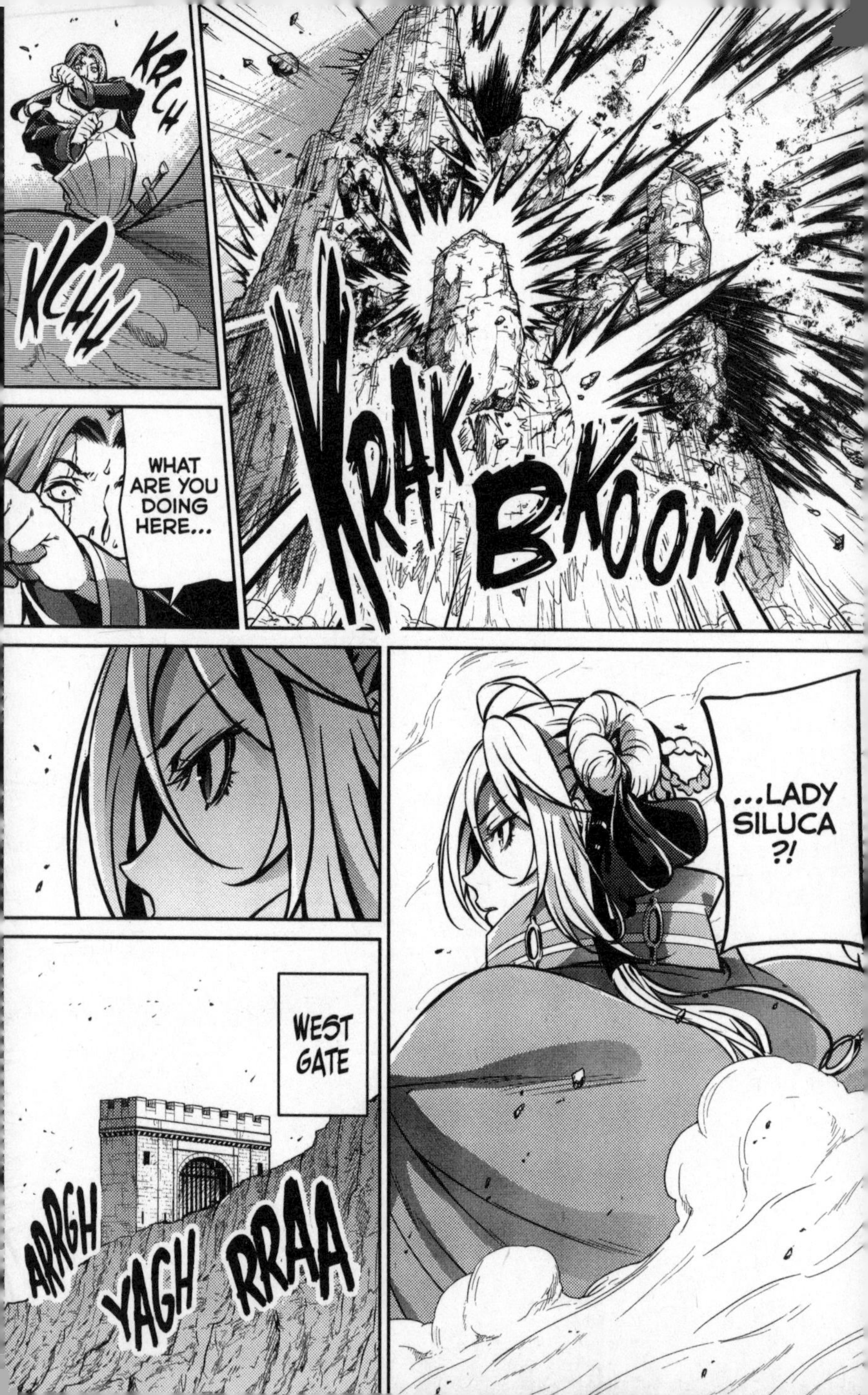
KRAK
BKOOM
KRCH
KCHH
WHAT ARE YOU DOING HERE...
...LADY SILUCA?!
WEST GATE
ARRGH
YAGH
RRAA

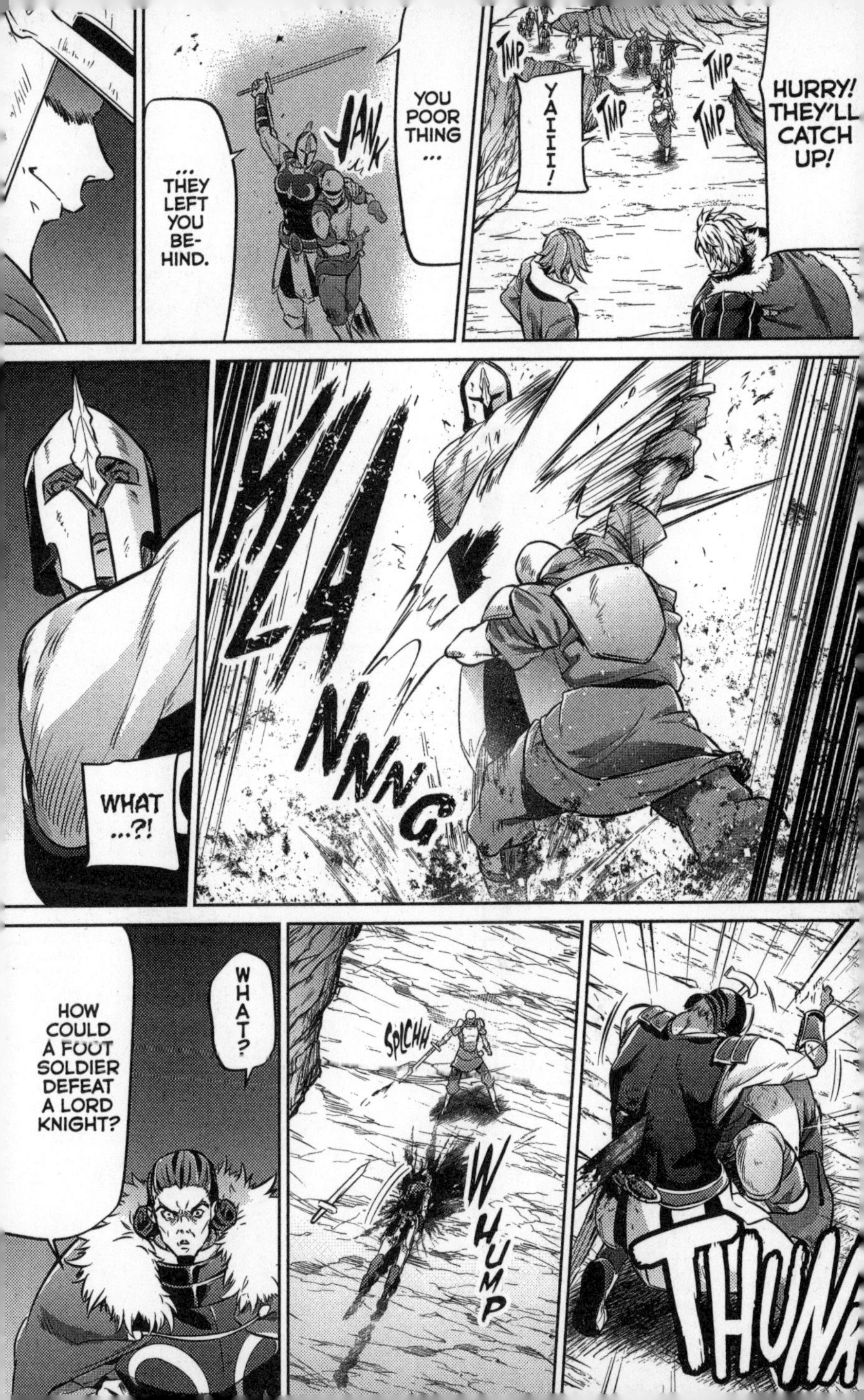
HURRY! THEY'LL CATCH UP!
TMP
TMP
TMP
TMP
YAIIII!
YOU POOR THING ...
JANK
... THEY LEFT YOU BE-HIND.
KLANNNG
WHAT ...?!
THUN
WHAT?
SPLCHH
WHUMP
HOW COULD A FOOT SOLDIER DEFEAT A LORD KNIGHT?

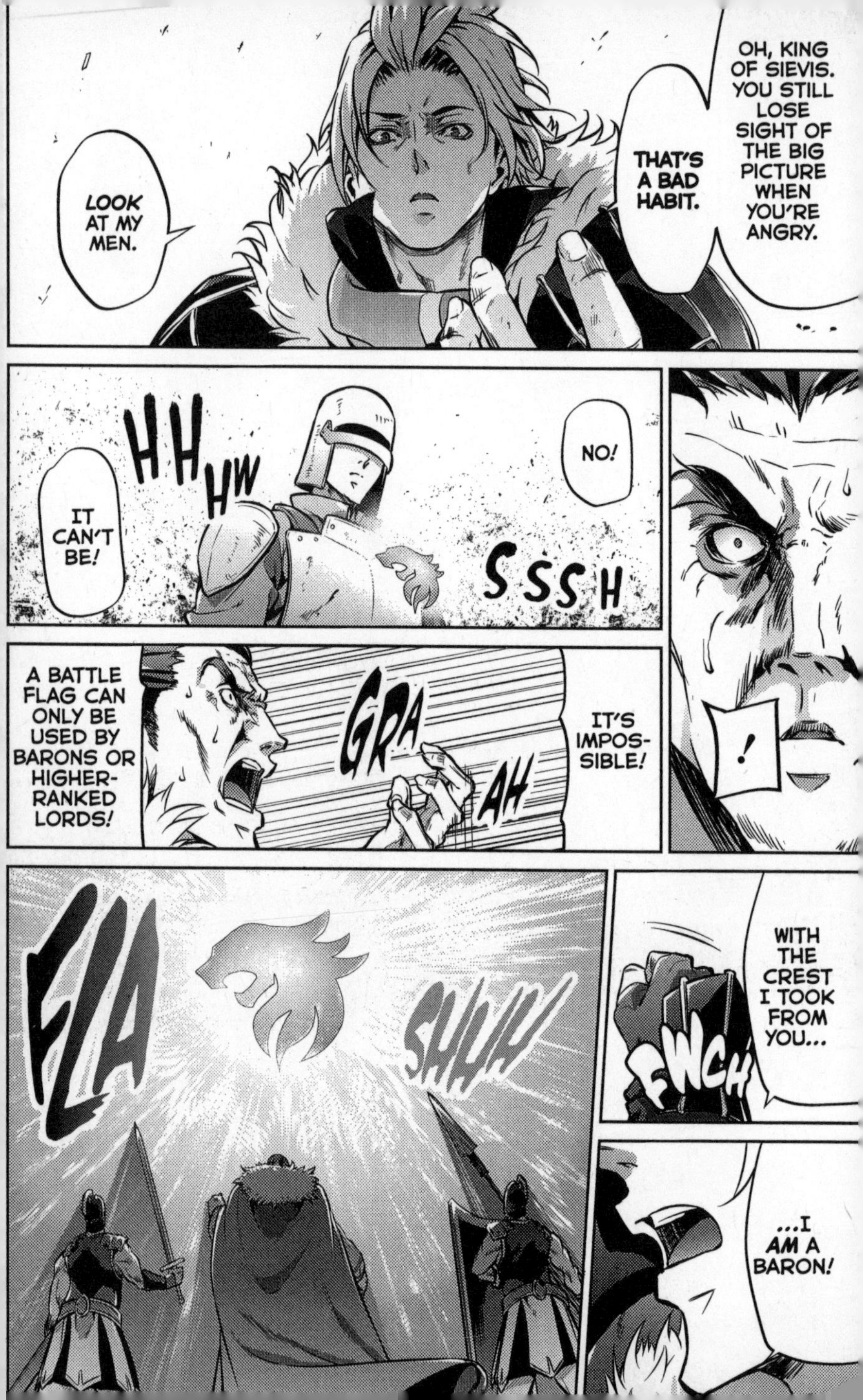
OH, KING OF SIEVIS. YOU STILL LOSE SIGHT OF THE BIG PICTURE WHEN YOU'RE ANGRY.
THAT'S A BAD HABIT.
LOOK AT MY MEN.
!
NO!
SSSH
HHHW
IT CAN'T BE!
IT'S IMPOSSIBLE!
GRAAH
A BATTLE FLAG CAN ONLY BE USED BY BARONS OR HIGHER-RANKED LORDS!
WITH THE CREST I TOOK FROM YOU...
FWCH
...I AM A BARON!
SHUH
FZA

WHAT?

HOW DID WE GET SURROUNDED?

OBVIOUSLY WE WEREN'T JUST RUNNING.

NOW THAT WE'VE LED YOU ONTO THIS NARROW ROAD...

...YOUR PHALANX FLAG IS USELESS.

YOU'RE NO MATCH FOR US. SIR LASSIC'S MEN ARE SPECIALIZED IN CHAOTIC FIGHTING.

THE SPARTAN.

KING OF SIEVIS. IT'S OVER.

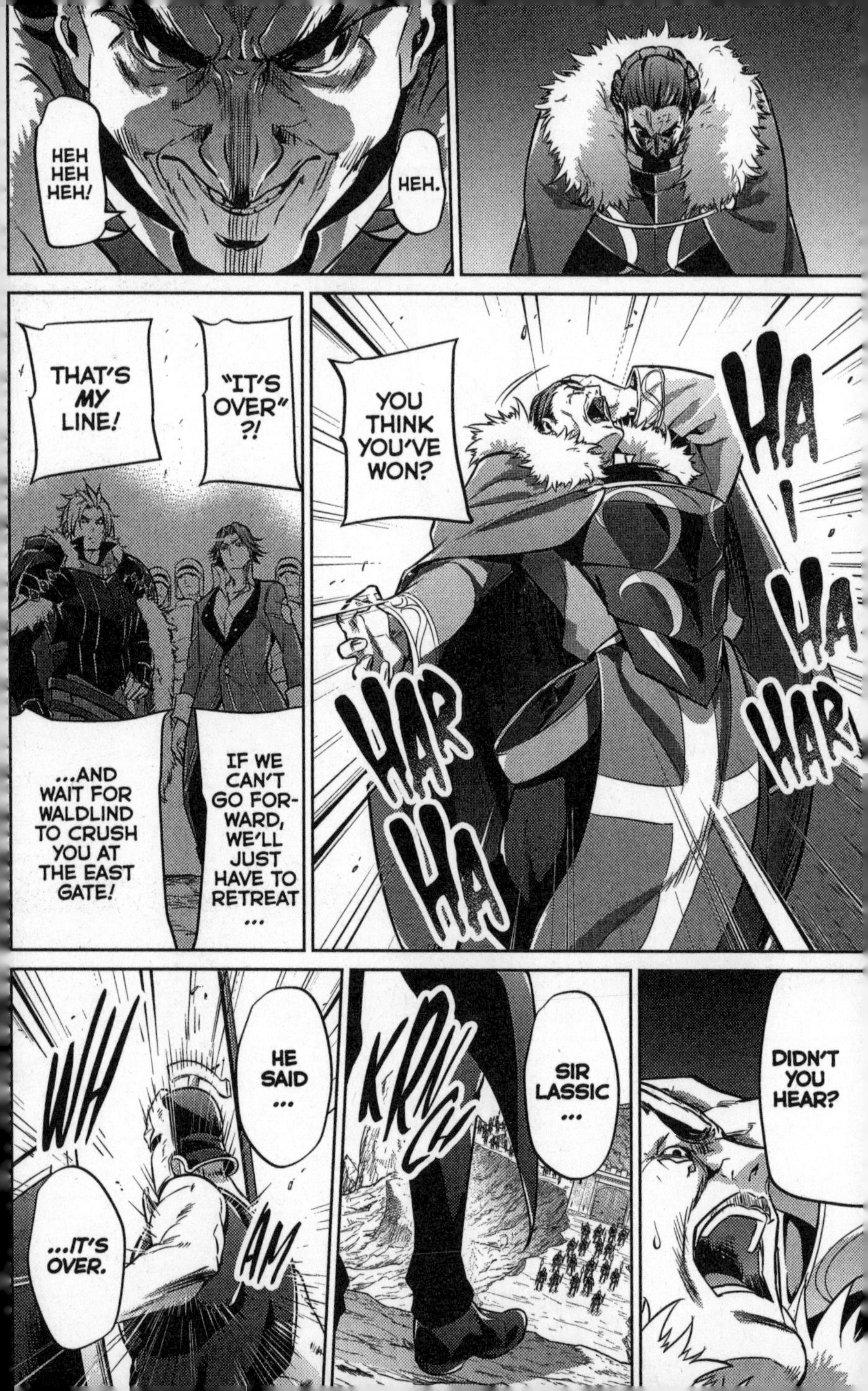
HEH.
HEH HEH HEH!
HA HA HA HAR!
YOU THINK YOU'VE WON?
HAR HA HA
"IT'S OVER" ?!
THAT'S *MY* LINE!
IF WE CAN'T GO FOR-WARD, WE'LL JUST HAVE TO RETREAT ...
...AND WAIT FOR WALDLIND TO CRUSH YOU AT THE EAST GATE!
DIDN'T YOU HEAR?
SIR LASSIC ...
KRNCH
HE SAID ...
WH
...IT'S OVER.
AM

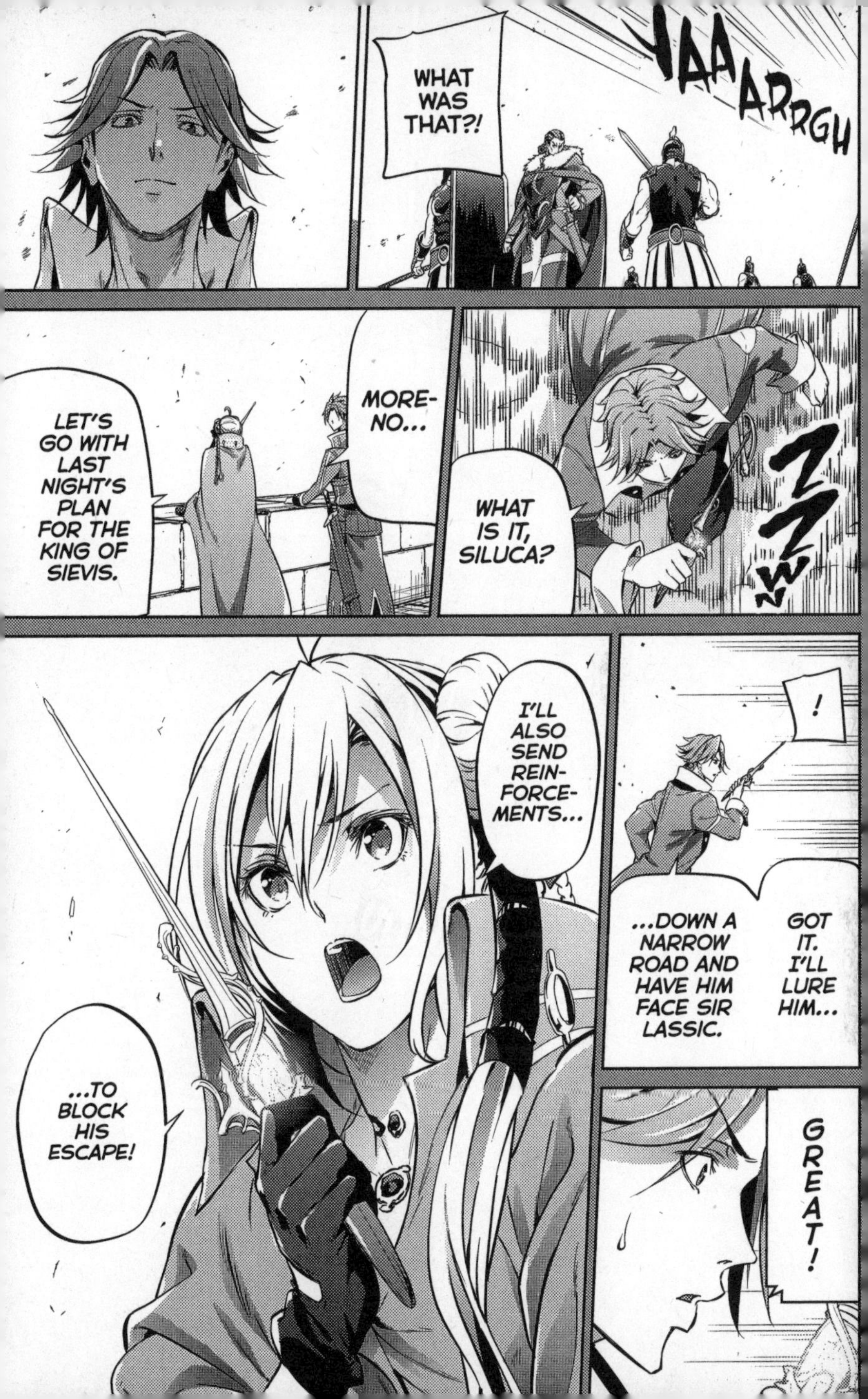
YAAARRGH
WHAT WAS THAT?!
MORE-NO...
WHAT IS IT, SILUCA?
ZZW
LET'S GO WITH LAST NIGHT'S PLAN FOR THE KING OF SIEVIS.
!
GOT IT. I'LL LURE HIM...
...DOWN A NARROW ROAD AND HAVE HIM FACE SIR LASSIC.
GREAT!
I'LL ALSO SEND REINFORCEMENTS...
...TO BLOCK HIS ESCAPE!

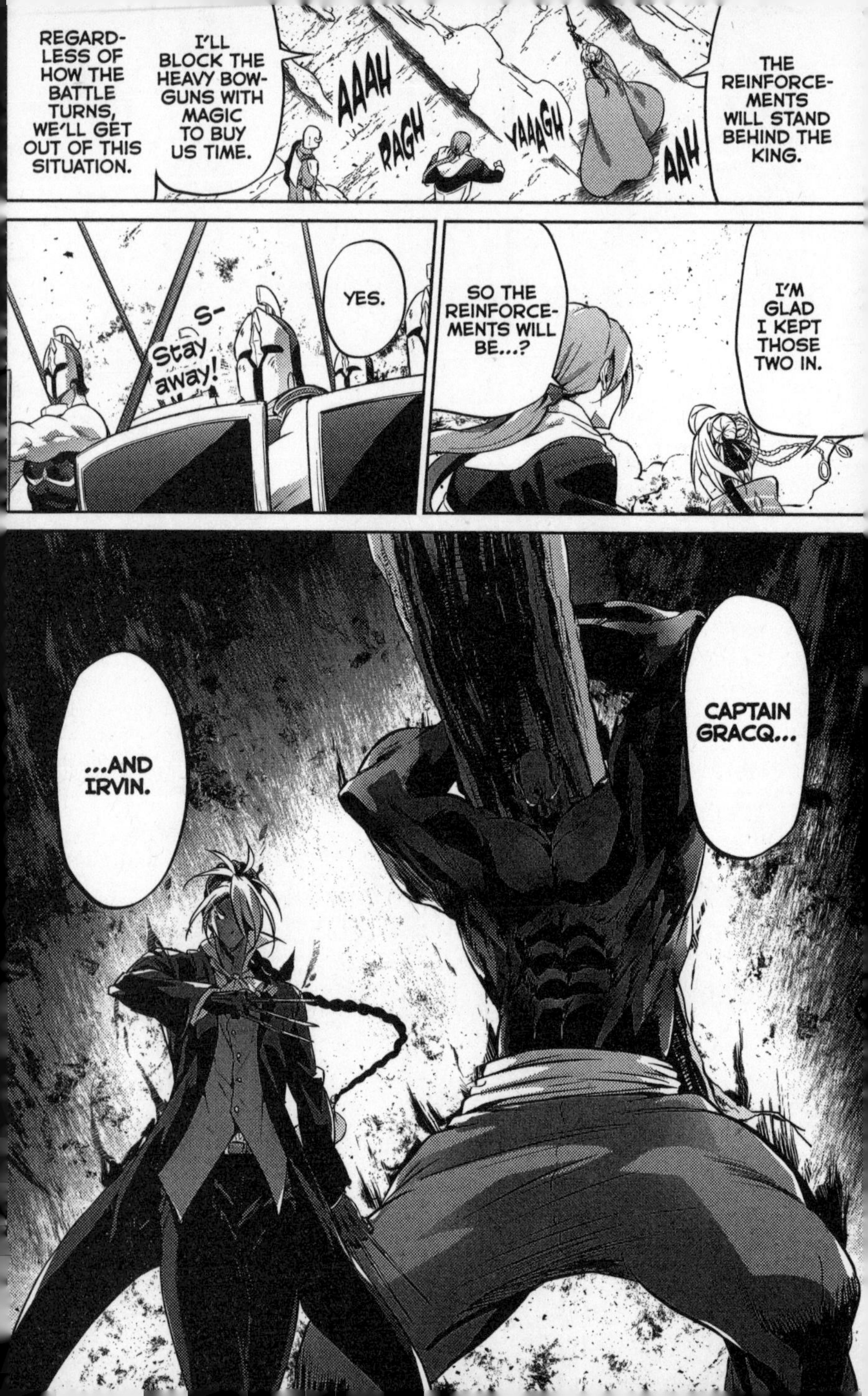
THE REINFORCEMENTS WILL STAND BEHIND THE KING.
AAH
YAAAGH
RAGH
AAAAH
I'LL BLOCK THE HEAVY BOWGUNS WITH MAGIC TO BUY US TIME.
REGARDLESS OF HOW THE BATTLE TURNS, WE'LL GET OUT OF THIS SITUATION.
I'M GLAD I KEPT THOSE TWO IN.
SO THE REINFORCEMENTS WILL BE...?
YES.
S- Stay away!
CAPTAIN GRACQ...
...AND IRVIN.

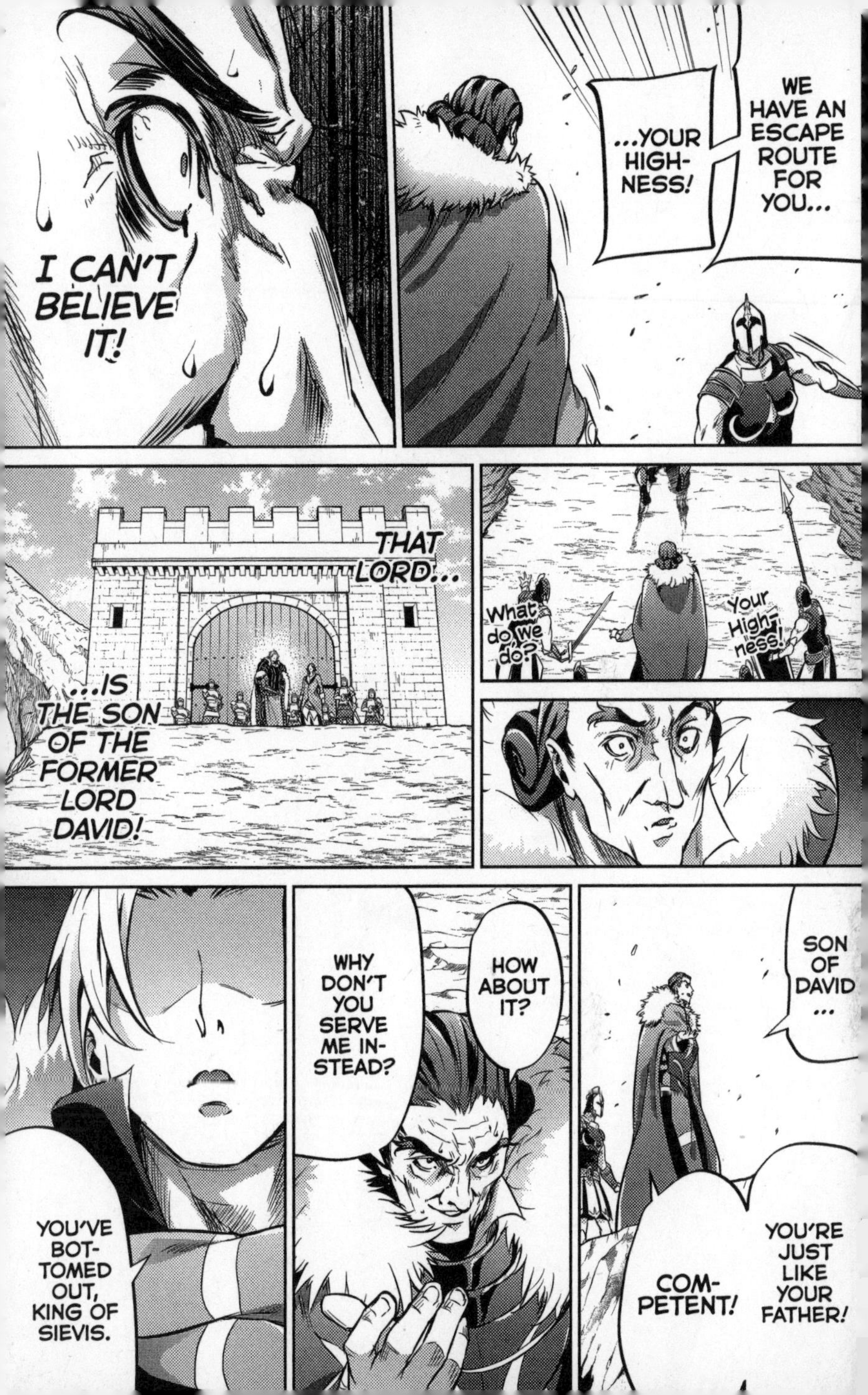
WE HAVE AN ESCAPE ROUTE FOR YOU...
...YOUR HIGHNESS!
I CAN'T BELIEVE IT!
Your Highness!
What do we do?
THAT LORD...
...IS THE SON OF THE FORMER LORD DAVID!
SON OF DAVID...
YOU'RE JUST LIKE YOUR FATHER!
COMPETENT!
HOW ABOUT IT?
WHY DON'T YOU SERVE ME INSTEAD?
YOU'VE BOTTOMED OUT, KING OF SIEVIS.

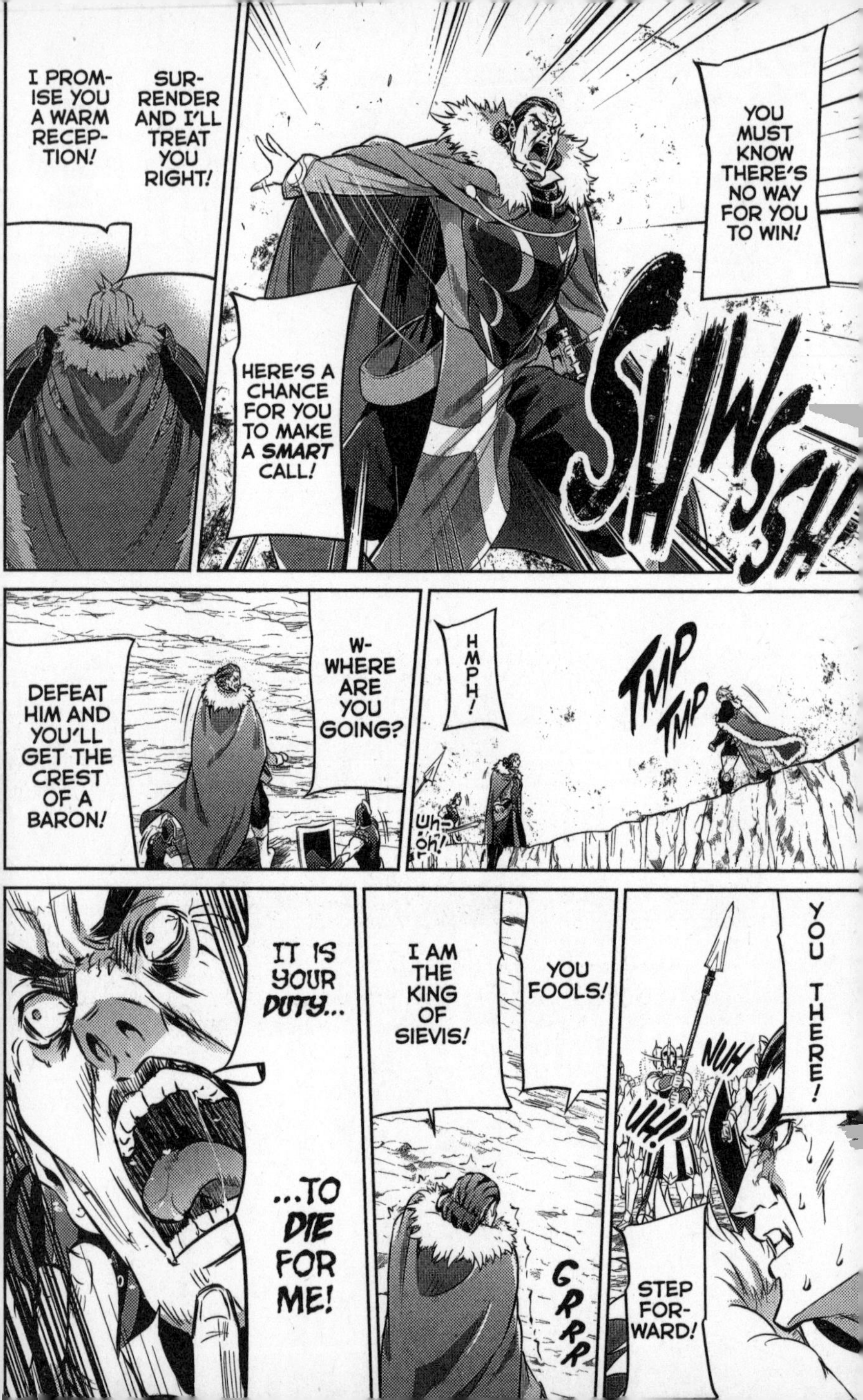
YOU MUST KNOW THERE'S NO WAY FOR YOU TO WIN!
HERE'S A CHANCE FOR YOU TO MAKE A SMART CALL!
SHWSH
SHH
SURRENDER AND I'LL TREAT YOU RIGHT!
I PROMISE YOU A WARM RECEPTION!
TMP TMP
HMPH!
Uh-oh!
W-WHERE ARE YOU GOING?
DEFEAT HIM AND YOU'LL GET THE CREST OF A BARON!
YOU THERE!
NUH UH!
STEP FORWARD!
YOU FOOLS!
I AM THE KING OF SIEVIS!
GRRR
IT IS YOUR DUTY...
...TO DIE FOR ME!

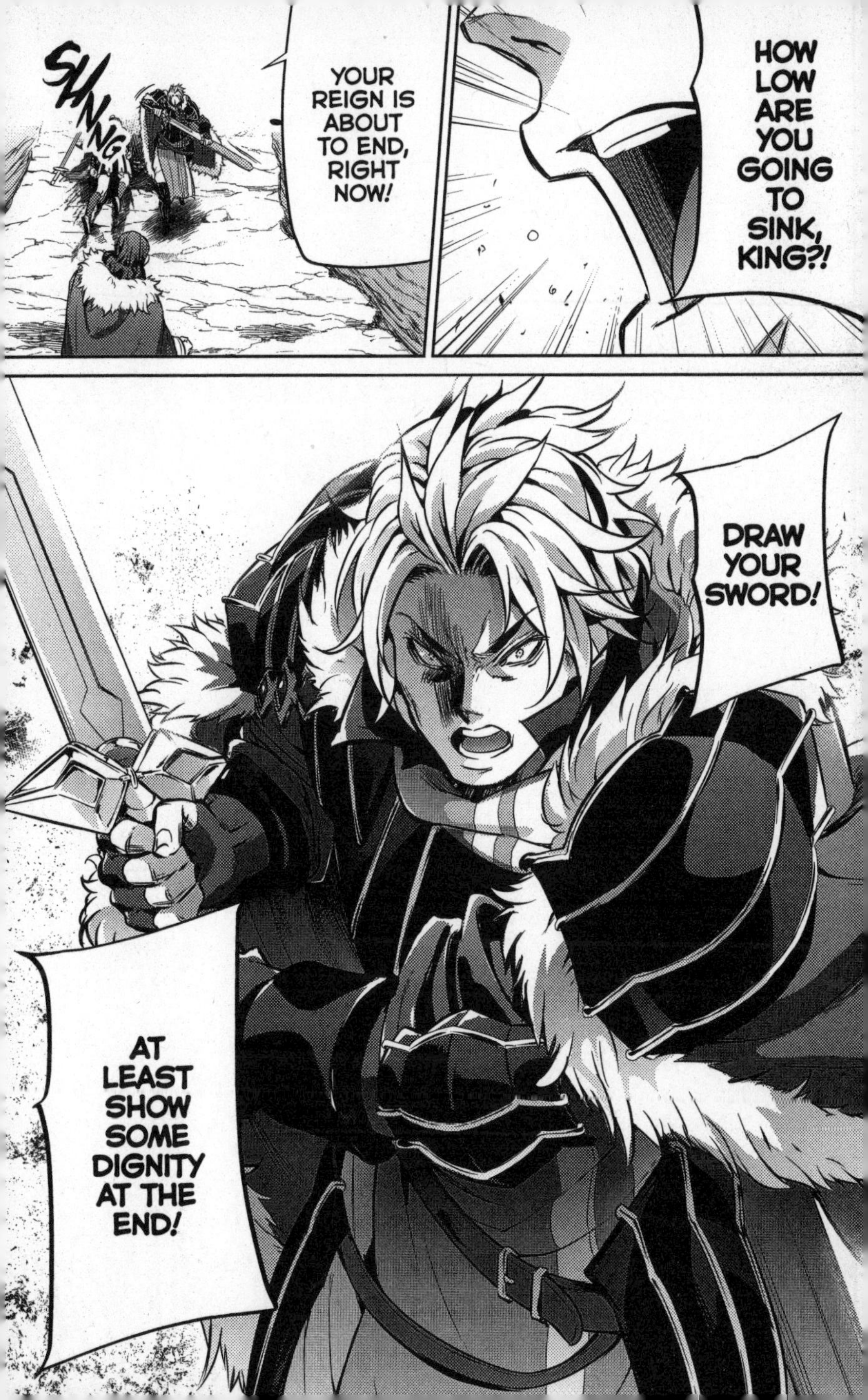
HOW LOW ARE YOU GOING TO SINK, KING?!
YOUR REIGN IS ABOUT TO END, RIGHT NOW!
SHNNG
DRAW YOUR SWORD!
AT LEAST SHOW SOME DIGNITY AT THE END!

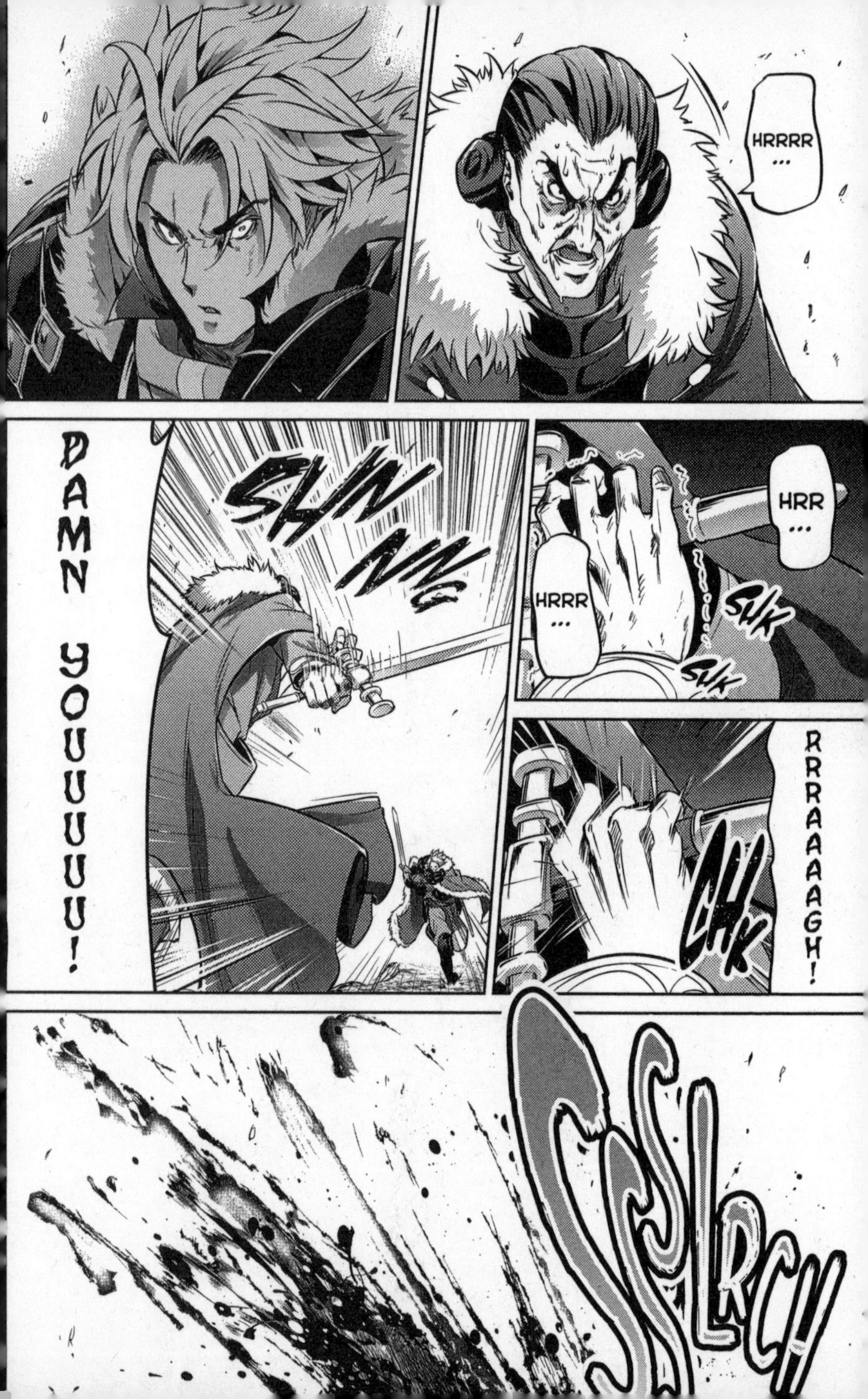
HRRRR ...
HRR ...
HRRR ...
SUK
SUK
RRRAAAAGH!
CHK
DAMN YOUUUUUU!
SHWING
SSSLRCH

RECORD OF
GRANCREST WAR
WAR

RECORD OF
GRANCREST
WAR

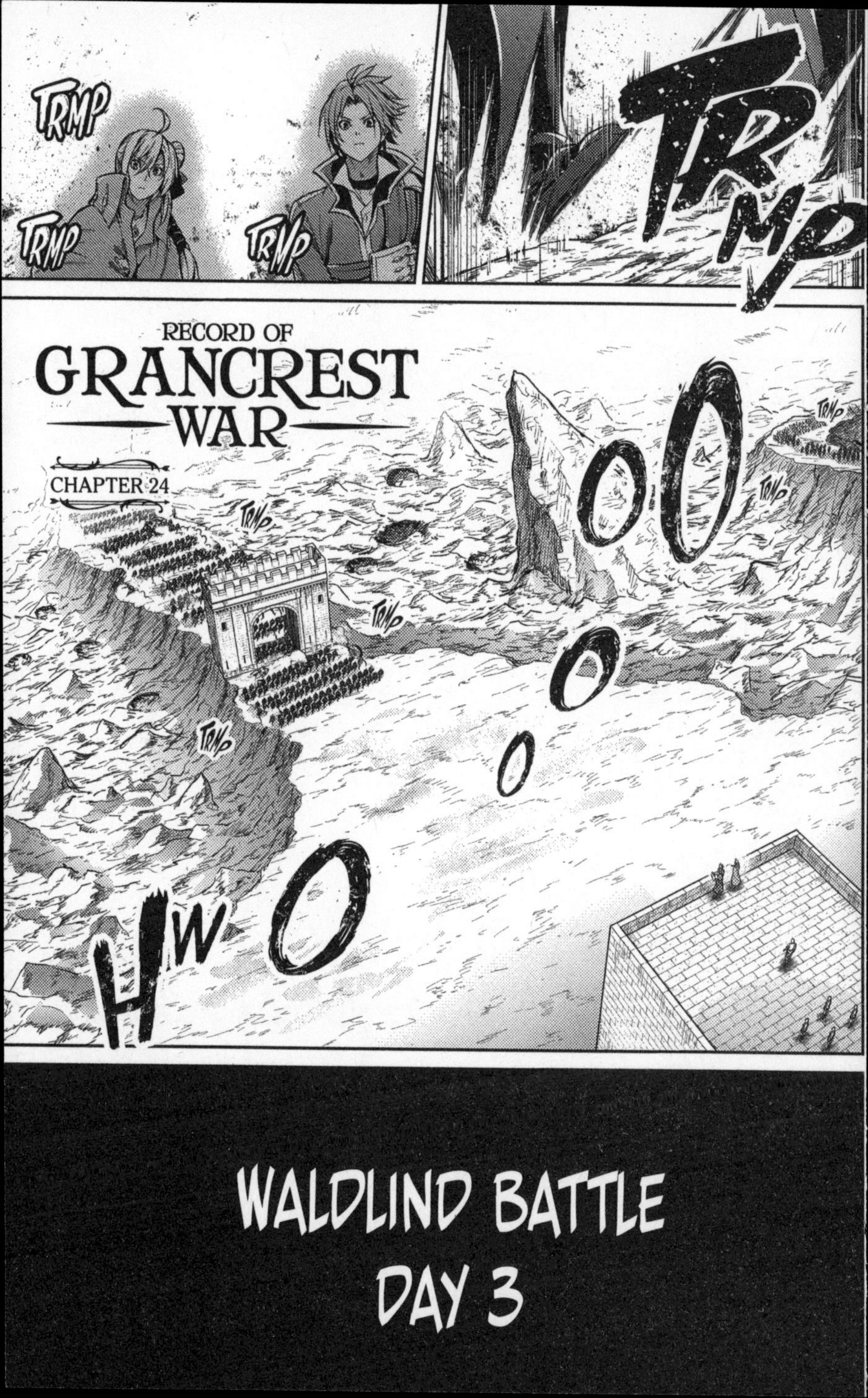
TRMP
TRMP
TRMP
TRMP
RECORD OF GRANCREST WAR
CHAPTER 24
TRMP
TRMP
TRMP
TRMP
TRMP
HWOOOOO

WALDLIND BATTLE DAY 3

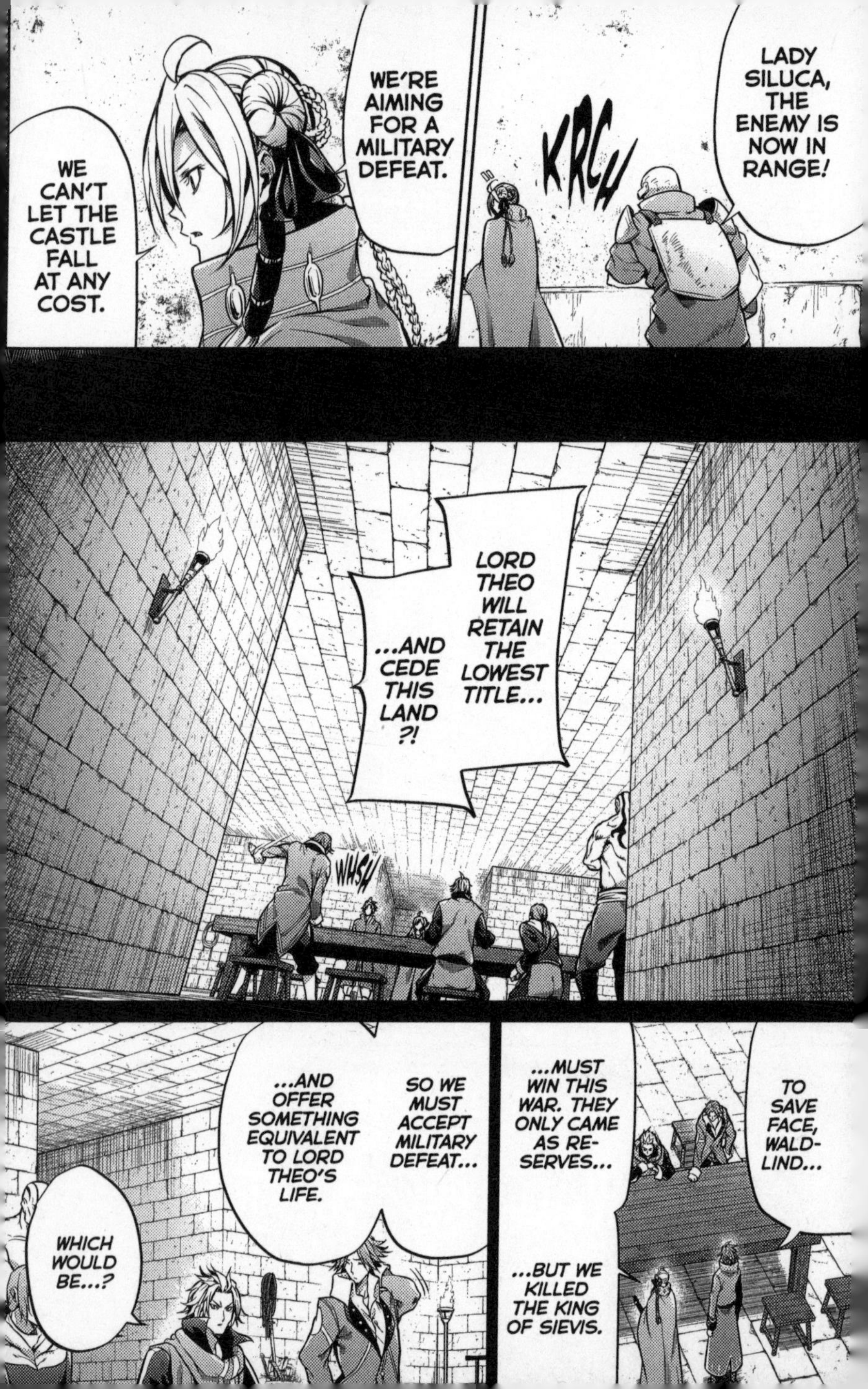
LADY SILUCA, THE ENEMY IS NOW IN RANGE!
KRCH
WE'RE AIMING FOR A MILITARY DEFEAT.
WE CAN'T LET THE CASTLE FALL AT ANY COST.
LORD THEO WILL RETAIN THE LOWEST TITLE...
...AND CEDE THIS LAND?!
WHSH
TO SAVE FACE, WALD-LIND...
...MUST WIN THIS WAR. THEY ONLY CAME AS RE-SERVES...
...BUT WE KILLED THE KING OF SIEVIS.
SO WE MUST ACCEPT MILITARY DEFEAT...
...AND OFFER SOMETHING EQUIVALENT TO LORD THEO'S LIFE.
WHICH WOULD BE...?

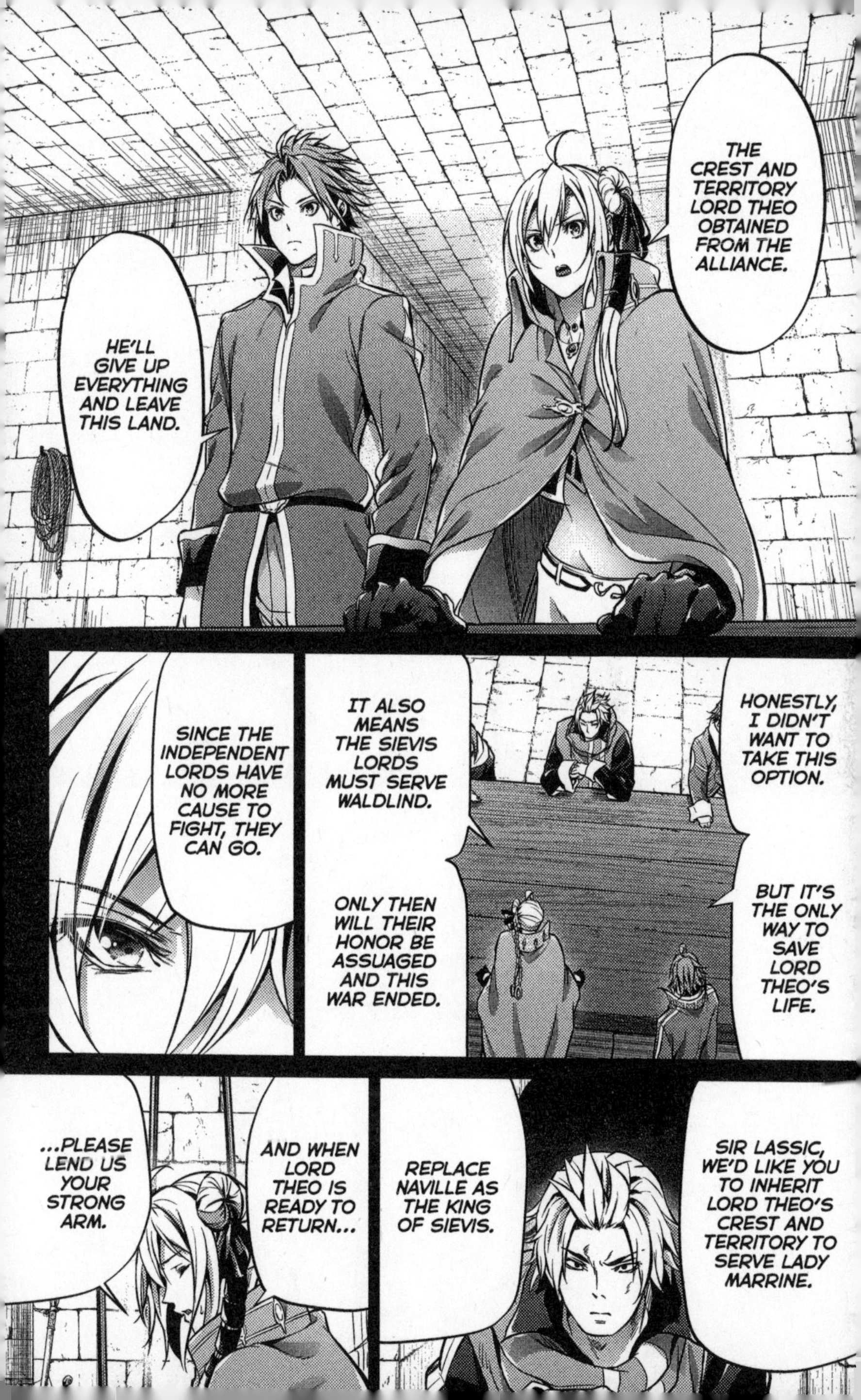
THE CREST AND TERRITORY LORD THEO OBTAINED FROM THE ALLIANCE.
HE'LL GIVE UP EVERYTHING AND LEAVE THIS LAND.
HONESTLY, I DIDN'T WANT TO TAKE THIS OPTION.
BUT IT'S THE ONLY WAY TO SAVE LORD THEO'S LIFE.
IT ALSO MEANS THE SIEVIS LORDS MUST SERVE WALDLIND.
ONLY THEN WILL THEIR HONOR BE ASSUAGED AND THIS WAR ENDED.
SINCE THE INDEPENDENT LORDS HAVE NO MORE CAUSE TO FIGHT, THEY CAN GO.
SIR LASSIC, WE'D LIKE YOU TO INHERIT LORD THEO'S CREST AND TERRITORY TO SERVE LADY MARRINE.
REPLACE NAVILLE AS THE KING OF SIEVIS.
AND WHEN LORD THEO IS READY TO RETURN...
...PLEASE LEND US YOUR STRONG ARM.

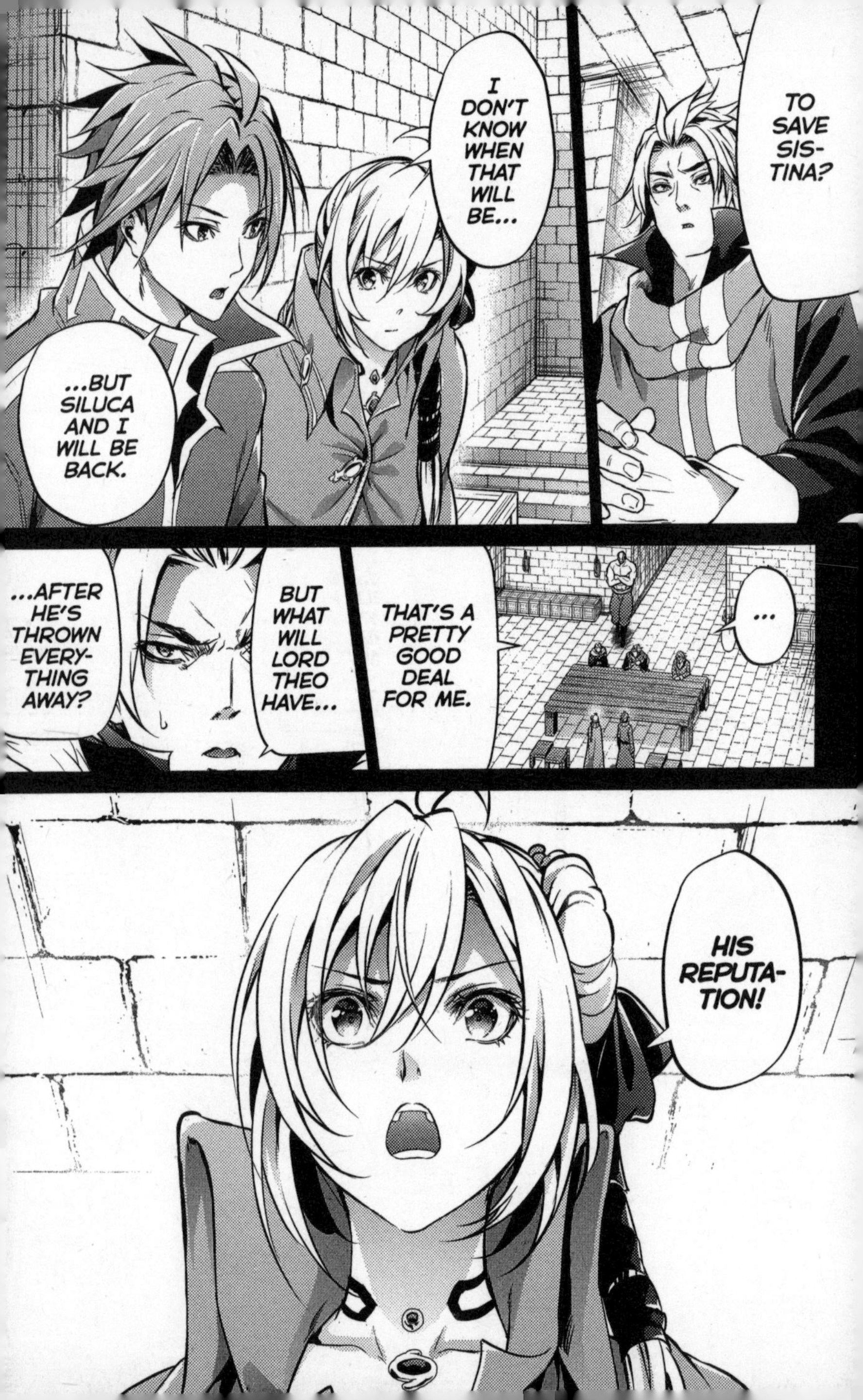
TO SAVE SIS-TINA?
I DON'T KNOW WHEN THAT WILL BE...
...BUT SILUCA AND I WILL BE BACK.
...
THAT'S A PRETTY GOOD DEAL FOR ME.
BUT WHAT WILL LORD THEO HAVE...
...AFTER HE'S THROWN EVERY-THING AWAY?
HIS REPUTA-TION!

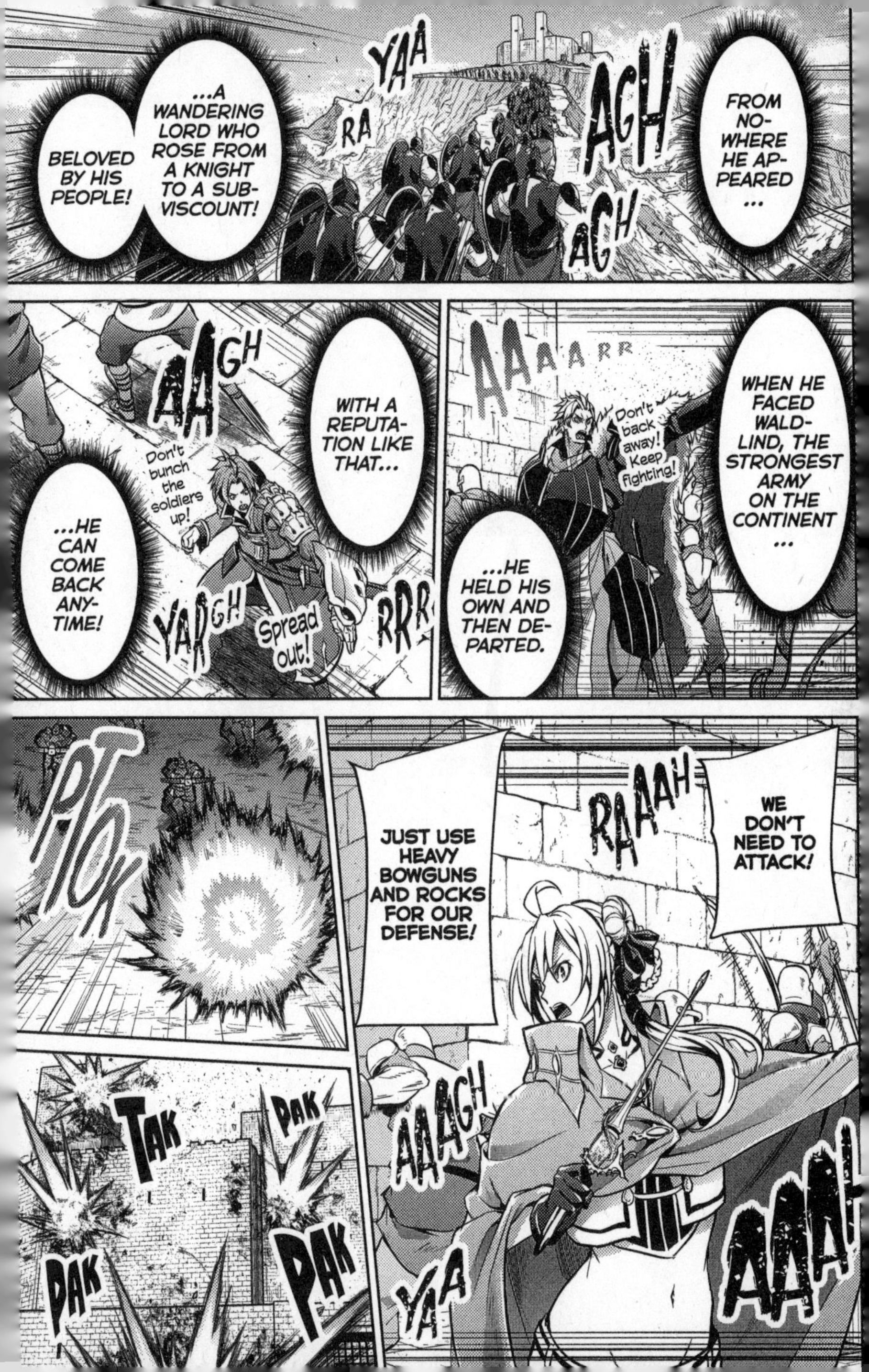
FROM NO-WHERE HE AP-PEARED...
AGH
AGH
...A WANDERING LORD WHO ROSE FROM A KNIGHT TO A SUB-VISCOUNT!
YAA
RA
BELOVED BY HIS PEOPLE!
WHEN HE FACED WALD-LIND, THE STRONGEST ARMY ON THE CONTINENT...
Don't back away! Keep fighting!
AAAARR
...HE HELD HIS OWN AND THEN DE-PARTED.
WITH A REPUTA-TION LIKE THAT...
AAGH
Don't bunch the soldiers up!
...HE CAN COME BACK ANY-TIME!
RRR
Spread out!
YAAGH
WE DON'T NEED TO ATTACK!
RAAAH
JUST USE HEAVY BOWGUNS AND ROCKS FOR OUR DEFENSE!
AAAGH
AAA
YAA
PTOK
DAK
TAK
DAK
PAK

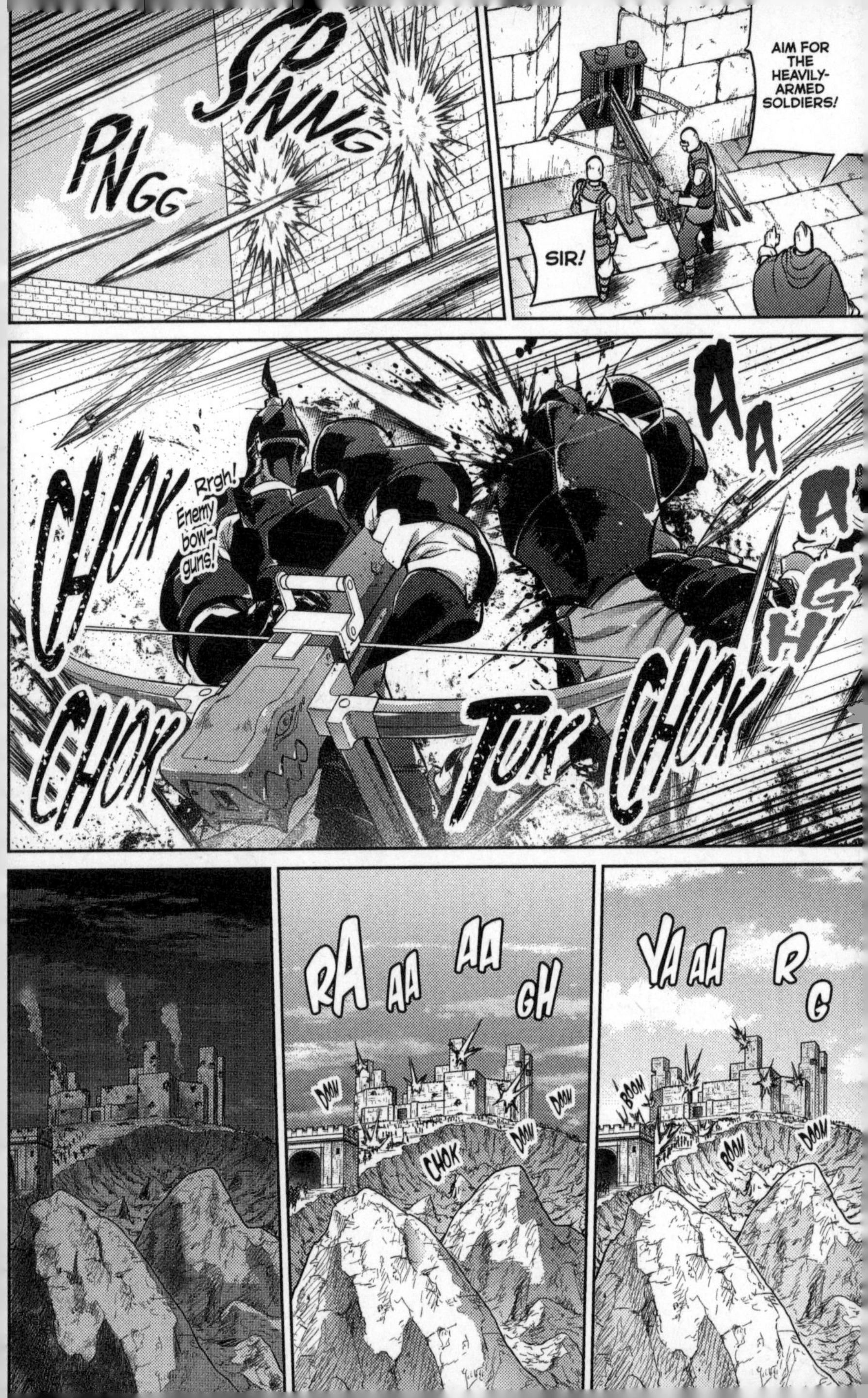
AIM FOR THE HEAVILY-ARMED SOLDIERS!
SIR!
SPNNG
PNGG
AAAGH
CHOK
Rrgh! Enemy bow-guns!
CHOK
TUK
CHOK
YAAARG
BOOM
BOOM
DOOM
RAAAAGH
DOOM
DOOM
DOOM
CHOK

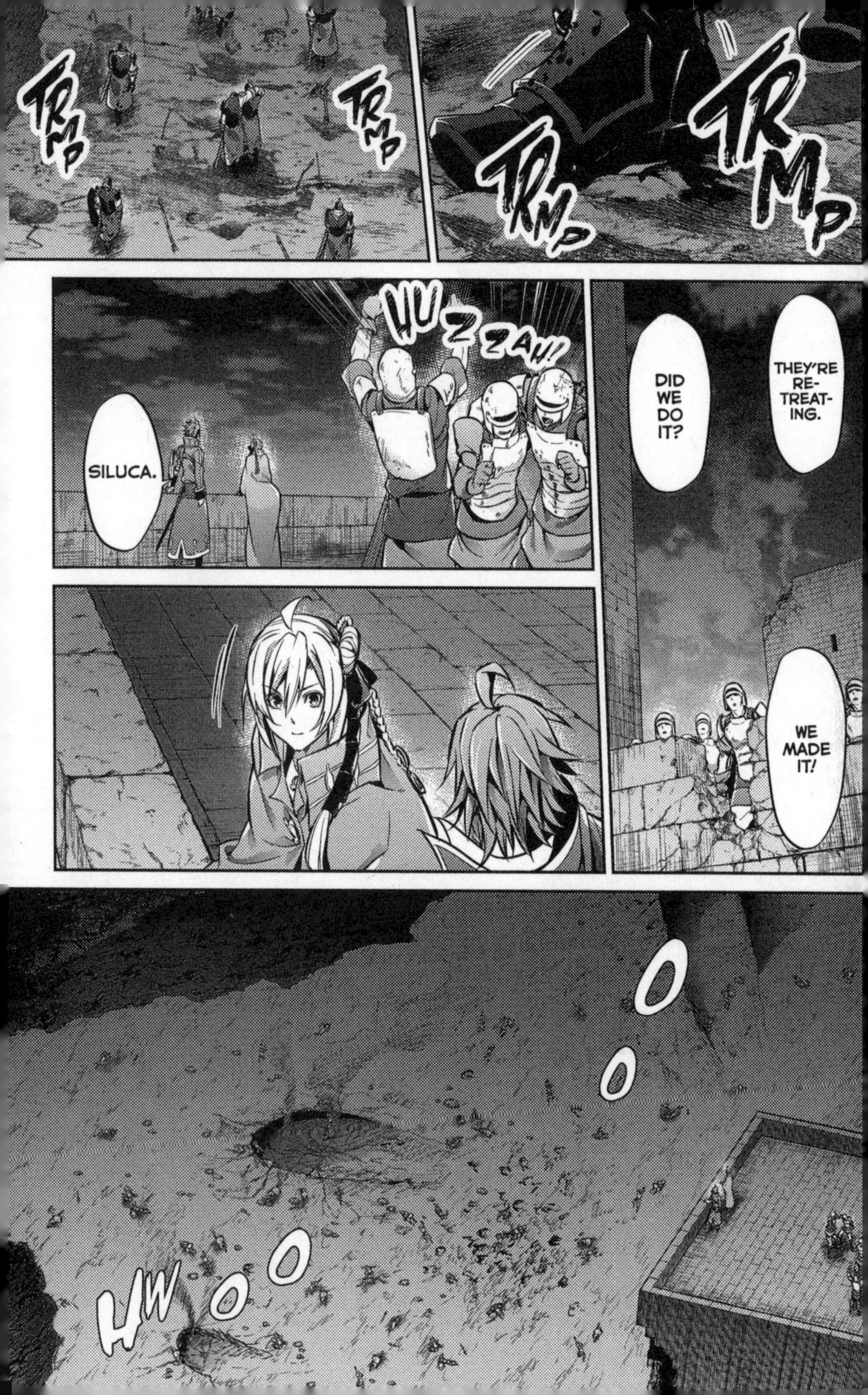
TRMP
TRMP
TRMP
TRMP
THEY'RE RE-TREAT-ING.
DID WE DO IT?
WE MADE IT!
HUZZAH!
SILUCA.
HWOOOO

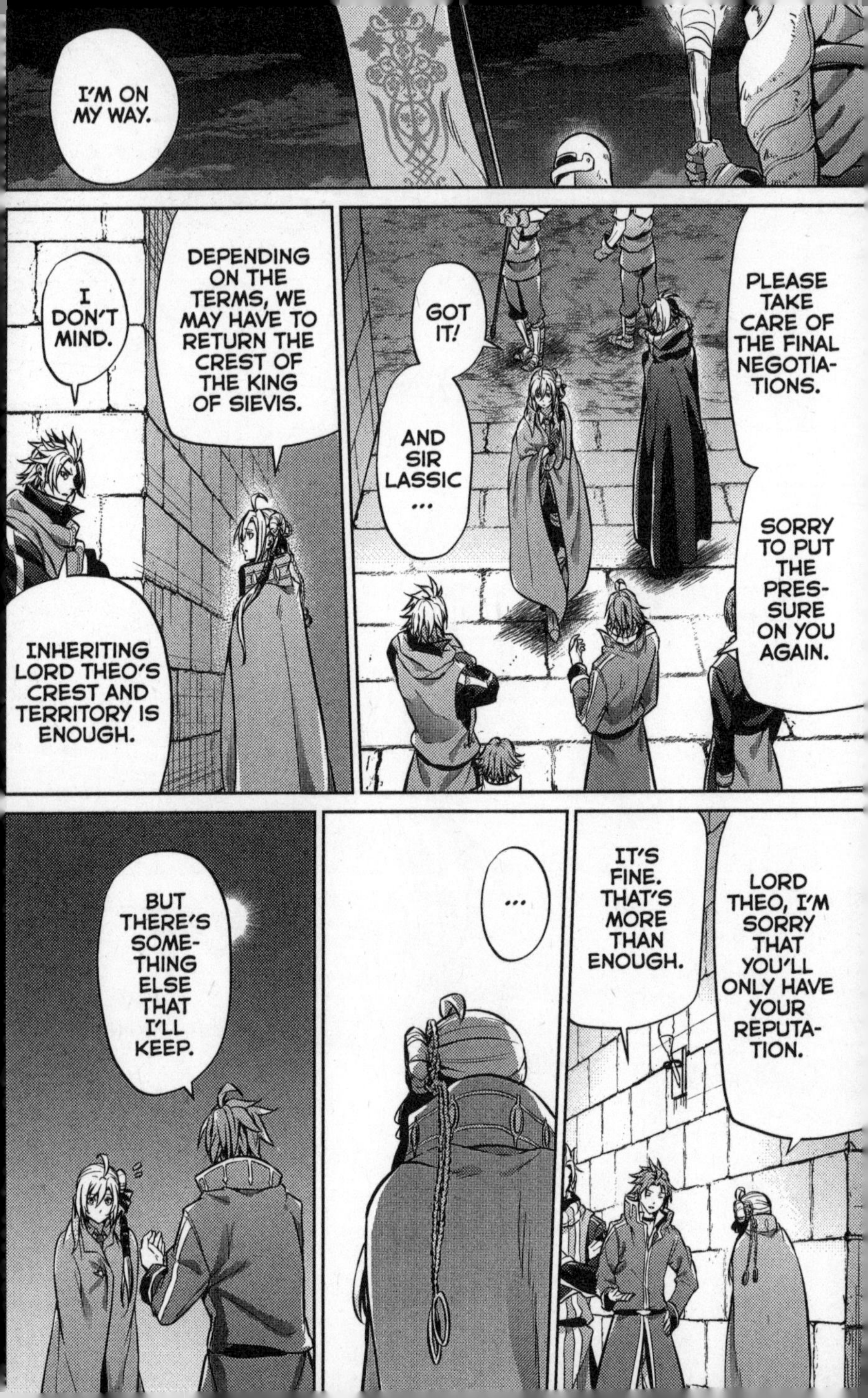
I'M ON MY WAY.
PLEASE TAKE CARE OF THE FINAL NEGOTIA-TIONS.
SORRY TO PUT THE PRES-SURE ON YOU AGAIN.
GOT IT!
AND SIR LASSIC ...
DEPENDING ON THE TERMS, WE MAY HAVE TO RETURN THE CREST OF THE KING OF SIEVIS.
I DON'T MIND.
INHERITING LORD THEO'S CREST AND TERRITORY IS ENOUGH.
LORD THEO, I'M SORRY THAT YOU'LL ONLY HAVE YOUR REPUTA-TION.
IT'S FINE. THAT'S MORE THAN ENOUGH.
...
BUT THERE'S SOME-THING ELSE THAT I'LL KEEP.

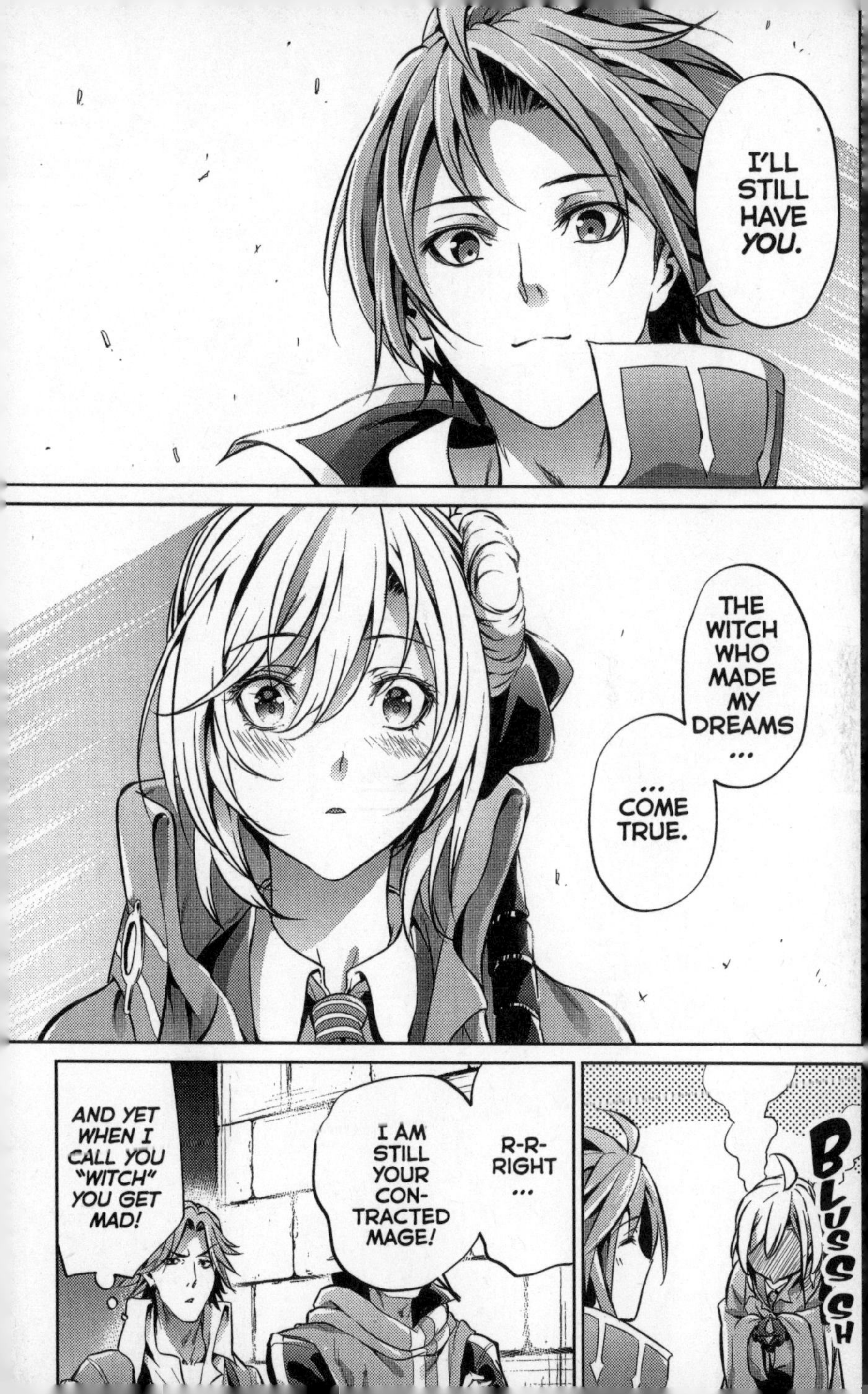
I'LL STILL HAVE YOU.
THE WITCH WHO MADE MY DREAMS...
...COME TRUE.
BLUSSH
R-R-RIGHT...
I AM STILL YOUR CONTRACTED MAGE!
AND YET WHEN I CALL YOU "WITCH" YOU GET MAD!

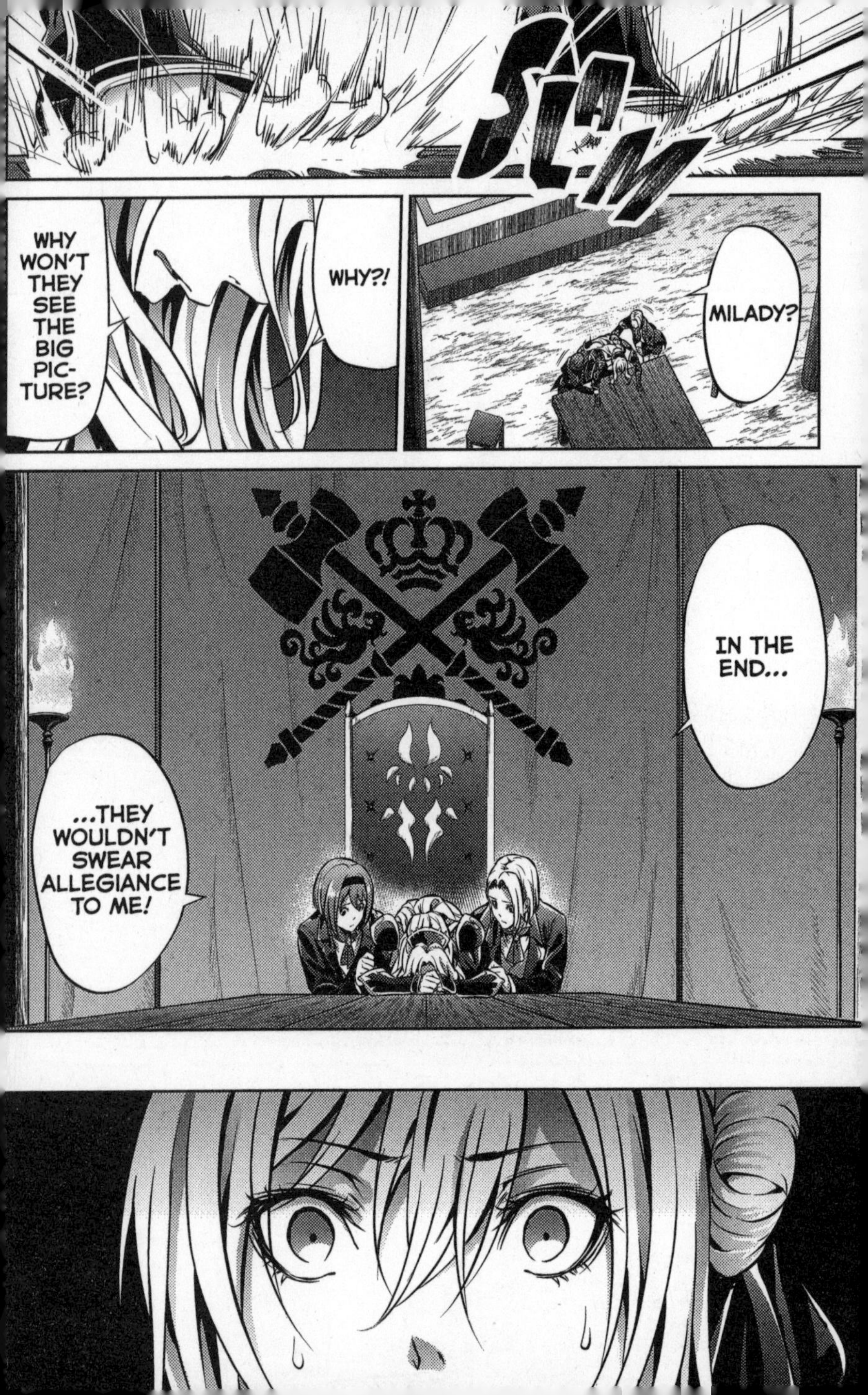
SLAM
MILADY?
WHY?!
WHY WON'T THEY SEE THE BIG PICTURE?
IN THE END...
...THEY WOULDN'T SWEAR ALLEGIANCE TO ME!

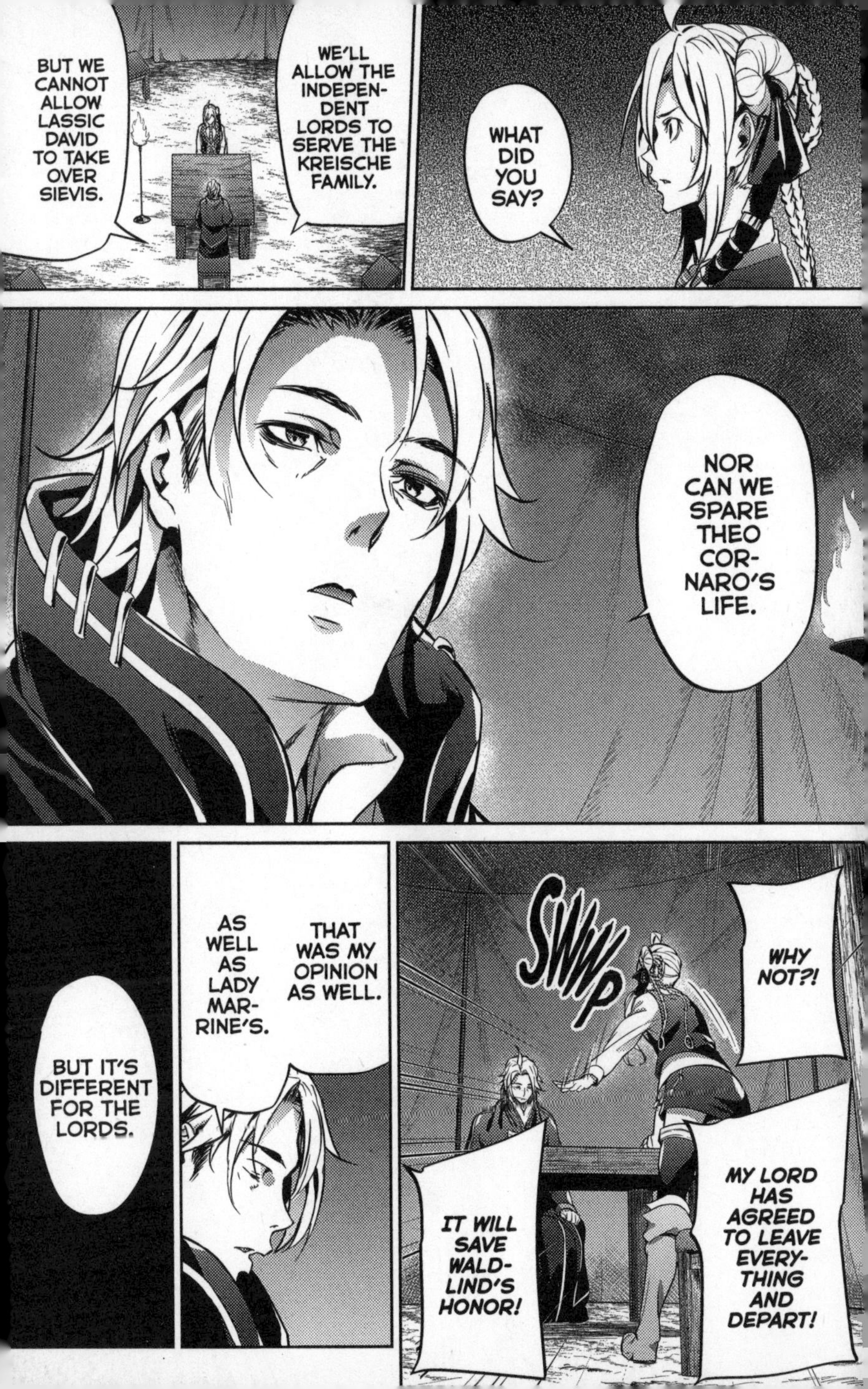
WHAT DID YOU SAY?
WE'LL ALLOW THE INDEPENDENT LORDS TO SERVE THE KREISCHE FAMILY.
BUT WE CANNOT ALLOW LASSIC DAVID TO TAKE OVER SIEVIS.
NOR CAN WE SPARE THEO CORNARO'S LIFE.
WHY NOT?!
SWWP
MY LORD HAS AGREED TO LEAVE EVERYTHING AND DEPART!
IT WILL SAVE WALDLIND'S HONOR!
THAT WAS MY OPINION AS WELL.
AS WELL AS LADY MARRINE'S.
BUT IT'S DIFFERENT FOR THE LORDS.

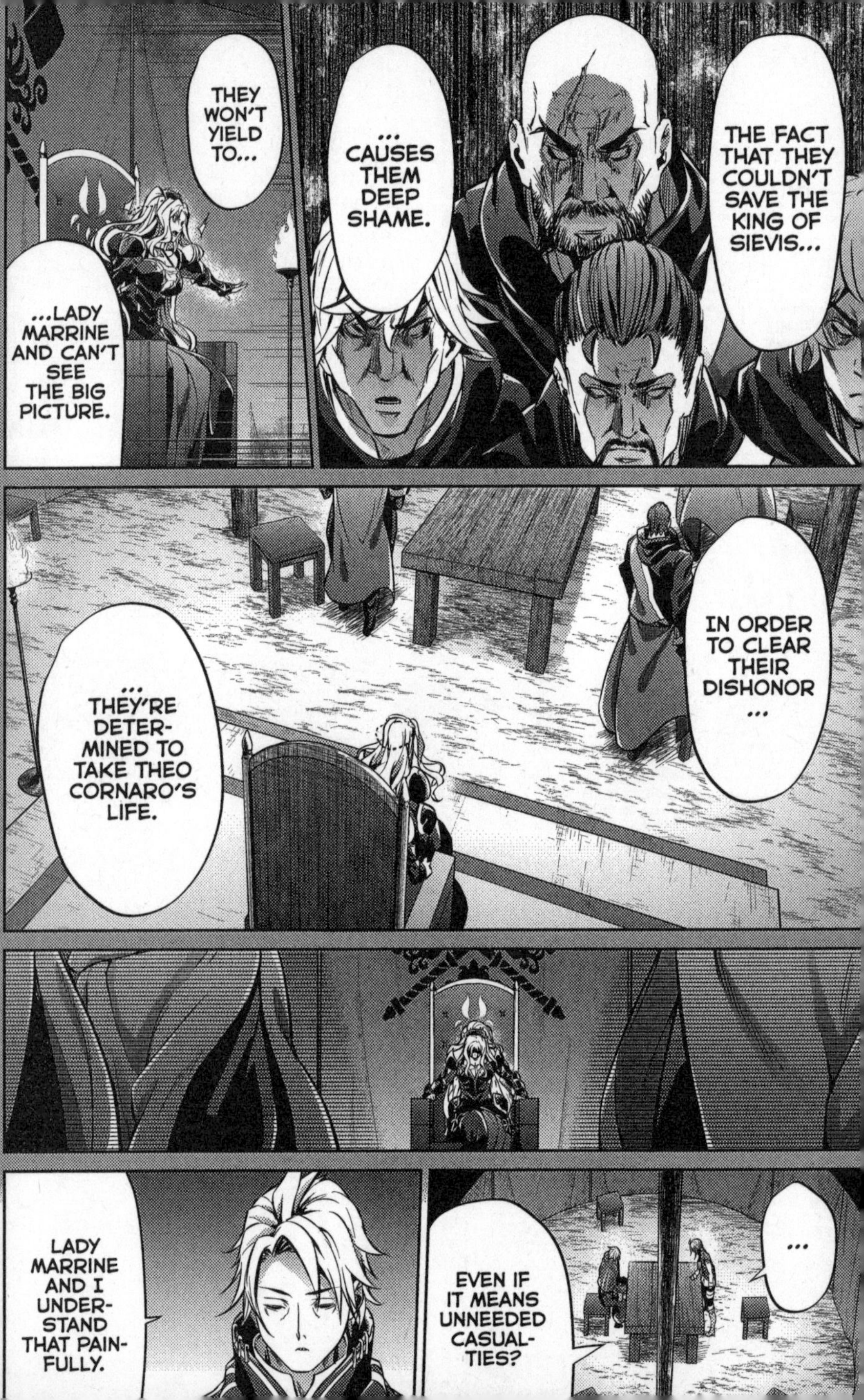
THE FACT THAT THEY COULDN'T SAVE THE KING OF SIEVIS...
...CAUSES THEM DEEP SHAME.
THEY WON'T YIELD TO...
...LADY MARRINE AND CAN'T SEE THE BIG PICTURE.
IN ORDER TO CLEAR THEIR DISHONOR...
...THEY'RE DETERMINED TO TAKE THEO CORNARO'S LIFE.
...
EVEN IF IT MEANS UNNEEDED CASUALTIES?
LADY MARRINE AND I UNDERSTAND THAT PAINFULLY.

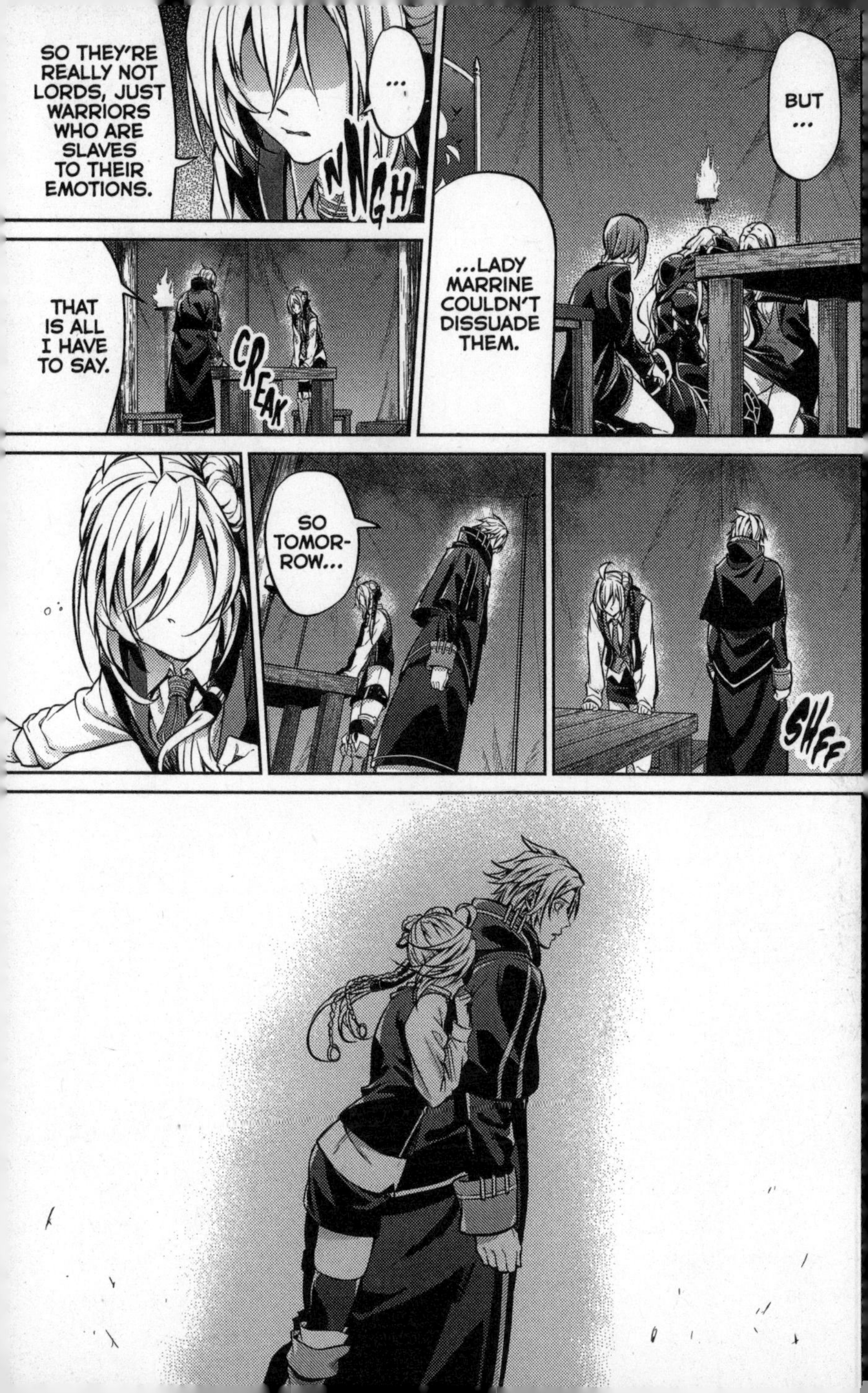
BUT ...
...LADY MARRINE COULDN'T DISSUADE THEM.
...
NNGH
SO THEY'RE REALLY NOT LORDS, JUST WARRIORS WHO ARE SLAVES TO THEIR EMOTIONS.
THAT IS ALL I HAVE TO SAY.
CREAK
SHFF
SO TOMORROW...

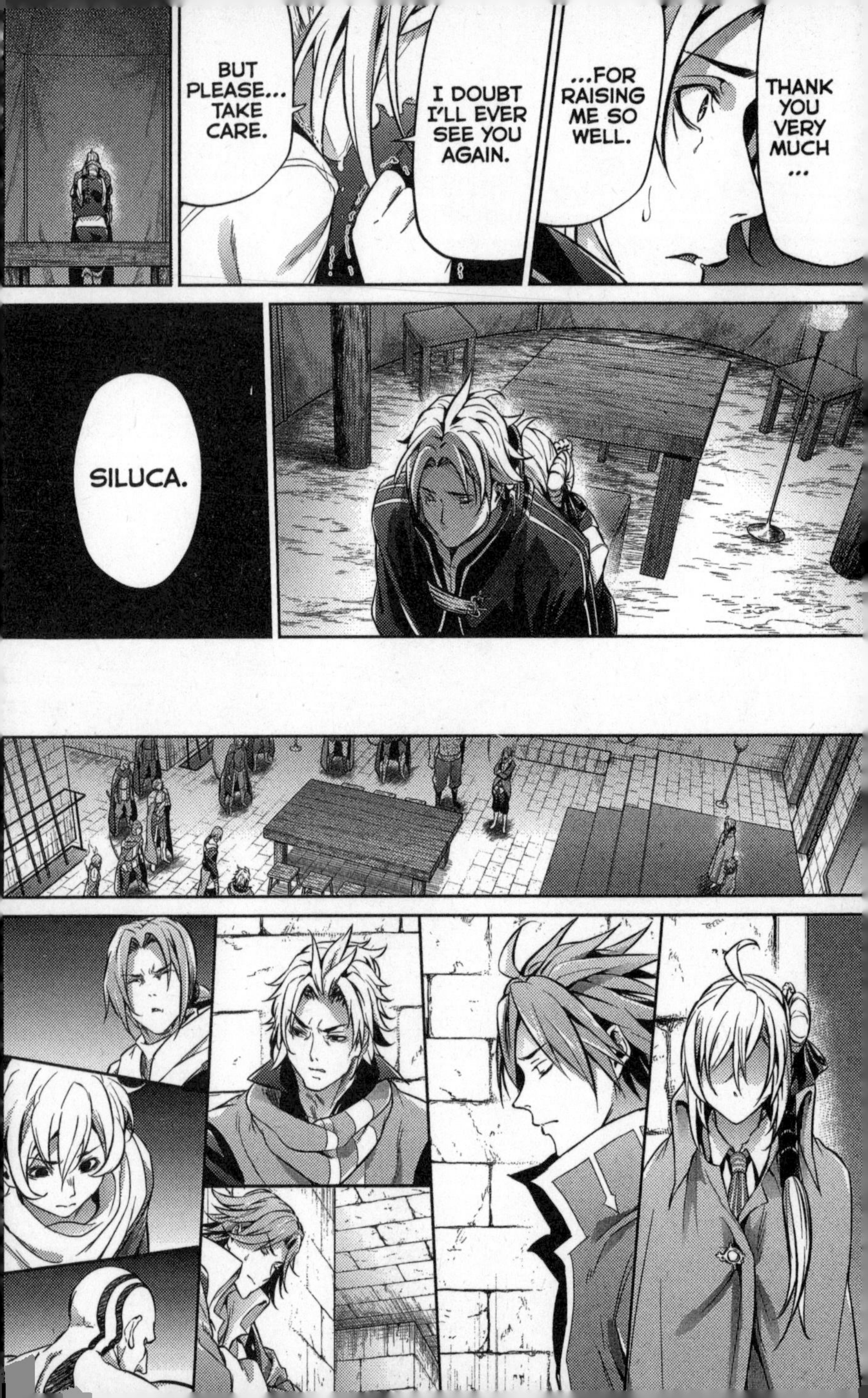
THANK YOU VERY MUCH...
...FOR RAISING ME SO WELL.
I DOUBT I'LL EVER SEE YOU AGAIN.
BUT PLEASE... TAKE CARE.
SILUCA.

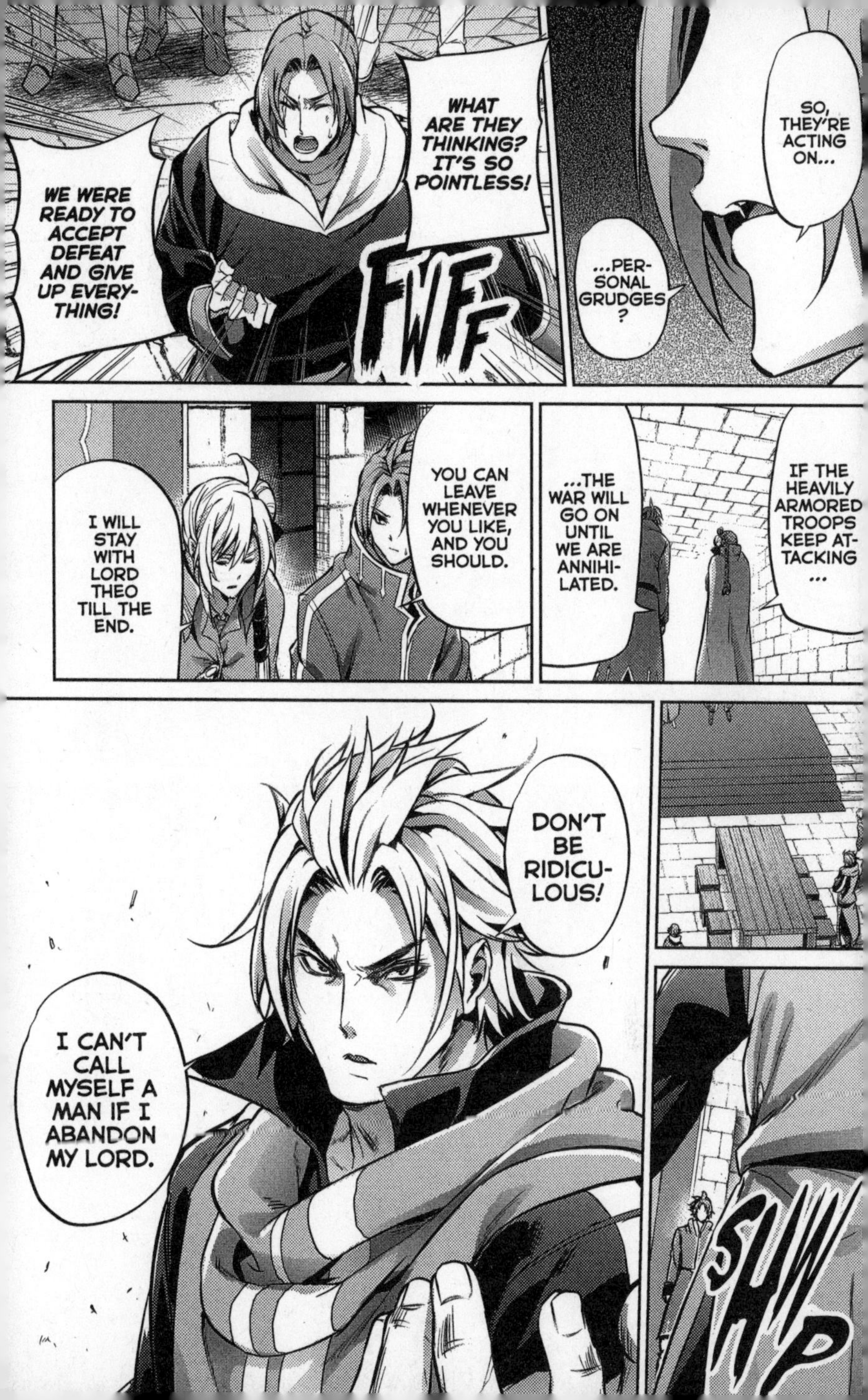
SO, THEY'RE ACTING ON...
...PERSONAL GRUDGES?
WHAT ARE THEY THINKING? IT'S SO POINTLESS!
FWF
WE WERE READY TO ACCEPT DEFEAT AND GIVE UP EVERYTHING!
IF THE HEAVILY ARMORED TROOPS KEEP ATTACKING...
...THE WAR WILL GO ON UNTIL WE ARE ANNIHILATED.
YOU CAN LEAVE WHENEVER YOU LIKE, AND YOU SHOULD.
I WILL STAY WITH LORD THEO TILL THE END.
SHWP
DON'T BE RIDICULOUS!
I CAN'T CALL MYSELF A MAN IF I ABANDON MY LORD.

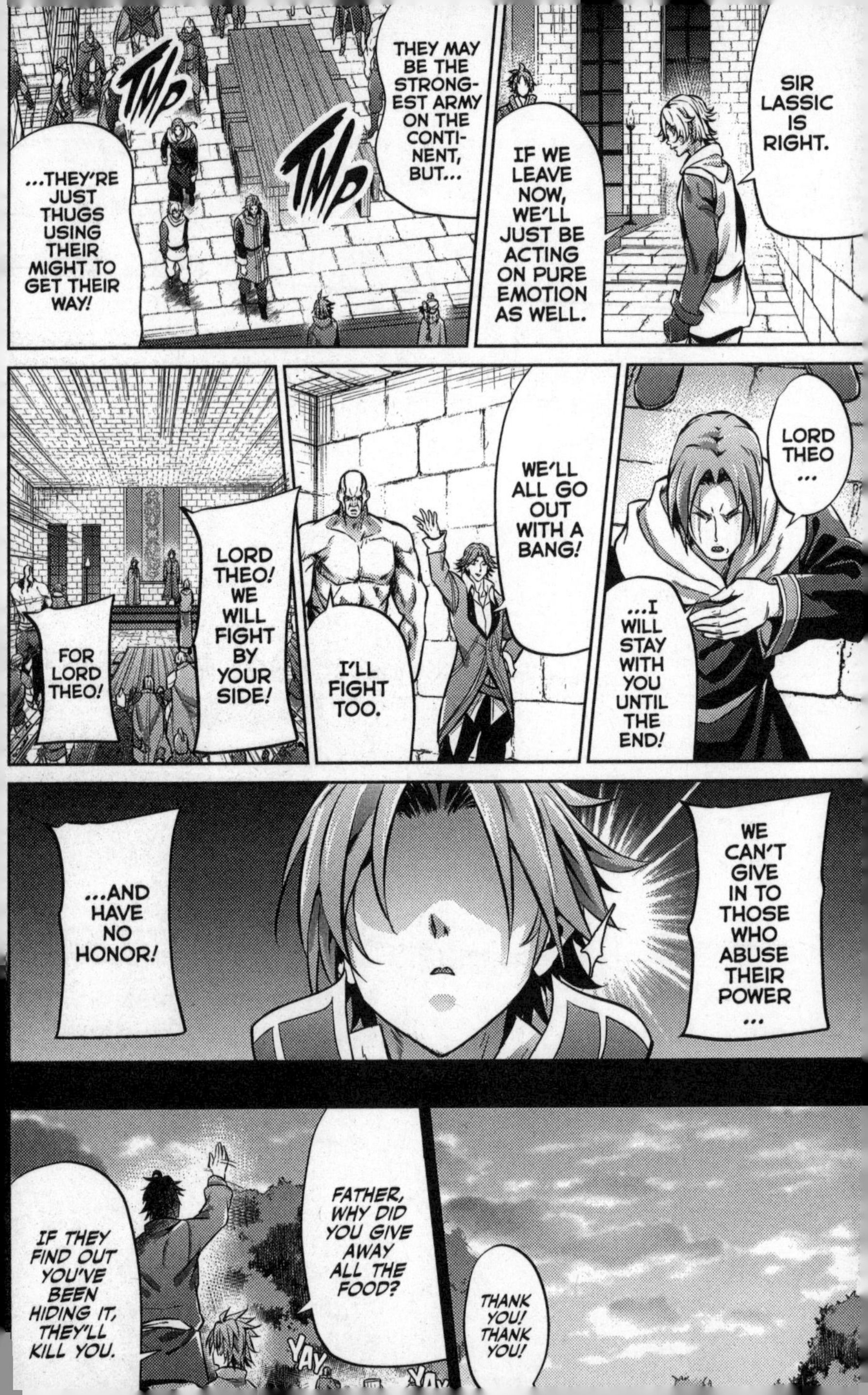
SIR LASSIC IS RIGHT.
IF WE LEAVE NOW, WE'LL JUST BE ACTING ON PURE EMOTION AS WELL.
THEY MAY BE THE STRONGEST ARMY ON THE CONTINENT, BUT...
TMP
TMP
...THEY'RE JUST THUGS USING THEIR MIGHT TO GET THEIR WAY!
LORD THEO...
...I WILL STAY WITH YOU UNTIL THE END!
WE'LL ALL GO OUT WITH A BANG!
I'LL FIGHT TOO.
LORD THEO! WE WILL FIGHT BY YOUR SIDE!
FOR LORD THEO!
WE CAN'T GIVE IN TO THOSE WHO ABUSE THEIR POWER...
...AND HAVE NO HONOR!
THANK YOU! THANK YOU!
FATHER, WHY DID YOU GIVE AWAY ALL THE FOOD?
YAY
YAY
IF THEY FIND OUT YOU'VE BEEN HIDING IT, THEY'LL KILL YOU.

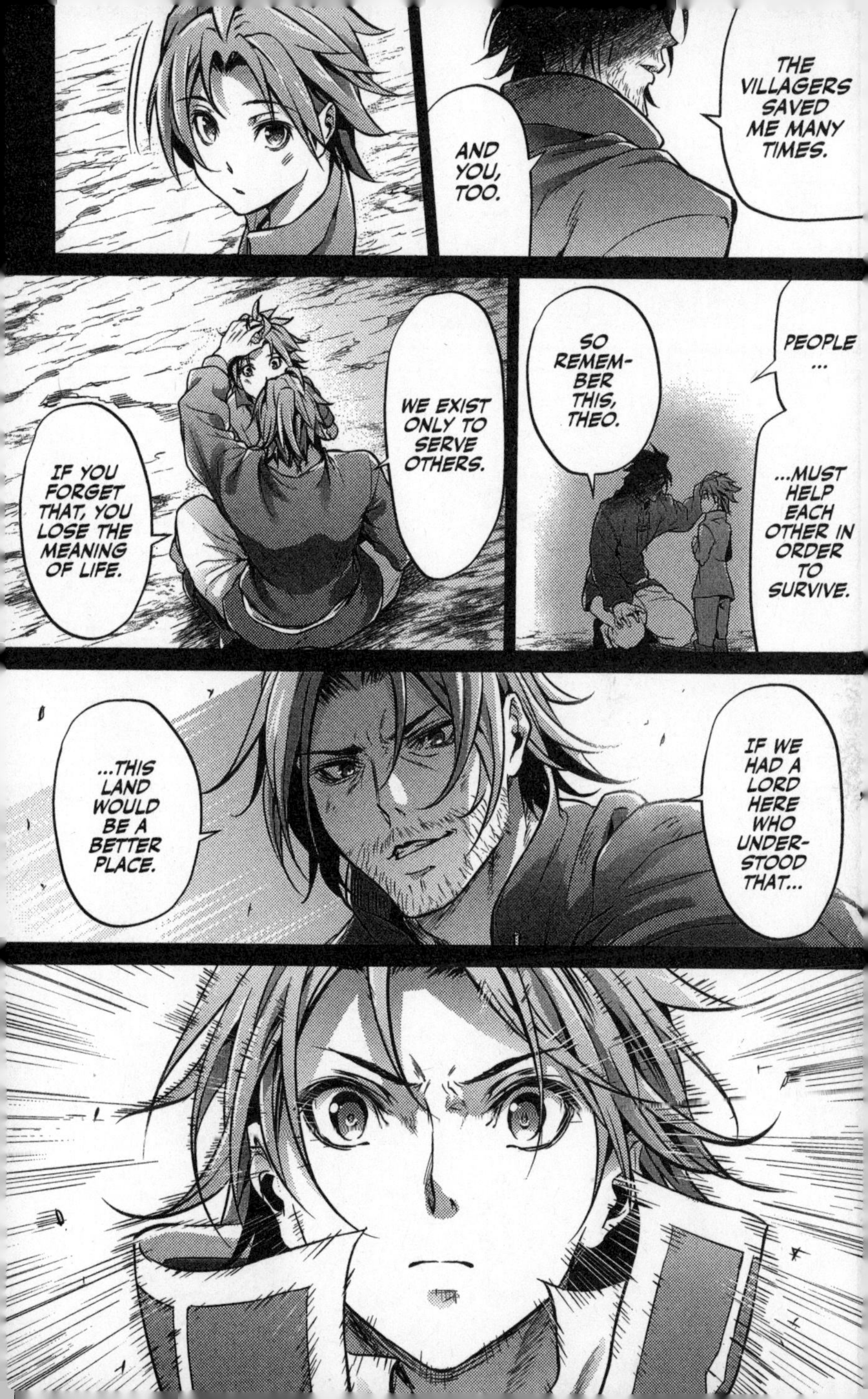
THE VILLAGERS SAVED ME MANY TIMES.
AND YOU, TOO.
PEOPLE ...
...MUST HELP EACH OTHER IN ORDER TO SURVIVE.
SO REMEMBER THIS, THEO.
WE EXIST ONLY TO SERVE OTHERS.
IF YOU FORGET THAT, YOU LOSE THE MEANING OF LIFE.
IF WE HAD A LORD HERE WHO UNDERSTOOD THAT...
...THIS LAND WOULD BE A BETTER PLACE.

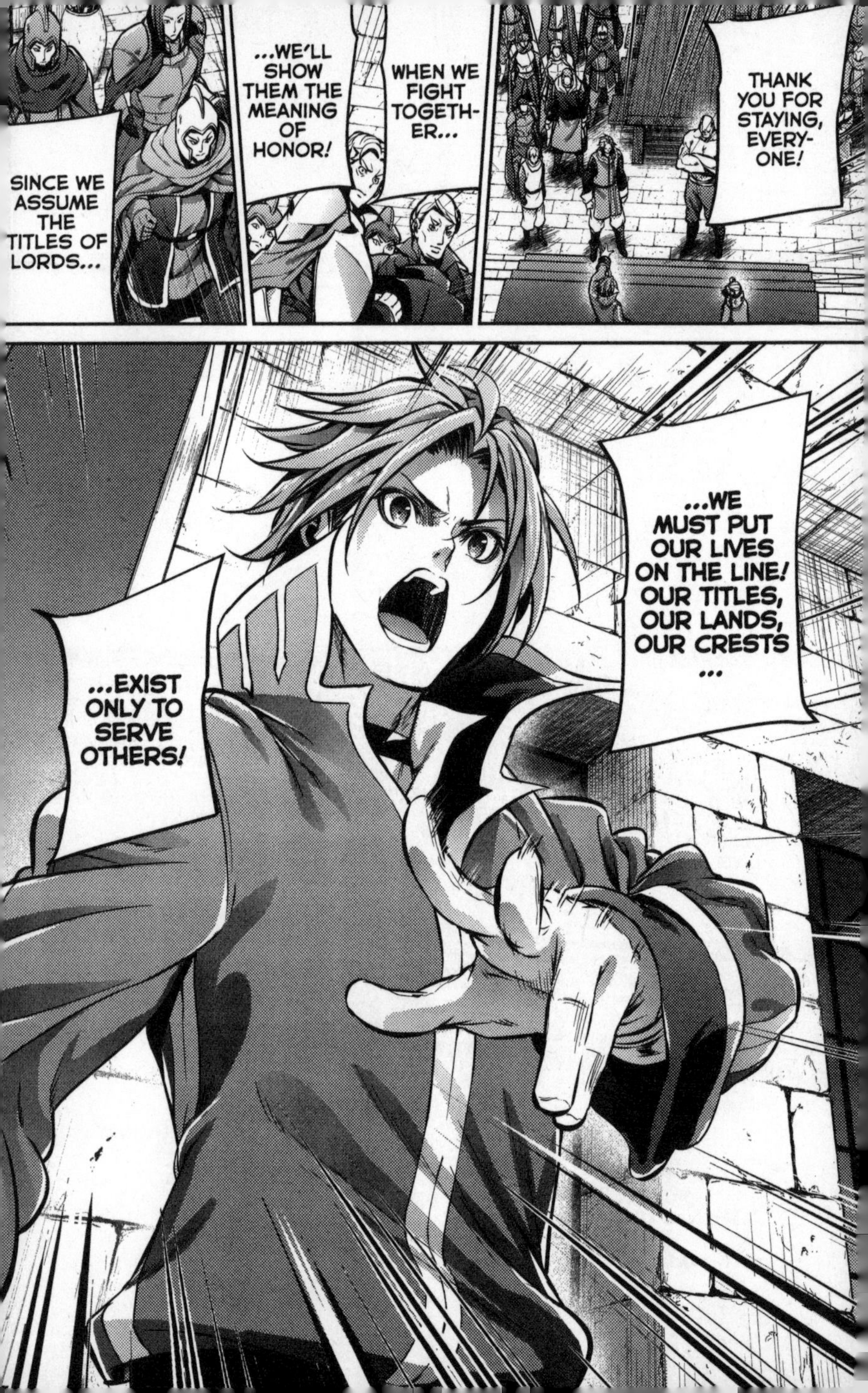
THANK YOU FOR STAYING, EVERY-ONE!
WHEN WE FIGHT TOGETH-ER...
...WE'LL SHOW THEM THE MEANING OF HONOR!
SINCE WE ASSUME THE TITLES OF LORDS...
...WE MUST PUT OUR LIVES ON THE LINE! OUR TITLES, OUR LANDS, OUR CRESTS...
...EXIST ONLY TO SERVE OTHERS!

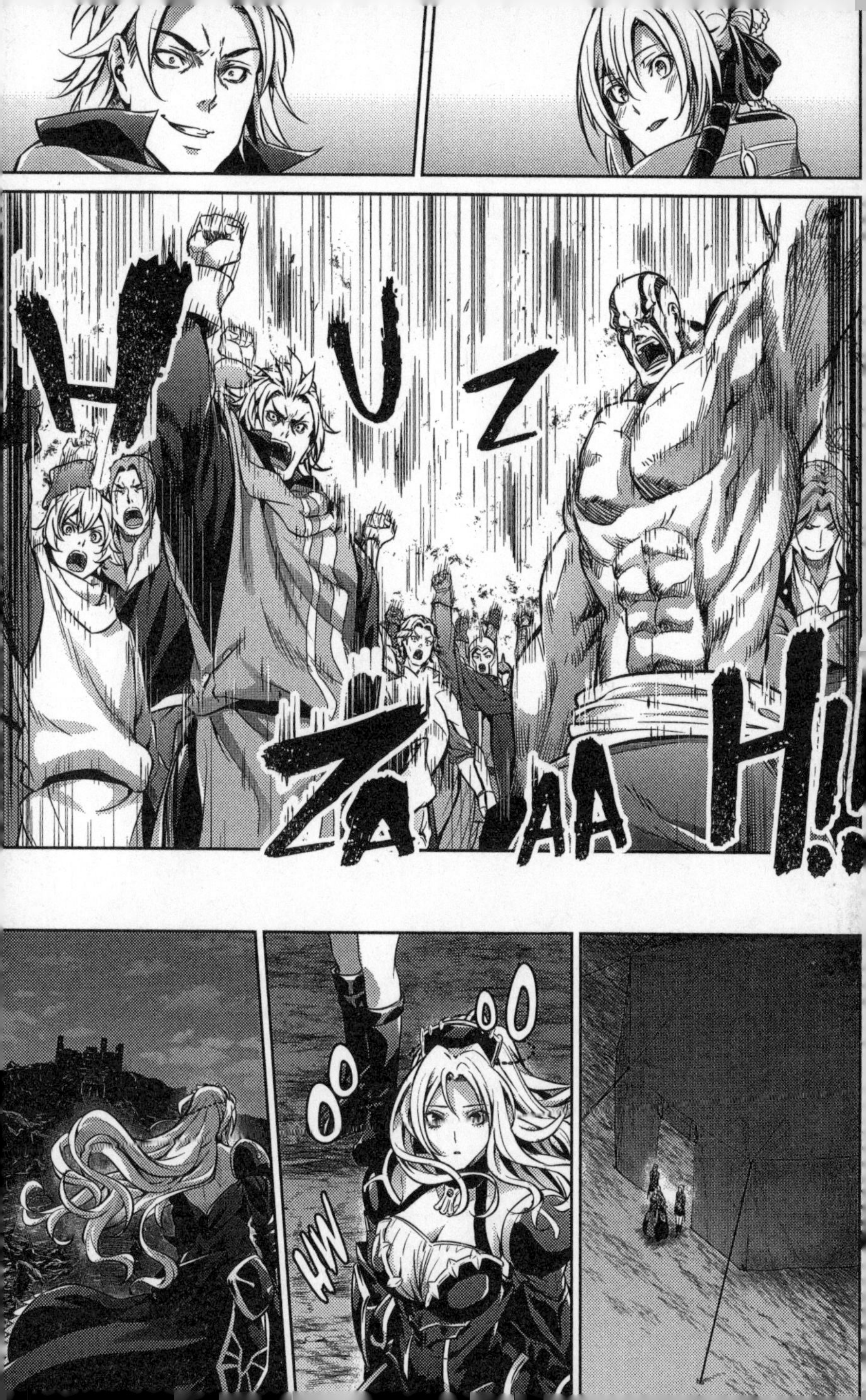
HUZZAAAH!!

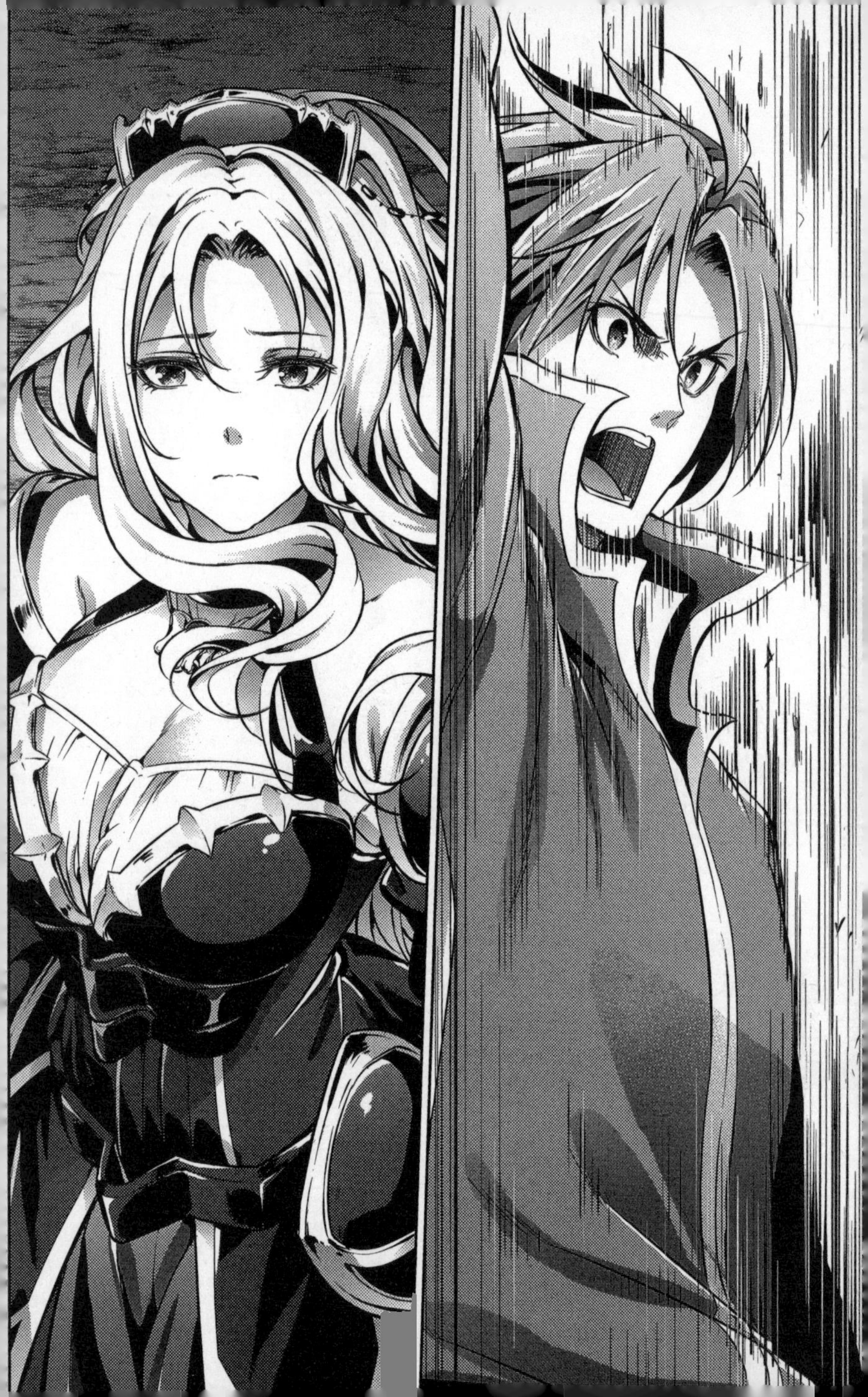

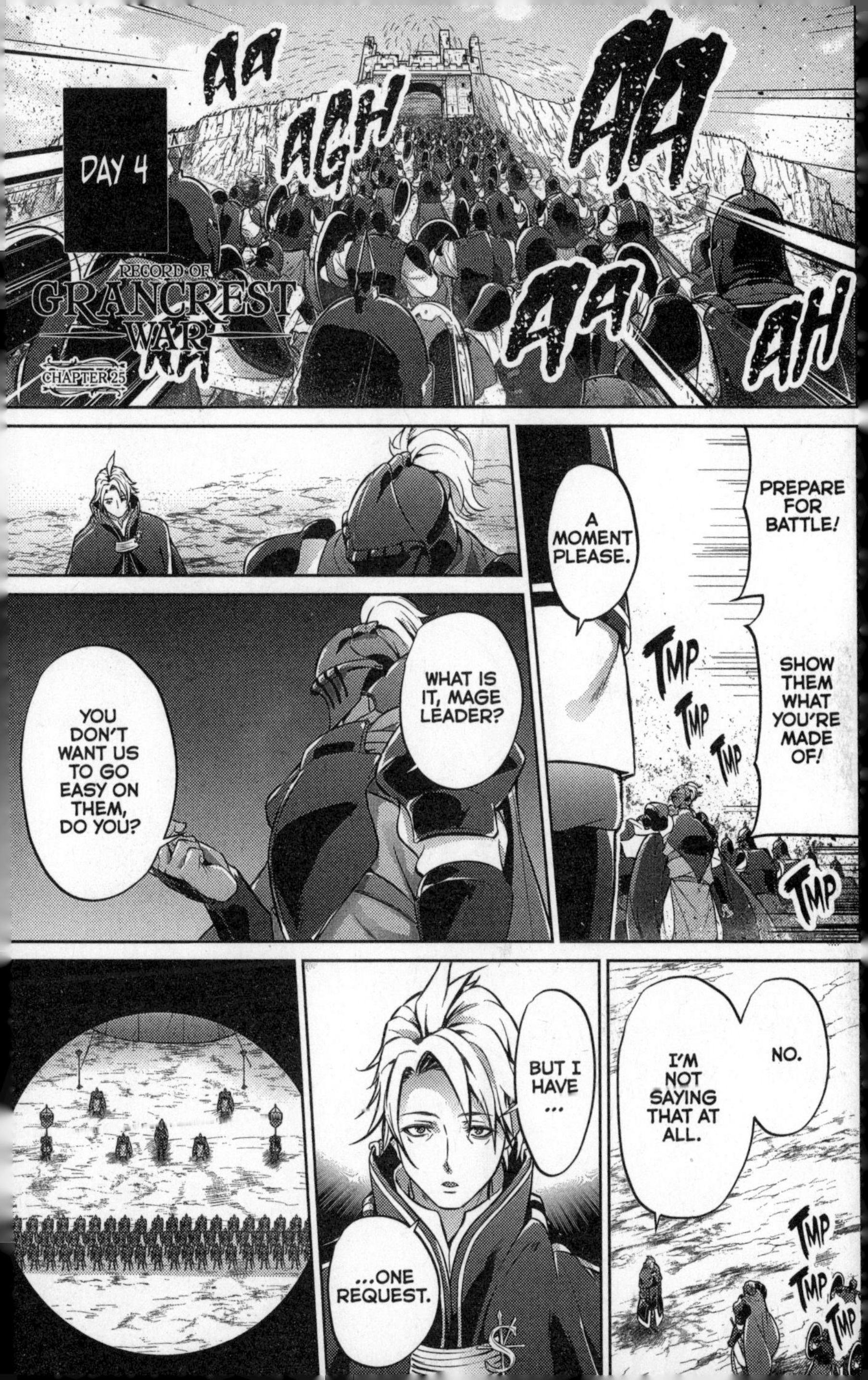
DAY 4
RECORD OF GRANCREST WAR
CHAPTER 25
AA AA AH
AA AGH
PREPARE FOR BATTLE!
A MOMENT PLEASE.
SHOW THEM WHAT YOU'RE MADE OF!
TMP TMP TMP TMP
WHAT IS IT, MAGE LEADER?
YOU DON'T WANT US TO GO EASY ON THEM, DO YOU?
NO.
I'M NOT SAYING THAT AT ALL.
TMP TMP TMP
BUT I HAVE ...
...ONE REQUEST.

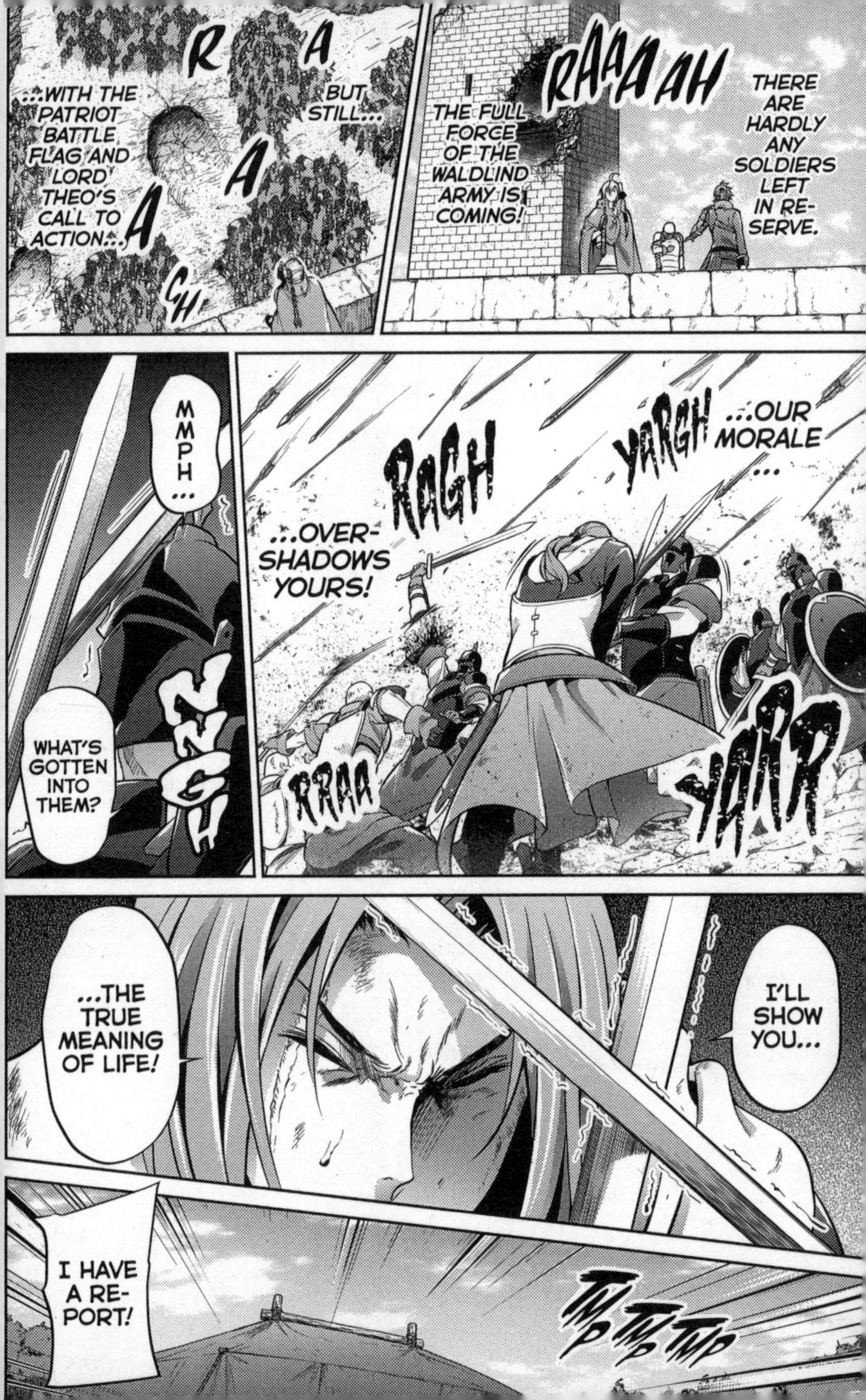
RAAAAAH
THERE ARE HARDLY ANY SOLDIERS LEFT IN RESERVE.
THE FULL FORCE OF THE WALDLIND ARMY IS COMING!
BUT STILL...
...WITH THE PATRIOT BATTLE FLAG AND LORD THEO'S CALL TO ACTION...
RAAAACH
...OUR MORALE...
YARGH
RAGH
...OVER-SHADOWS YOURS!
YARR
RRAA
MMPH...
NNGH
WHAT'S GOTTEN INTO THEM?
I'LL SHOW YOU...
...THE TRUE MEANING OF LIFE!
TMP TMP TMP
I HAVE A RE-PORT!

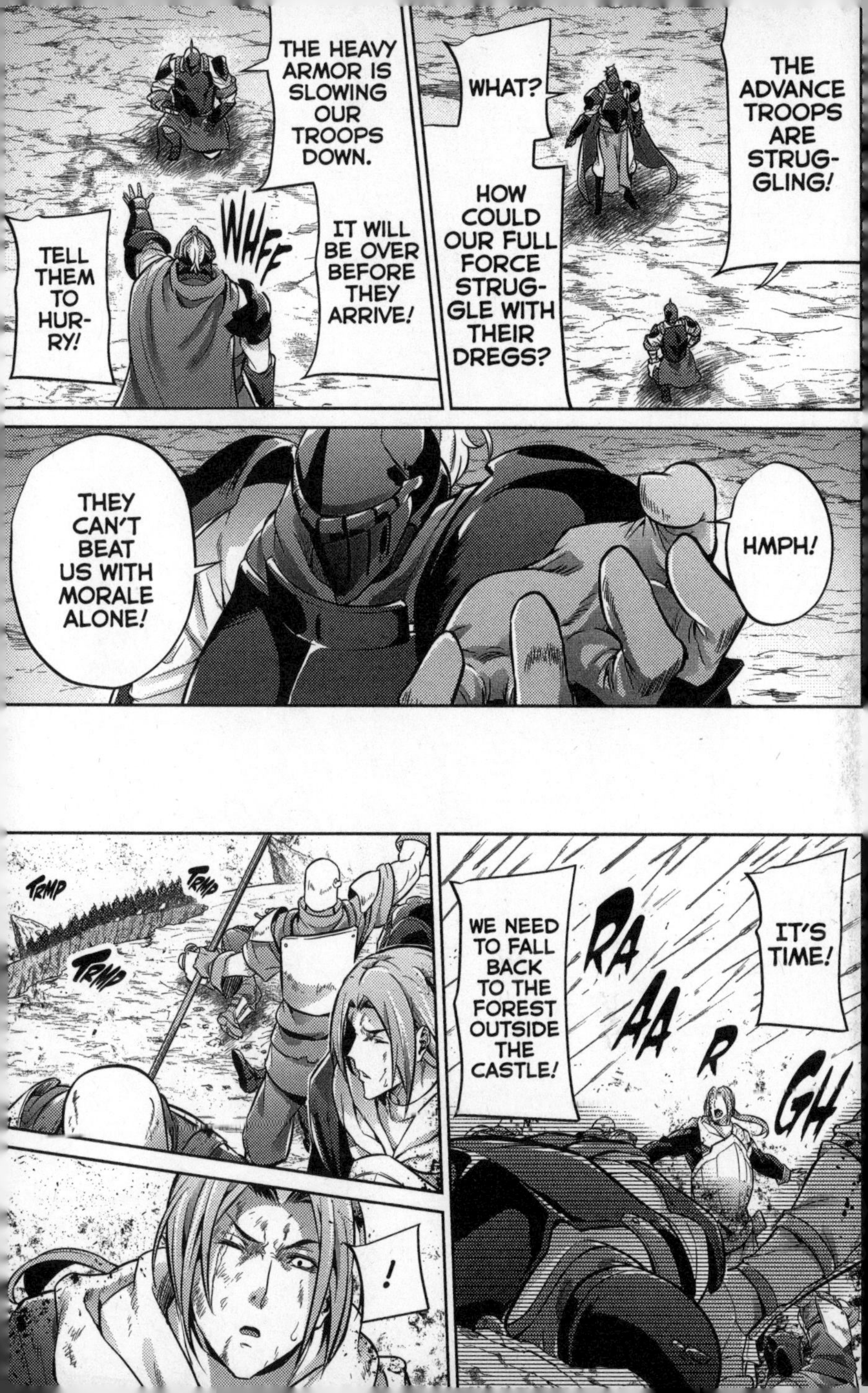
THE ADVANCE TROOPS ARE STRUGGLING!
WHAT?
HOW COULD OUR FULL FORCE STRUGGLE WITH THEIR DREGS?
THE HEAVY ARMOR IS SLOWING OUR TROOPS DOWN.
IT WILL BE OVER BEFORE THEY ARRIVE!
WHFF
TELL THEM TO HURRY!
HMPH!
THEY CAN'T BEAT US WITH MORALE ALONE!
IT'S TIME!
RAAARGH
WE NEED TO FALL BACK TO THE FOREST OUTSIDE THE CASTLE!
TRMP
TRMP
TRMP
!

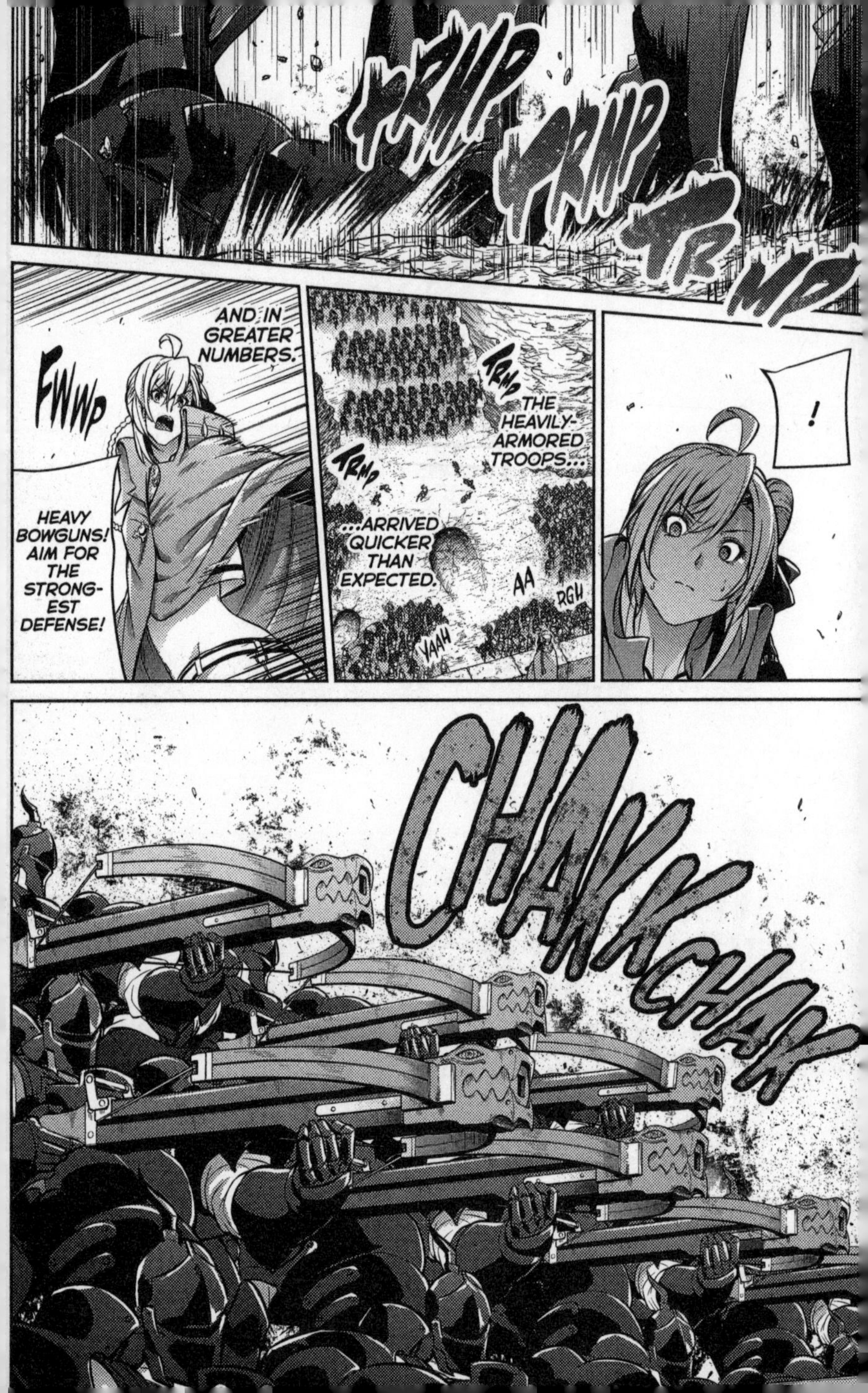
TRMP
TRMP
TRMP
!
TRMP
THE HEAVILY-ARMORED TROOPS...
TRMP
...ARRIVED QUICKER THAN EXPECTED.
AARGH
YAAH
AND IN GREATER NUMBERS.
FWWP
HEAVY BOWGUNS! AIM FOR THE STRONGEST DEFENSE!
CHAKCHAK

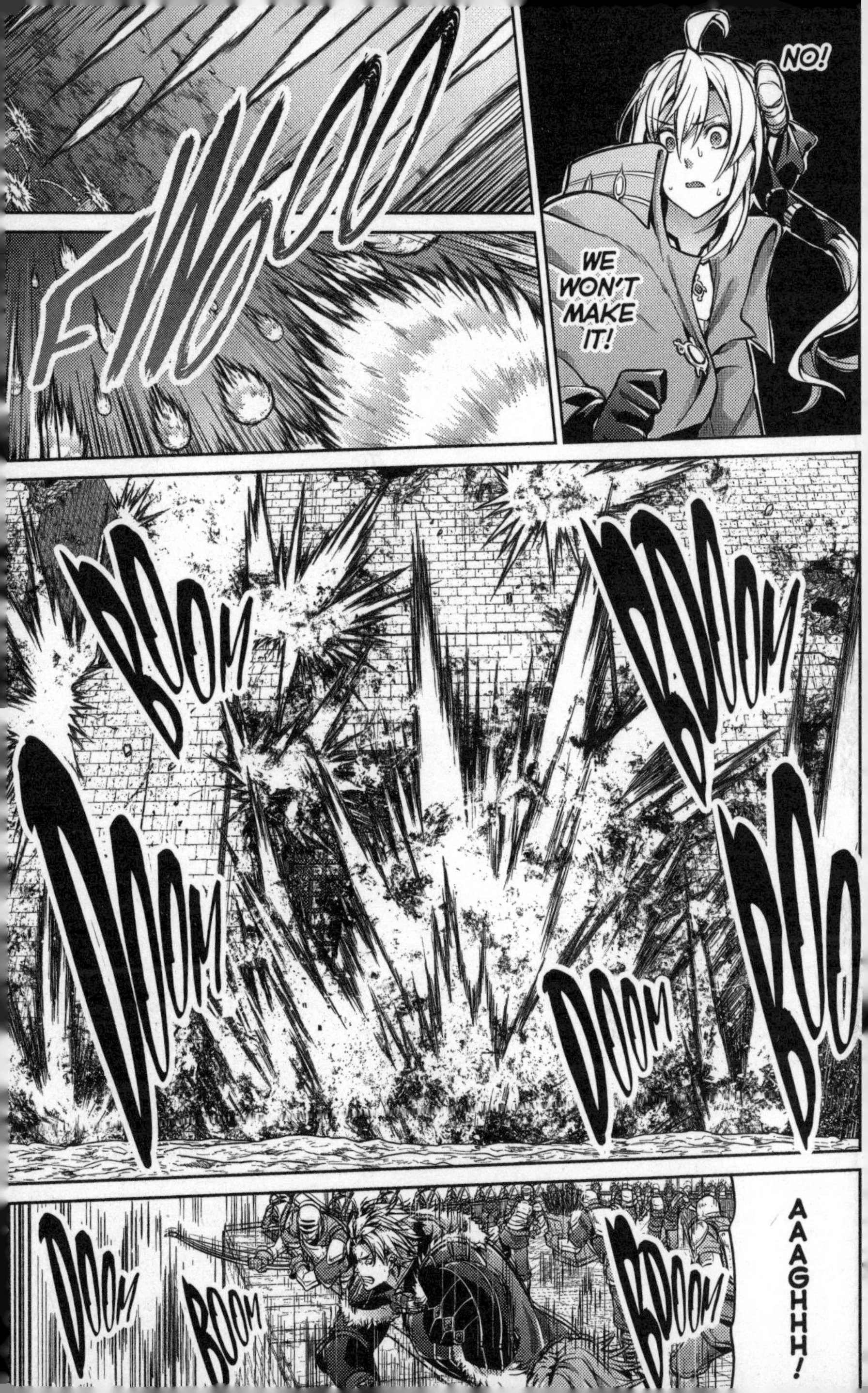
NO!
WE WON'T MAKE IT!
BOOOM
BOO
DOOM
BOOM
DOOOM!
AAAGHHH!
BOOOM
BOOM
DOOM

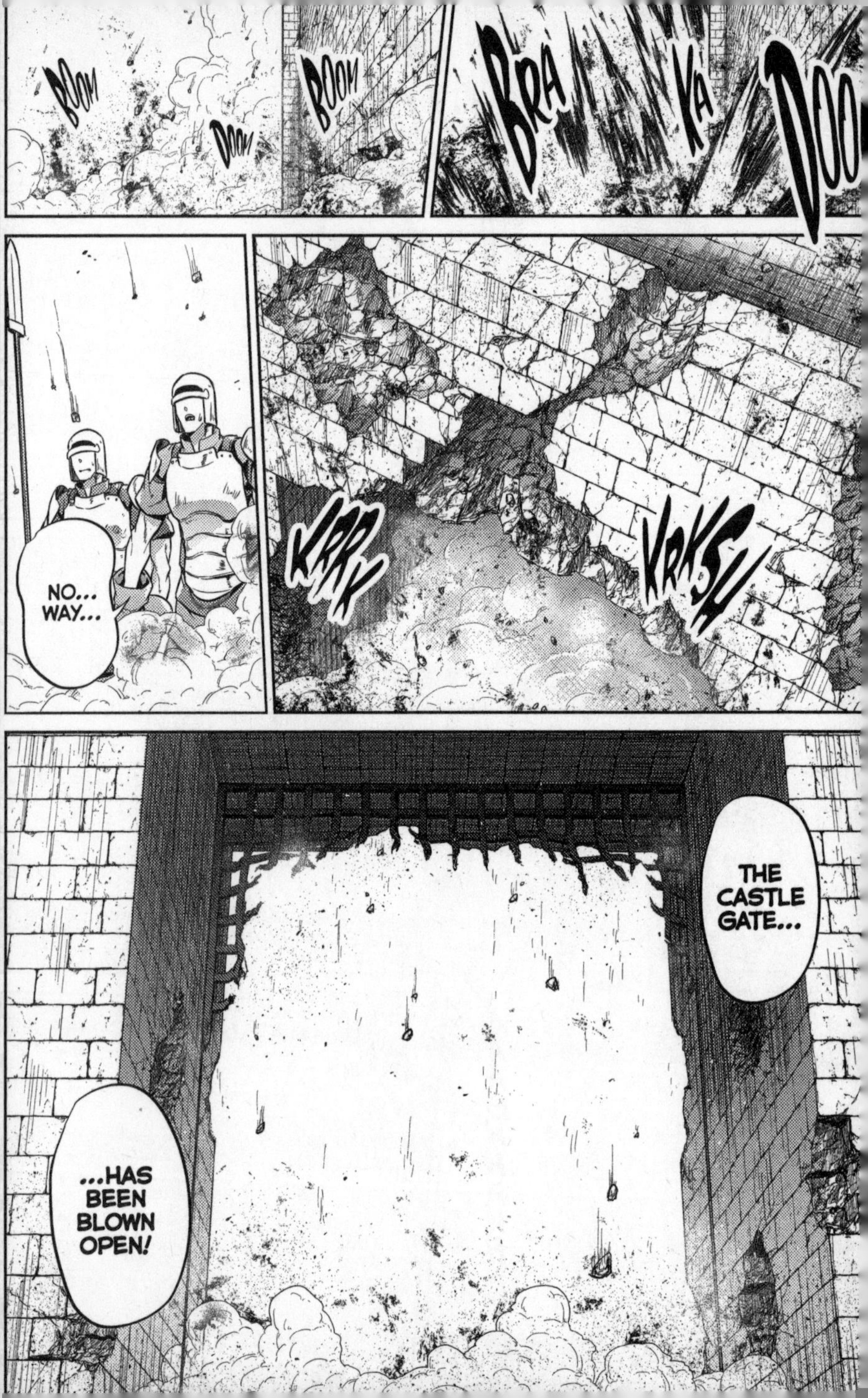
BRA
KA
DOO
BOOM
BOOM
DOOM
KRKSH
KRRK
NO... WAY...
THE CASTLE GATE...
...HAS BEEN BLOWN OPEN!

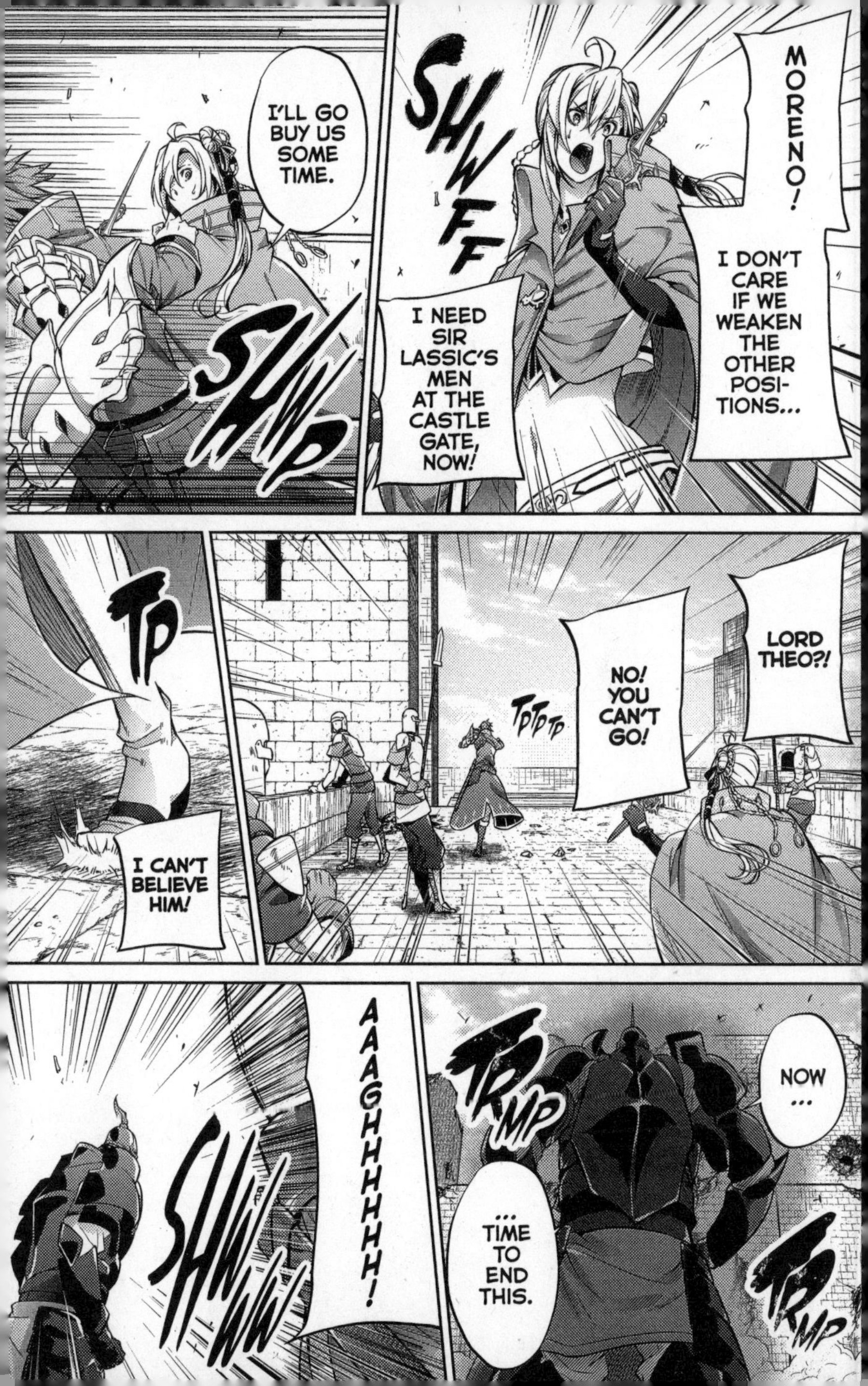
MORENO!
I DON'T CARE IF WE WEAKEN THE OTHER POSI-TIONS...
SHWFF
I NEED SIR LASSIC'S MEN AT THE CASTLE GATE, NOW!
I'LL GO BUY US SOME TIME.
SHWP
LORD THEO?!
NO! YOU CAN'T GO!
TPTPTPTP
TP
I CAN'T BELIEVE HIM!
NOW...
TRMP
...TIME TO END THIS.
TRMP
AAAGHHHHHHH!
SHWWW

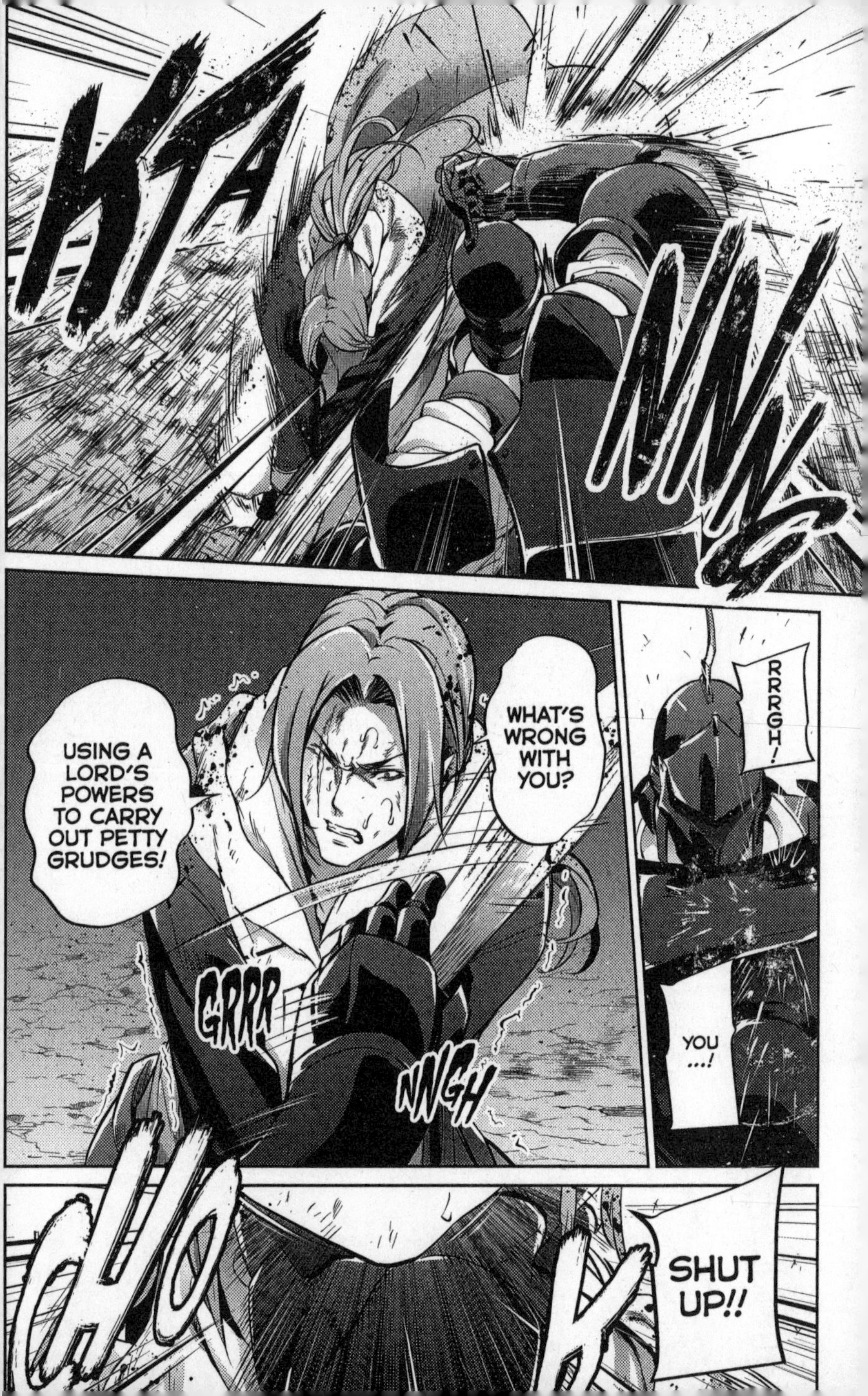
KTA
NNNG
RRRGH!
YOU ...!
WHAT'S WRONG WITH YOU?
USING A LORD'S POWERS TO CARRY OUT PETTY GRUDGES!
GRRR
NNGH
SHUT UP!!
CHOK

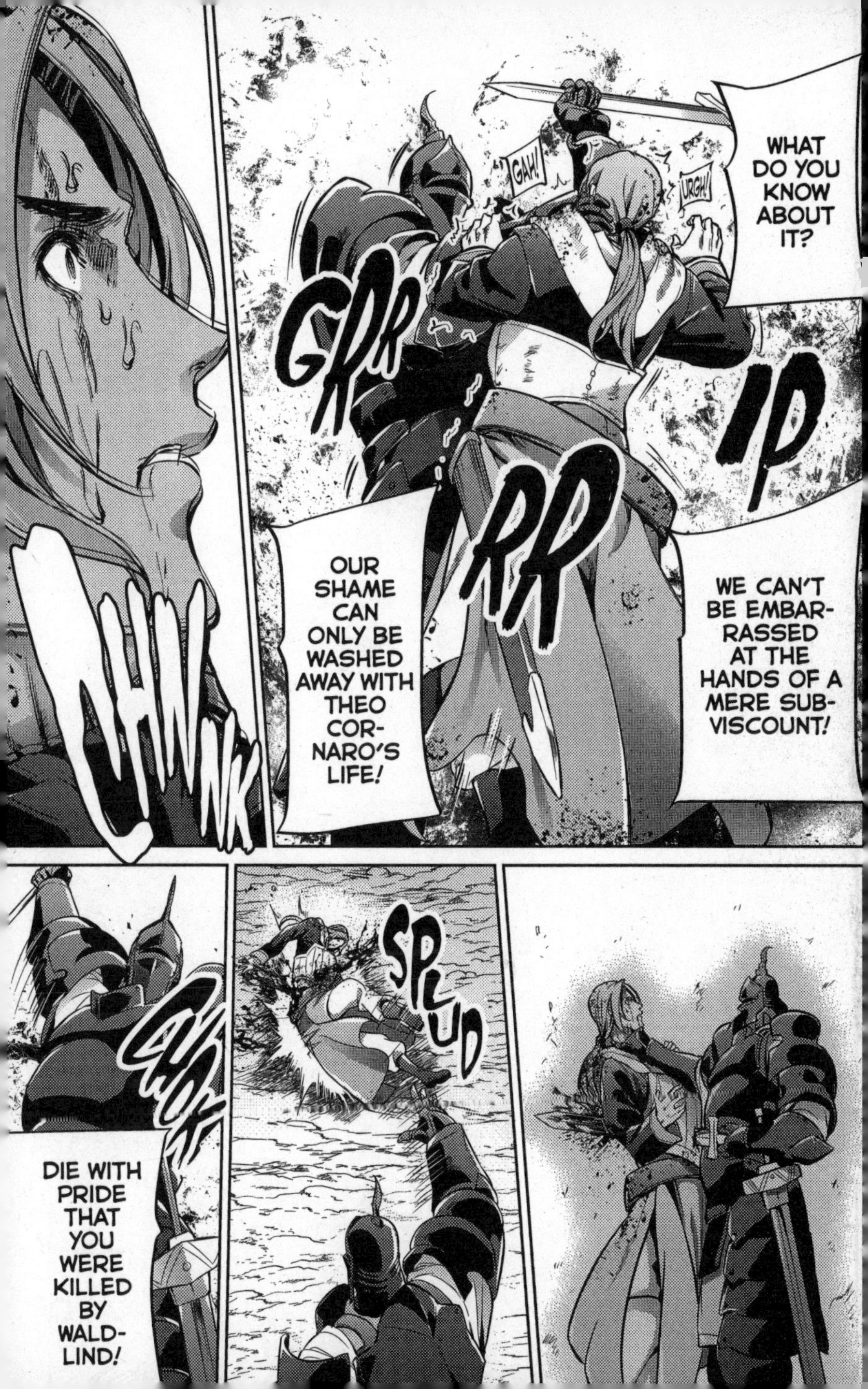

WHAT DO YOU KNOW ABOUT IT?
¡URGH!
GAH!
GRR
RRIP
WE CAN'T BE EMBARRASSED AT THE HANDS OF A MERE SUB-VISCOUNT!
OUR SHAME CAN ONLY BE WASHED AWAY WITH THEO CORNARO'S LIFE!
CHANNK
SPLUD
CHOK
DIE WITH PRIDE THAT YOU WERE KILLED BY WALDLIND!

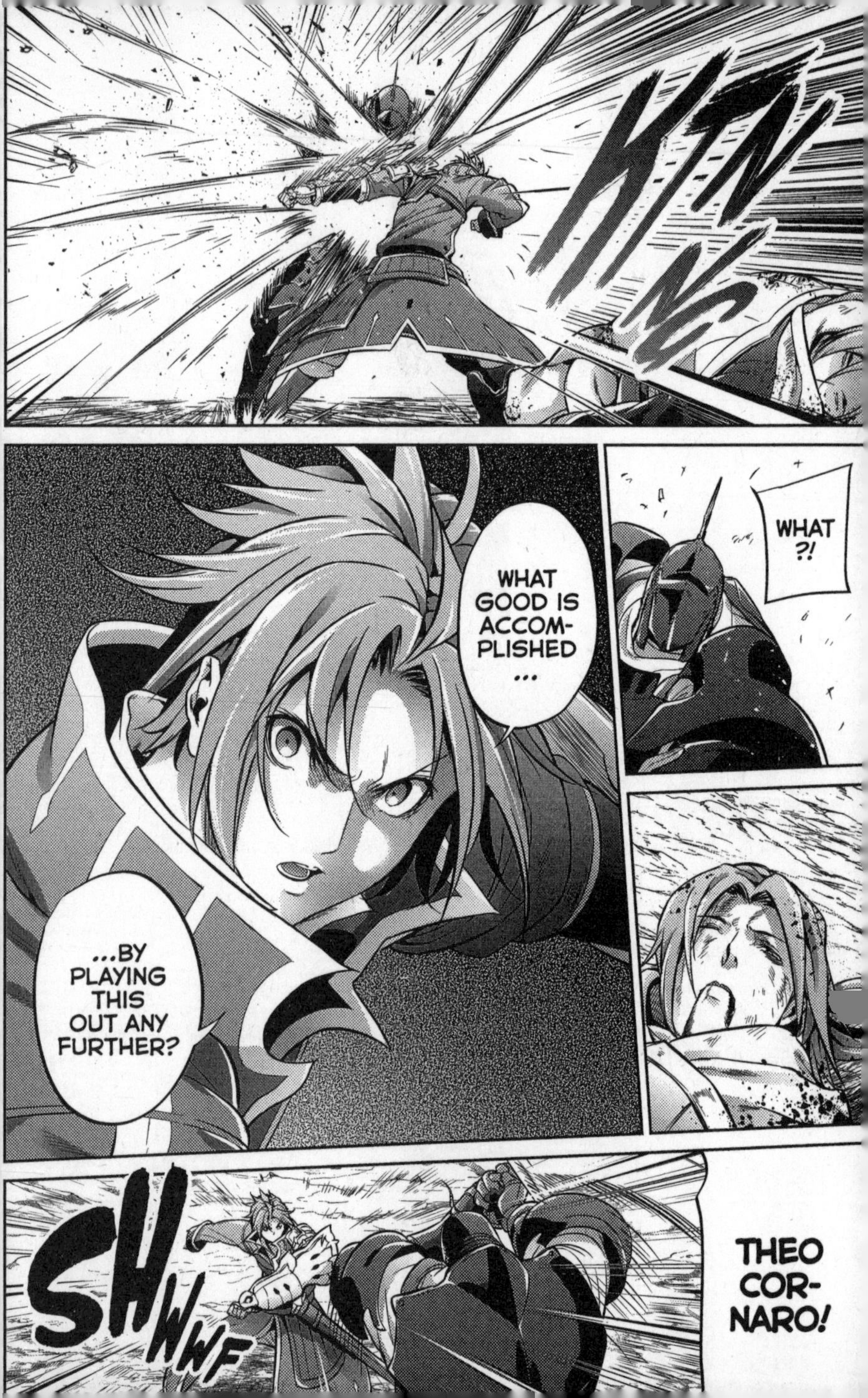
WHAT ?!
WHAT GOOD IS ACCOMPLISHED ...
...BY PLAYING THIS OUT ANY FURTHER?
THEO COR-NARO!
SHWWF

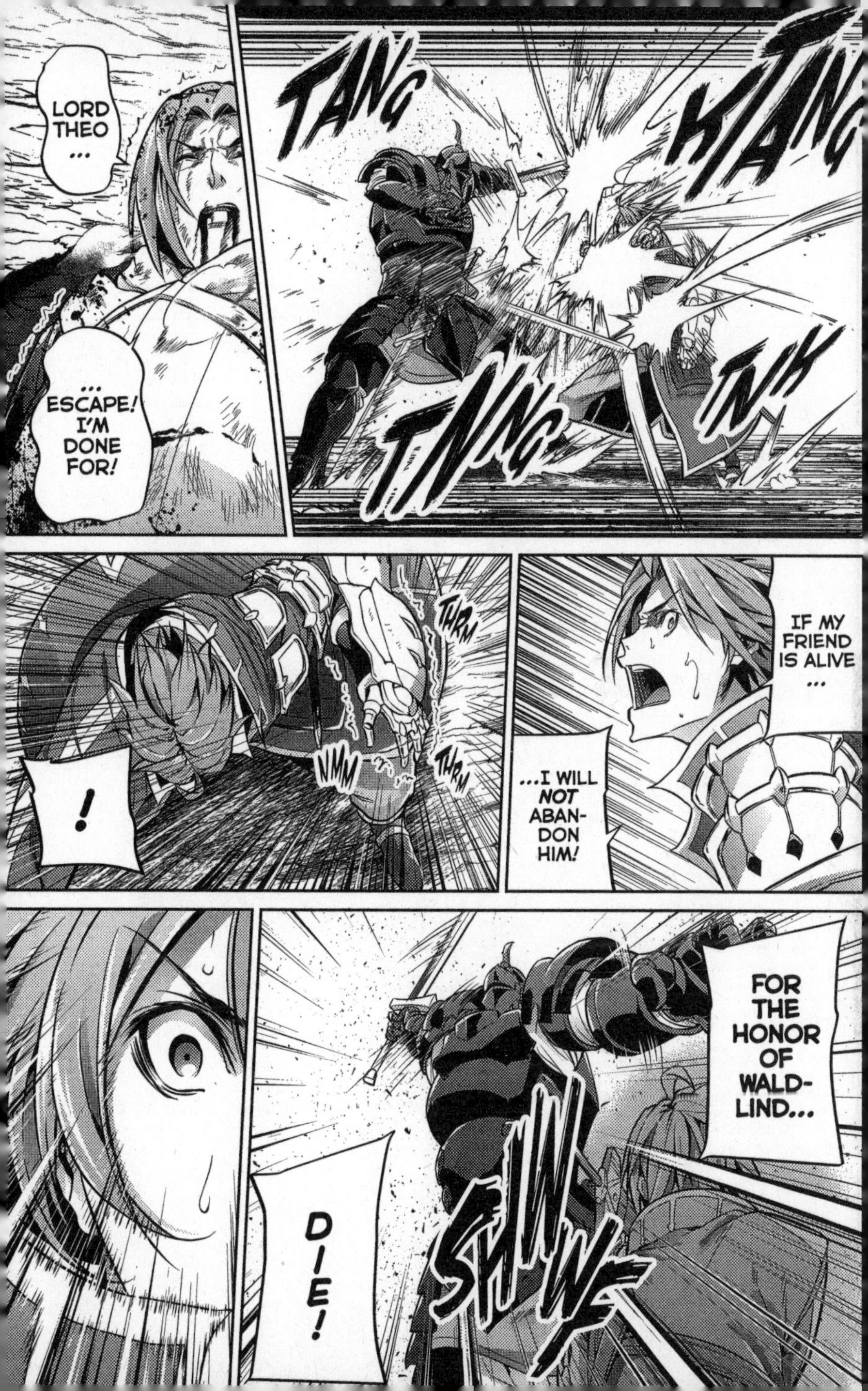
KYANG
TANG
INK
TING
LORD THEO ...
... ESCAPE! I'M DONE FOR!
IF MY FRIEND IS ALIVE ...
...I WILL *NOT* ABAN-DON HIM!
THRM
THRM
NMM
!
FOR THE HONOR OF WALD-LIND...
SHNK
DIE!

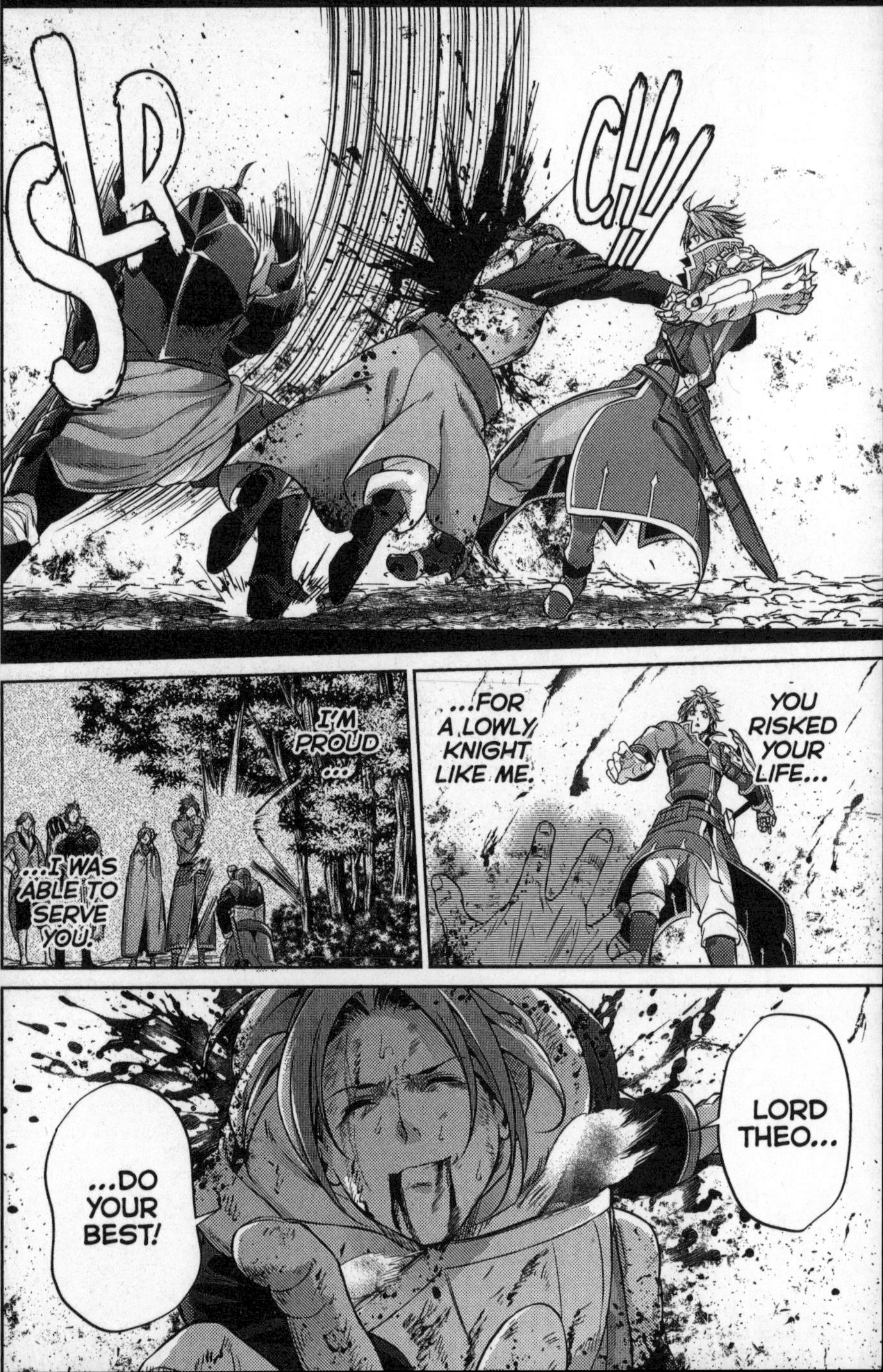
SLR
CH!!
YOU RISKED YOUR LIFE...
...FOR A LOWLY KNIGHT LIKE ME.
I'M PROUD...
...I WAS ABLE TO SERVE YOU.
LORD THEO...
...DO YOUR BEST!

RISE!

SHWE—

LORD THEO, WE NEED TO FALL BACK!

SIR NEE-MAN!

THMMP

KRAASH

WELL...

TRMP

KCH

CHNK

KCH

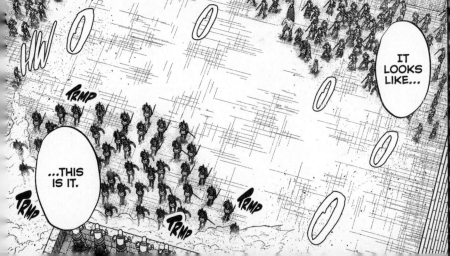

IT LOOKS LIKE...

TRMP

...THIS IS IT.

TRMP

TRMP

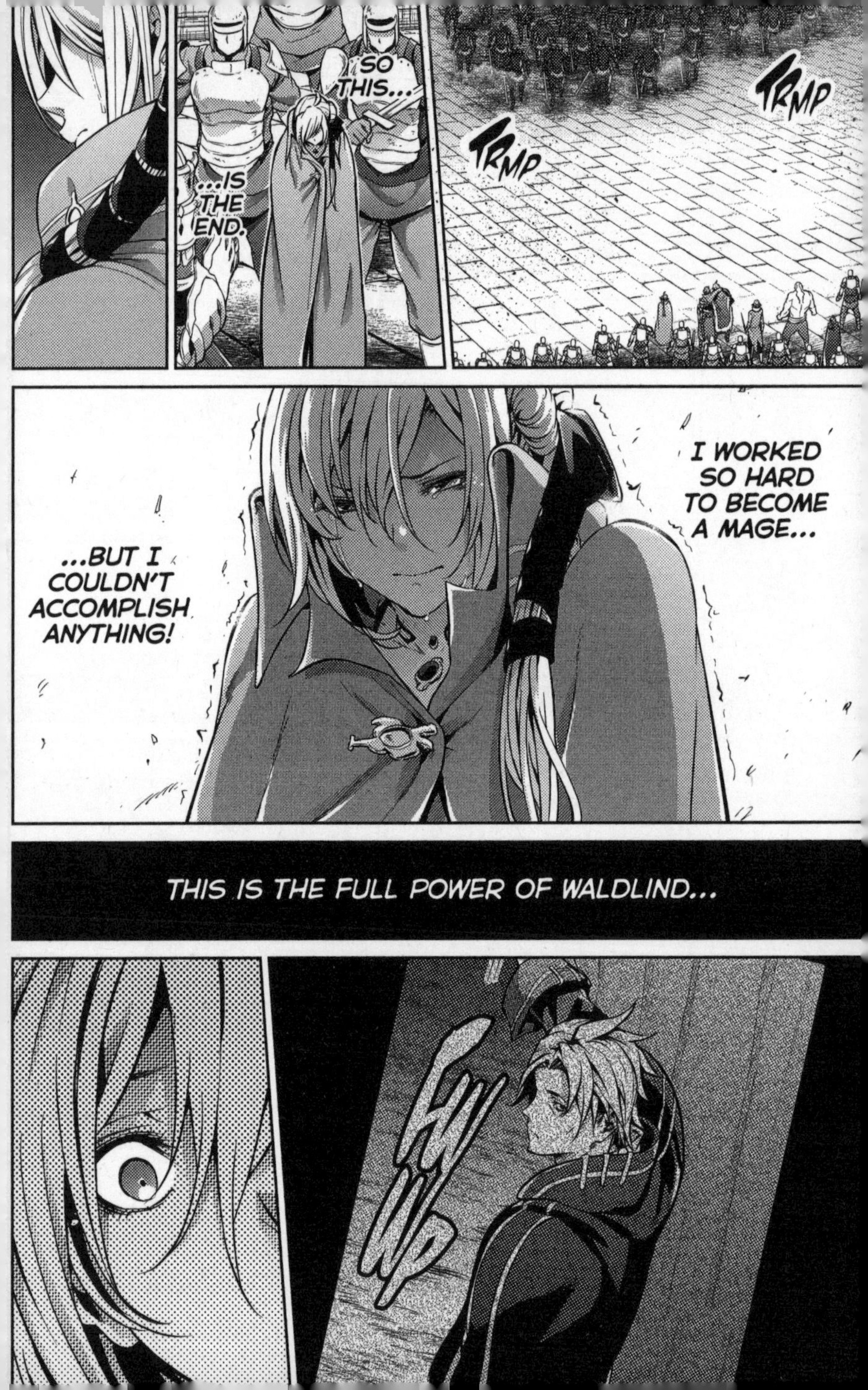
TRMP
TRMP
SO THIS...
...IS THE END.
I WORKED SO HARD TO BECOME A MAGE...
...BUT I COULDN'T ACCOMPLISH ANYTHING!
THIS IS THE FULL POWER OF WALDLIND...

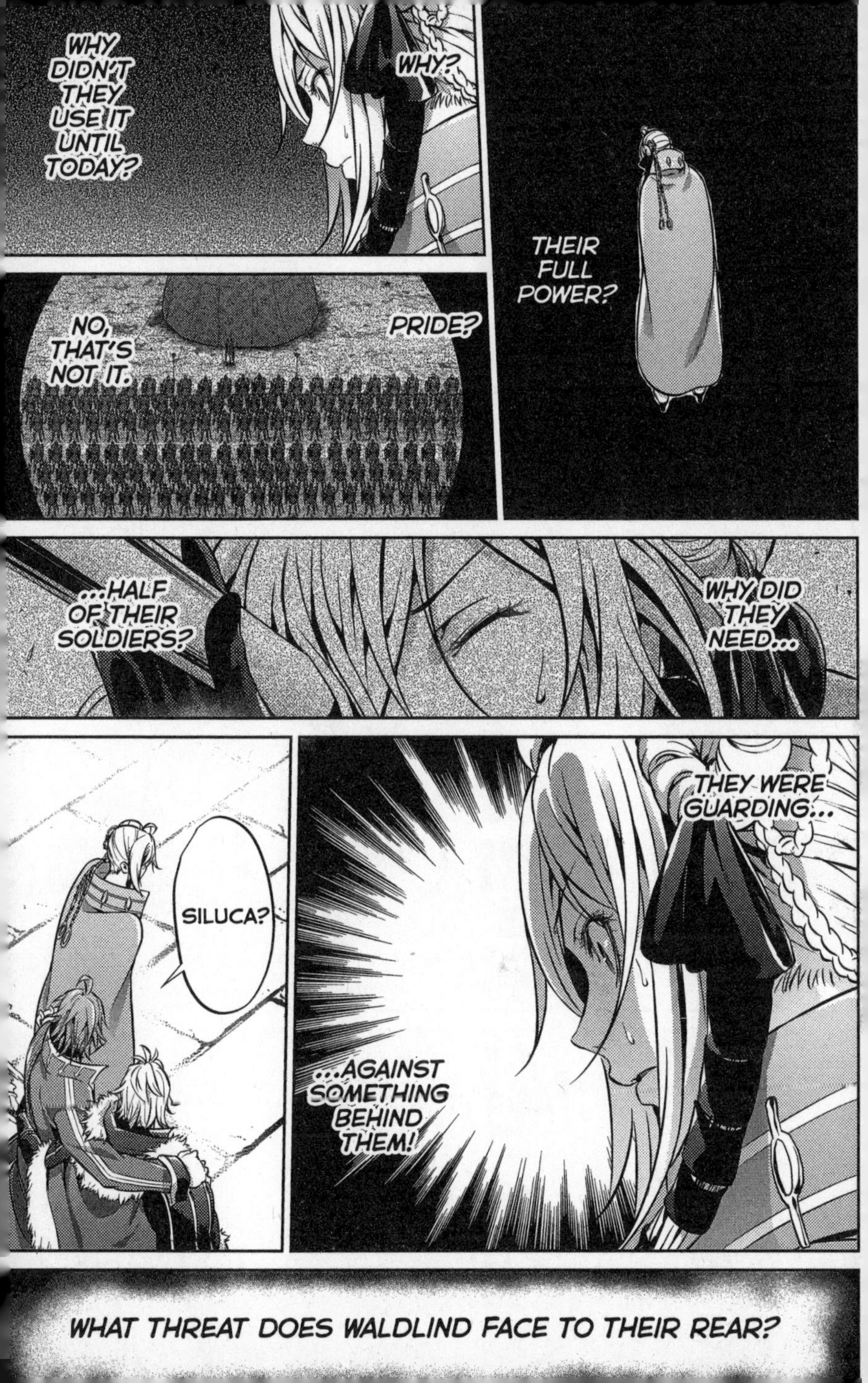
THEIR FULL POWER?
WHY?
WHY DIDN'T THEY USE IT UNTIL TODAY?
PRIDE?
NO, THAT'S NOT IT.
WHY DID THEY NEED...
...HALF OF THEIR SOLDIERS?
THEY WERE GUARDING...
...AGAINST SOMETHING BEHIND THEM!
SILUCA?
WHAT THREAT DOES WALDLIND FACE TO THEIR REAR?

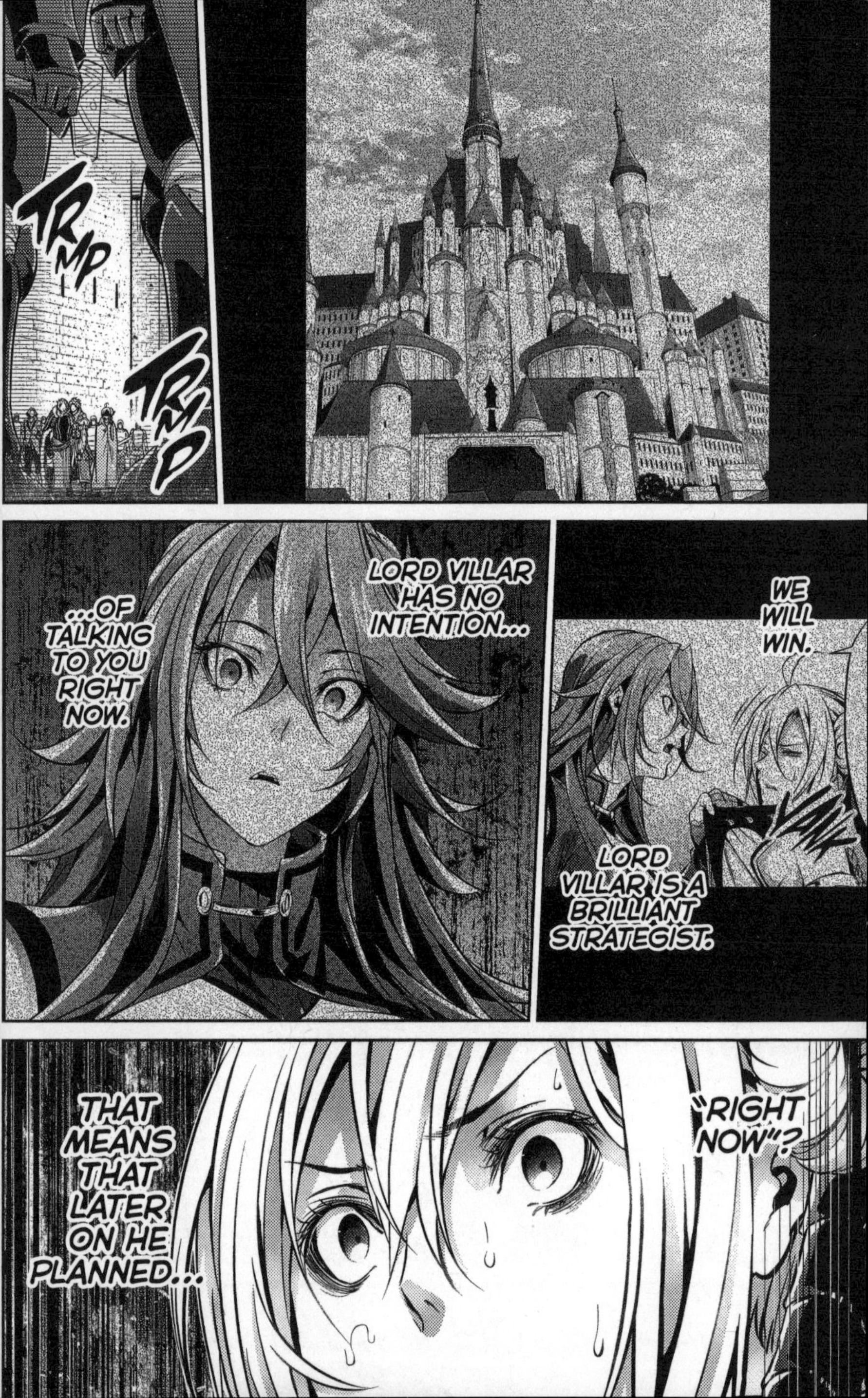
TRMP
TRMP
WE WILL WIN.
LORD VILLAR IS A BRILLIANT STRATEGIST.
LORD VILLAR HAS NO INTENTION...
...OF TALKING TO YOU RIGHT NOW.
"RIGHT NOW"?
THAT MEANS THAT LATER ON HE PLANNED...

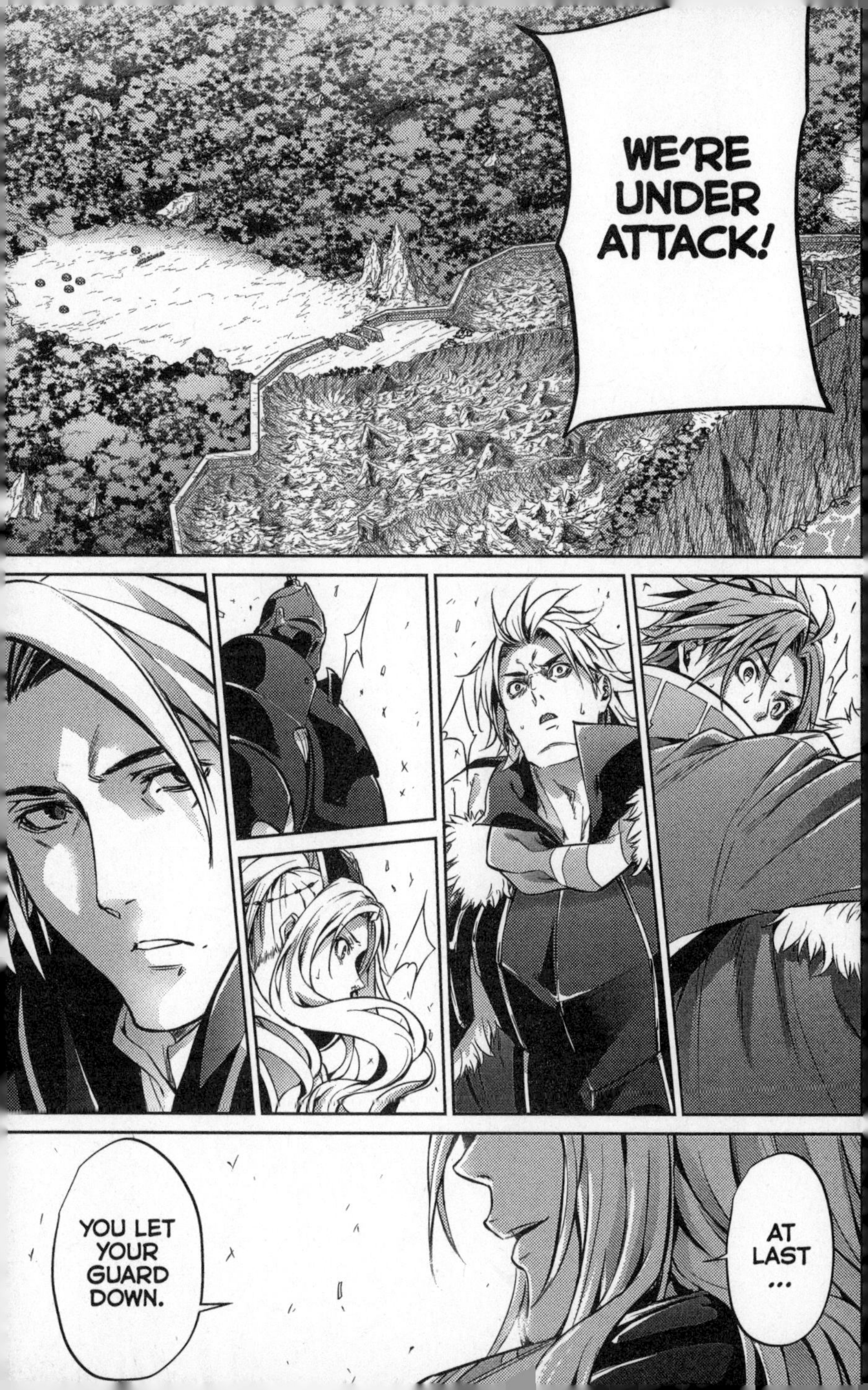
WE'RE UNDER ATTACK!
AT LAST ...
YOU LET YOUR GUARD DOWN.

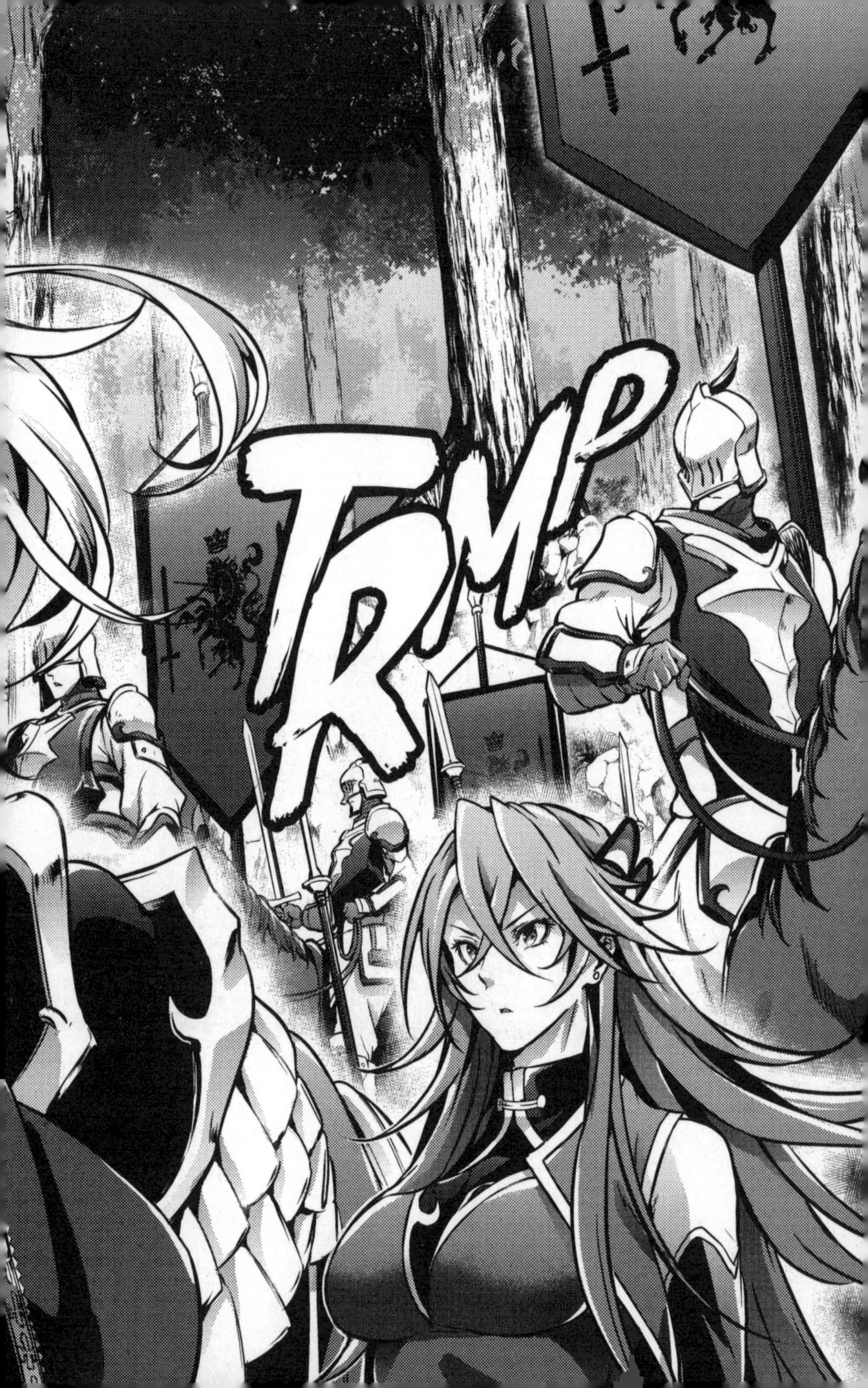
TRMP

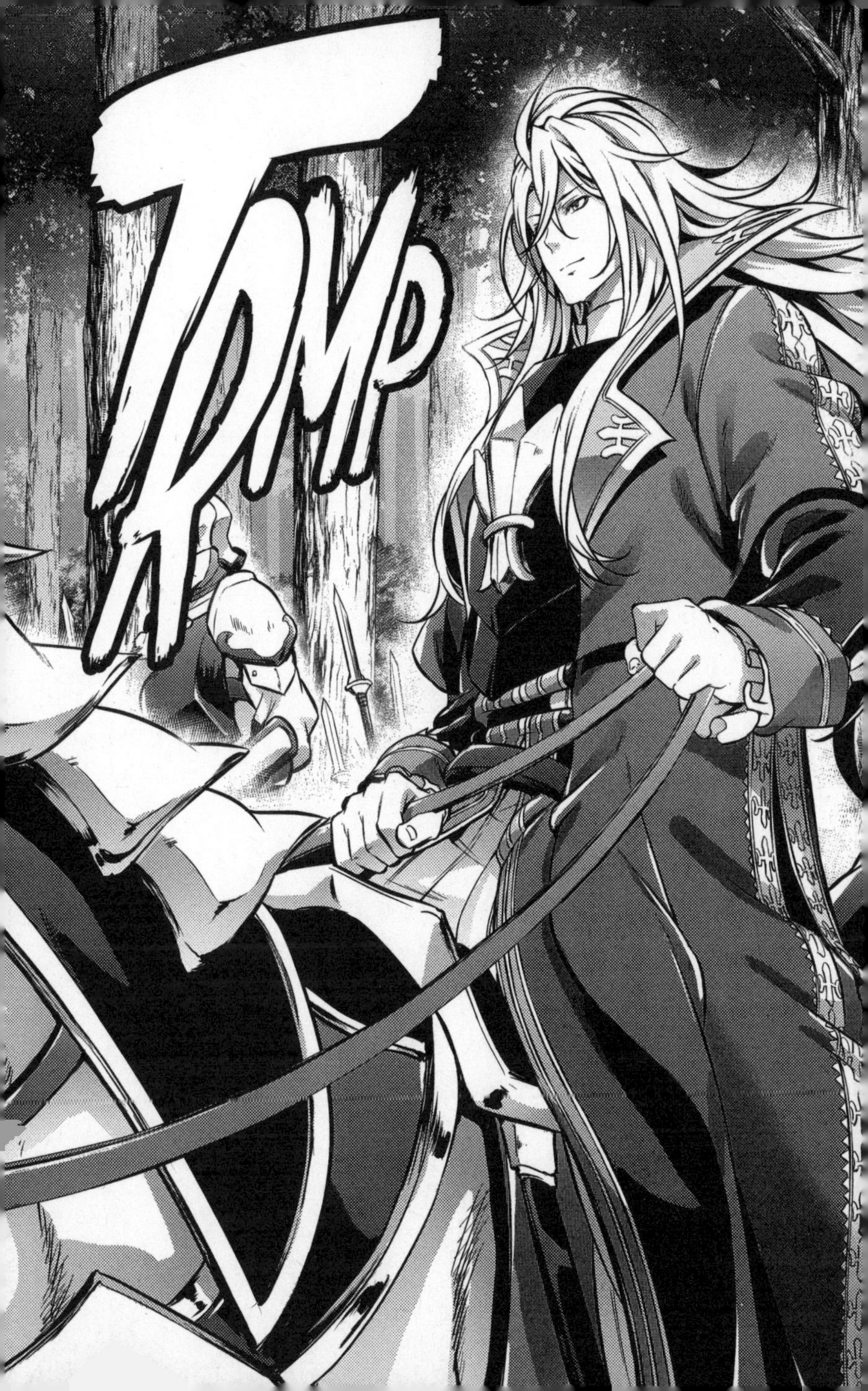
TOMP

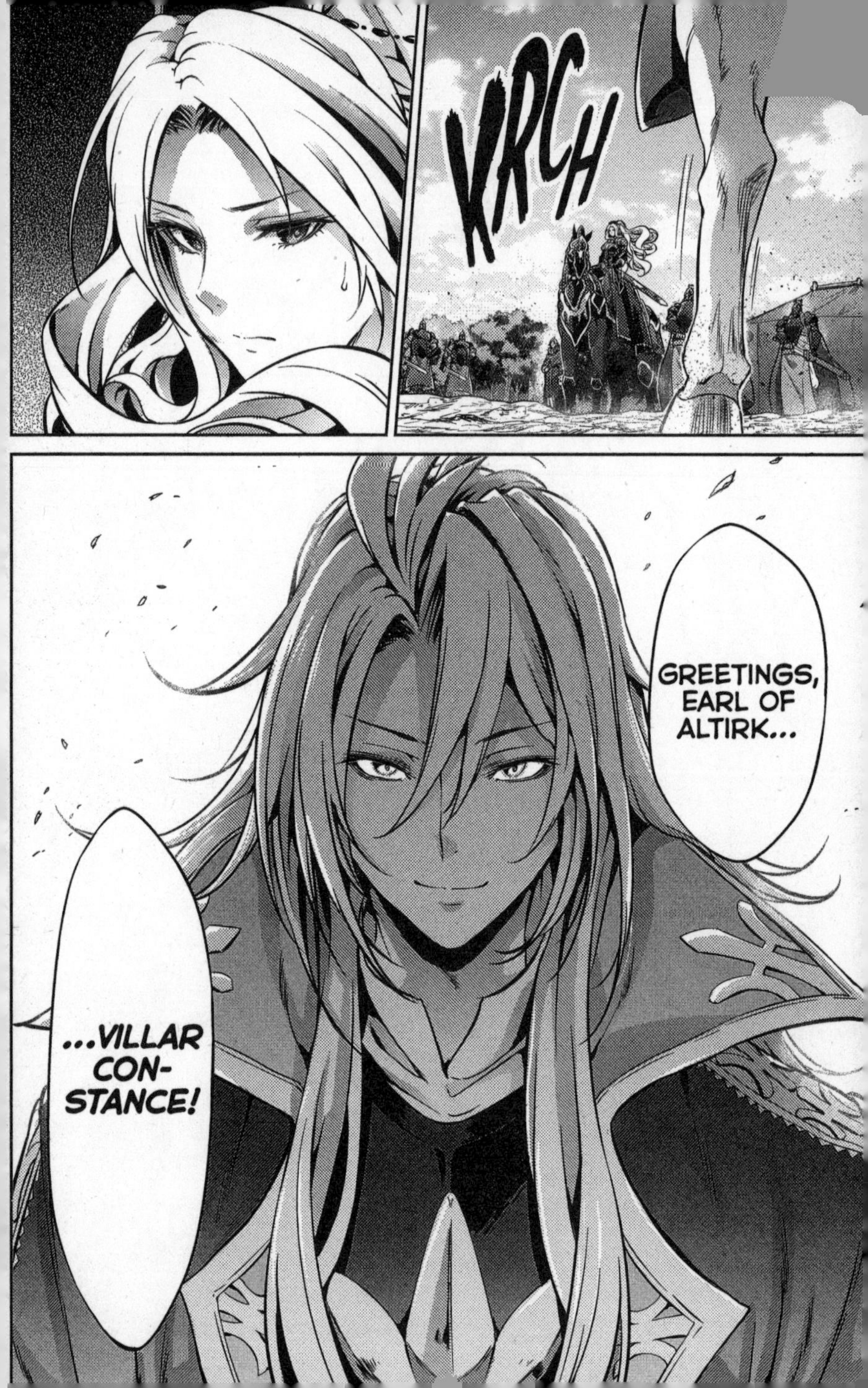
KRCH
GREETINGS, EARL OF ALTIRK...
...VILLAR CON-STANCE!

THANK YOU FOR PICKING UP VOLUME 4.
THIS IS YOTSUBA.

THE ORIGINAL NOVEL SERIES RAN IN TEN VOLUMES. THE ANIME SHOULD COVER THE STORY THROUGH THE NINTH NOVEL BY THE END OF MAY. (I'M WRITING THIS AFTERWORD IN APRIL.)

AND YET THE MANGA'S STORY IS STILL HOVERING AROUND THE END OF THE FIRST NOVEL. LOL. THE NEXT MANGA VOLUME WILL FINALLY CARRY THE STORY INTO THE SECOND NOVEL.

WHILE I WATCH THE ANIME, I KEEP THINKING, "ARGH! I WANT TO DRAW THAT PART SOON!" BUT THEN I REALIZE HOW FAR AWAY THAT IS FOR US!

ANYWAY, THE MANGA VERSION IS GOING SLOWLY, BUT I HOPE YOU STAY PATIENT AND KEEP READING.

I HOPE TO SEE YOU AGAIN IN VOLUME 5!

MAKOTO YOTSUBA

四葉真

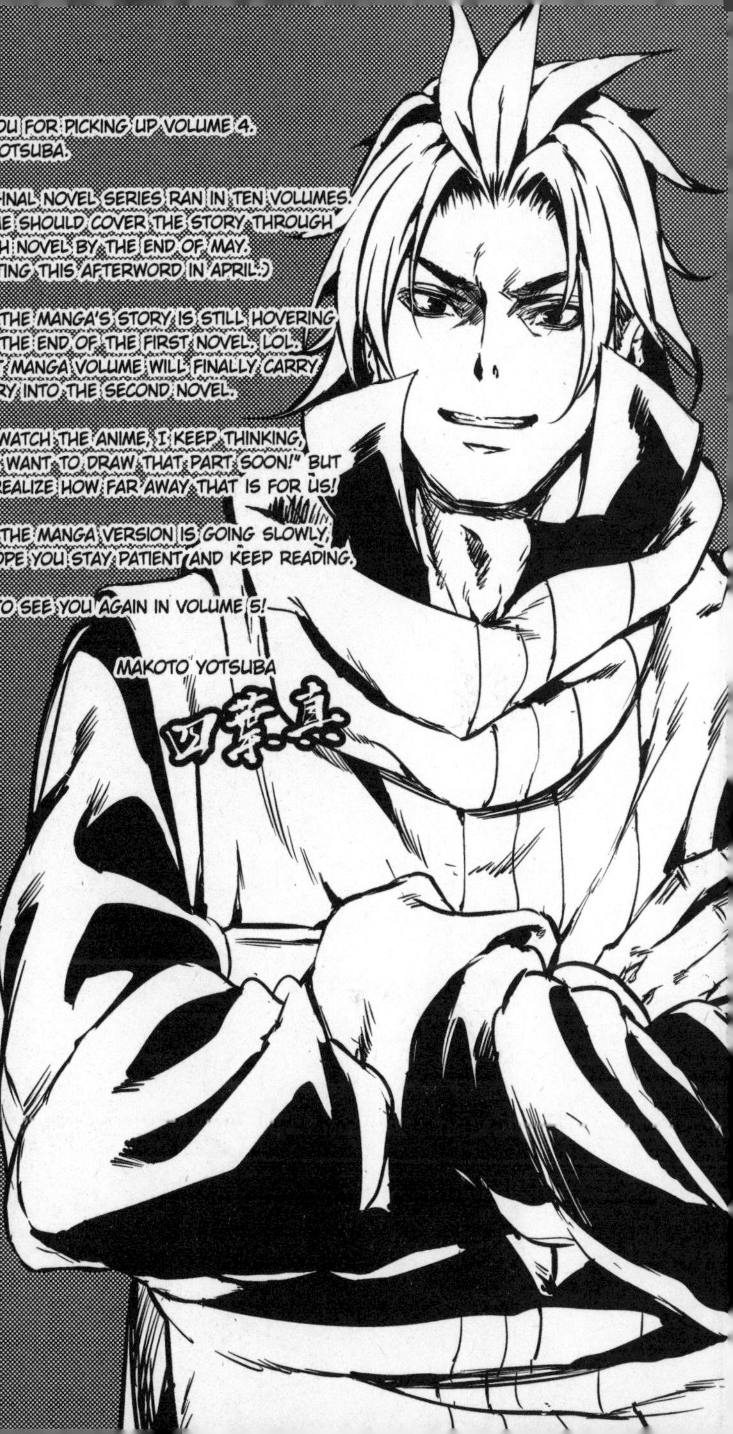

RECORD OF GRANCREST WAR

VOLUME 4

Original Story by **Ryo Mizuno**
Story & Art by **Makoto Yotsuba**
Character Design by **Miyuu**

Translation: **Satsuki Yamashita**
Touch-Up Art & Lettering: **James Gaubatz**
English Adaptation: **Stan!**
Design: **Julian [JR] Robinson**
Editor: **David Brothers**

GRANCREST SENKI by Ryo Mizuno,
Makoto Yotsuba, Miyuu
© 2016 Ryo Mizuno · Miyuu / KADOKAWA
© Makoto Yotsuba 2018
All rights reserved.
First published in Japan in 2018 by
HAKUSENSHA, Inc., Tokyo.
English language translation rights arranged with
HAKUSENSHA, Inc., Tokyo.

Printed in the U.S.A.

Published by VIZ Media, LLC
P.O. Box 77010
San Francisco, CA 94107

10 9 8 7 6 5 4 3 2 1
First printing, August 2019

viz.com

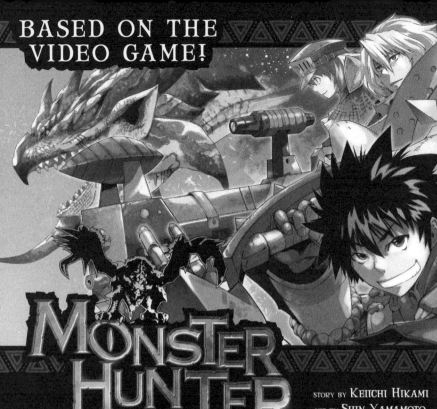

YOU'RE READING
THE WRONG WAY

Record of Grancrest War reads from right to left, starting in the upper-right corner. Japanese is read from right to left, meaning that action, sound effects, and word-balloon order are completely reversed from English order.